EMOTIONS IN HISTORY

General Editors

UTE FREVERT   THOMAS DIXON

Love, Honour, and Jealousy

An Intimate History of the Italian Economic Miracle

NIAMH CULLEN

OXFORD
UNIVERSITY PRESS

OXFORD
UNIVERSITY PRESS

Great Clarendon Street, Oxford, OX2 6DP,
United Kingdom

Oxford University Press is a department of the University of Oxford.
It furthers the University's objective of excellence in research, scholarship,
and education by publishing worldwide. Oxford is a registered trade mark of
Oxford University Press in the UK and in certain other countries

First Edition published in 2019

Impression: 1

Published in the United States of America by Oxford University Press
198 Madison Avenue, New York, NY 10016, United States of America

British Library Cataloguing in Publication Data
Data available

Library of Congress Control Number: 2018963165

ISBN 978-0-19-884037-4

Printed and bound by
CPI Group (UK) Ltd, Croydon, CR0 4YY

This book is for Patrick and Robin

Acknowledgements

This book was researched and written over many years and in many different places in Ireland, Italy, and the UK. I have benefitted from the support and advice of colleagues and friends at many stages along the way, all helping to make it a better book.

I was able to begin the research for this book with a Irish Research Council-Marie Skłodowska Curie CARA co-fund fellowship in 2011. This award enabled me to spend two years at the University of Milan as a visiting fellow and I am grateful to Emanuela Scarpellini for her support during my time there. At University College Dublin I am thankful to David Kerr who offered advice and support over many years, and who introduced me to the Archivio del Diario which proved to be an invaluable resource for this book. I am also thankful to Judith Devlin, Ivar McGrath, and the postdoctoral community at UCD, who offered support and friendship during my time there. Ciara Meehan has been an especially supportive friend and colleague, with whom I shared many discussions about gender history and popular culture. In 2013 I was a visiting fellow at the Modern European History Research Centre at Oxford and I am grateful to Jane Garnett who was so supportive during my time there.

The final chapters of this book were completed during my time at the University of Southampton and I am extremely grateful to my colleagues there for the very generous support, guidance, and friendship that they offered during these final stages. I am especially grateful to Eve Colpus, Neil Gregor, and Joan Tumblety for taking the time to read my draft work and for their insightful and constructive feedback. My final-year students at Southampton were also exposed to some of the ideas and materials that make up this book through my teaching, and our seminar discussions also helped me to refine and rethink some of the ideas in the book.

I am very grateful to my editors at OUP, who have been so helpful and encouraging throughout this process. First of all I would like to acknowledge the support of the 'Emotions in History' series editors, Thomas Dixon and Ute Frevert, for their interest in the book and for their advice and encouragement. At OUP I am very thankful to Robert Faber for his initial support of the manuscript, while it has been a pleasure to work with Christina Wipf-Perry, who has been so helpful in the later stages of its preparation. I am also extremely grateful to the two anonymous readers of the manuscript, both for their thoughtful comments and critiques and for their encouragement. Any errors that remain are of course my own.

Much of the research for this book was carried out in the Archivio del Diario, Italy's National Diary Archive, in Pieve Santo Stefano in Tuscany, and huge thanks are owed to the archival staff who were so welcoming and helpful to me during my time there. I am especially grateful to Cristina Cangi who has put an enormous amount of time and effort into securing authors' permissions for this book. Thanks are also due to Antonella Brandizzi who supplied the images included here. *Grazie mille.*

I also made use of many other archives and libraries in Italy while researching this book. I am especially thankful to the staff of the archive of the UDI (Unione Donne in Italia) organization in Rome, to the Istituto Ernesto de Martino in Florence, and to the Archivio di Stato in Turin. I am also grateful to the staff at the Biblioteca Braidense, the Fondazione Mondadori in Milan, the Biblioteca Nazionale di Roma, the Biblioteca Nationale di Firenze, and the historical archive of the Camera dei deputati in Rome.

Both the Cullen and Walsh families have been hugely supportive during the writing of this book. Special thanks are due to my sister Maria for her help in reading the final manuscript and to Fergal for his assistance with maps. Finally, but most of all, thanks are due to Patrick for his tireless support, intellectual and otherwise, and to our son Robin.

Contents

List of Figures	xi
List of Abbreviations	xiii
Note on Sources and Translations	xv
Introduction	1
1. 'Who to Choose?' Finding a Suitable Marriage Partner	20
2. 'Forgive Me, Love...It Was Stronger than I am': Negotiating Intimacy and Sexuality	53
3. Where Violence and Love Meet: Honour and Italian Society	92
4. 'Love Means Jealousy': A Jealousy Epidemic in Post-war Italy?	129
5. 'The Marriage Outlaws': Experiences of Marriage Breakdown Before Divorce	160
Conclusion: Individuals, Families, and Nation	193
Appendices	201
Bibliography	203
Index	213

List of Figures

I.1. Map of Italy   8

1.1. Page from memoir of Laura Massini, describing her wedding   28

1.2. The importance of the *corredo* in getting married   40

2.1. The 1959 photo story 'My Unknown Love'   67

2.2. Beach cover image of *Grand Hotel*   68

3.1. 'Love in White Overalls'   93

3.2. Franca Viola   108

3.3. Map of Sicily   110

3.4. Newspaper feature about the impending trial of Filippo Melodia   115

4.1. Scribbled note 'love means jealousy'   134

4.2. *The Magnificent Cuckold*   141

4.3. 'Jealousy'   156

List of Abbreviations

ADN   Archivio Diaristico Nazionale (National Diary Archive)
PCI   Partito Comunista Italiano (Italian Communist Party)
UDI   Unione Donne Italiane (Union of Italian Women). UDI is now known as
        Unione Donne in Italia (Union of Women in Italy)

Note on Sources and Translations

Quotations from memoirs and diaries held at the Archivio Diaristico Nazionale (ADN) are quoted with the permission of the authors or their families. In cases where it was not possible to contact the authors or their relatives, no direct citations or identifying details have been included by request of the ADN. In these cases the text is identified only by first name and shelfmark.

Several of the diaries and memoirs conserved at the ADN were subsequently published. In these cases it is indicated that the published version originated in a text held at the ADN and that they are thus included in the sample set.

All translations from Italian are my own otherwise indicated. In my translations from the diaries and memoirs, I have tried to keep as closely as possible to the original punctuation and syntax of the Italian text in order to best convey the rhythms of the original text and to represent the author's voice as accurately as possible. Translation is always an imperfect task and necessarily involves some measure of interpretation; any errors are of course my own.

Introduction

The day of my wedding even though I seemed happy. I was despairing thinking of what was ahead of me. It was an obsession. I remember that I was preparing the final details of the lunch, all alone, when they had already rung the bells for the wedding mass [. . .] I got dressed in a great hurry because I was going to be late otherwise.

Even though I very much loved the man I was marrying, to me it seemed it was the day of my hanging. Once I arrived in the church, I saw everything double, I had a splitting headache. I didn't say anything to anyone.[1]

This is how Amalia Molinelli wrote about her wedding at the age of 22. Her words are strikingly candid and even shocking for a woman who presented herself as happily married in middle age. Amalia was born in 1928 to a peasant family in the northern Italian province of Emilia-Romagna and described a happy rural adolescence, going to dances regularly at weekends. As a young woman she had worked as a domestic servant in nearby Genoa but she disliked the city, preferring the openness of the rural landscape. Amalia married a local man in 1950. As the wedding drew close, she was terrified of going to live with her husband's family after the marriage, as was customary in the rural north. The main emotion in her account of the wedding is fear, although it was one that she kept hidden from everybody on the day. At the same time, she was careful to mention how much she loved her husband, the man to whom she would stay married for more than thirty years.

Despite the brutally honest description of how she felt on her wedding day, Amalia's memoir was nevertheless a carefully constructed narrative of her life. Her childhood education did not go beyond elementary school as was typical then for rural girls, and she wrote her memoir between 1976 and 1982, after having returned to education to gain her middle school diploma. By this time she was married for over twenty-five years and described herself as a house-wife. Even though the fear and anxiety she felt on her wedding day betrays her

---

[1] Amalia Molinelli, *I pensieri vagabondi di Amalia* (Milan, 2002), p. 43. A copy is also kept at the Archivio Diaristico Nazionale (ADN).

deep ambivalence at that point, it seemed in writing her memoir that love had to be a part of the narrative of marriage. In 1950, marriage in Italy was still firmly seen as a lifelong commitment and any debates about divorce were far from her consciousness as a young woman.

Almost ten years later, Livia Colasanti would have a very different experience of romantic partnership. Born in 1937 to a middle-class family in Rome, Livia's childhood was urban and affluent. She remembered long periods of leisure in her childhood with the family spending summers on the beach at Ostia, just outside Rome. Her early teenage years were also marked by the rise of consumerism and popular culture; particularly fashion and music. At 15 she began work, while also taking a secretarial course at night and starting what she described as a good, solid job at the age of 21. She had met her partner Dario the previous year in 1957. He was married, although separated. In 1964 Livia became pregnant and went to live with Dario. Although her immediate family accepted the situation, a wedding reception was held in order to save face in front of the extended family, with the fiction that a private ceremony had taken place beforehand. The 'farce' involved a full reception in a bar facing the Tiber, and a honeymoon in Florence. Uneasy recalling it even many years later in her memoir, Livia compared the staged wedding to 'a comedy, a scenario from a 1950s film', and likened herself and Dario to the couple in a posed publicity photograph of a bride and groom in St Peter's Square. The growing media focus on marriage and romantic love in film, music, and advertising evident by the 1960s was, in her view, at odds with the reality of her situation.

She left Dario nine months after her daughter was born. She asked 'how could I have lived with a man who was unfaithful, who did not share my politics and who even mocked my views [. . .]?'.[2] In Livia's memoir, the notion of romantic love provided a measure against which her own relationship was tested and failed, unlike in Amalia's narrative where love was presented as a seamless and barely examined component of the marriage. The commercialization of romantic love only highlighted the discordance of the staged wedding of Livia and Dario. Livia's memoir contained a much clearer notion of what an ideal romantic partnership would include, and she was certain that her own experience with Dario did not live up to her ideals. The differences between Amalia's and Livia's attitudes towards marriage and love are a sharp illustration of an Italy in transformation, not just in material circumstances but in attitudes, expectations, and feelings. Although both women wrote their memoirs in middle age, their attitudes were clearly shaped by the world in which they came of age. In Amalia's case this was the rural north where the needs of family were placed above all else, while in 1960s Rome, Livia could

---

[2] Livia Colasanti, 'Il sapore della cioccolata', MP/10, ADN.

have a job and enjoy fashion, popular music, and film. Crucially, the two women differed not just in their experiences but in how they made sense of their lives and their futures. Unlike Amalia, Livia was able to imagine that her life could be different.

This book will explore the story not just of how practices of courtship and marriage changed in Italy between 1945 and 1974, but how it became possible for Italian men and women to think about their lives, emotions, and their choices differently. It will do so by drawing closely on a large body of mostly memoirs and diaries, set against the context of the popular culture that these men and women absorbed in their youth and young adulthood. In its focus on the ordinary lives of Italians, this book aims to write a social history of emotions during Italy's economic miracle. In doing so it pays an important debt to the growing number of historians investigating the modern history of love, courtship, and marriage, including Claire Langhamer, Simon Szreter, and Kate Fisher on England, Dagmar Herzog on sexuality in Europe, Hester Vaizey, Paul Betts, and Josie McLellan on modern Germany, and Rebecca Pulju and Sarah Fishman on France.[3] Emotions have also been commanding attention in modern Italian history, notably with the work of Mark Seymour and Penny Morris.[4] Meanwhile the work of Anna Tonelli and Maria Porzio on the politics of love and sexuality and of Enrica Asquer on middle-class life during the economic boom, make valuable contributions to the history of

[3] Claire Langhamer, *The English in Love: The Intimate Story of an Emotional Revolution* (Oxford, 2013); Simon Szreter and Kate Fisher, *Sex Before the Sexual Revolution: Intimate Life in England 1918–1973* (Cambridge, 2010); Dagmar Herzog, *Sexuality in Europe: A Twentieth Century History* (Cambridge, 2011); Hester Vaizey, *Surviving Hitler's War: Family Life in Germany, 1939–1948* (London, 2010); Josie McLellan, *Love in the Time of Communism: Intimacy and Sexuality in the GDR* (Cambridge, 2011); Paul Betts, *Within Walls: Private Life in the German Democratic Republic* (Oxford, 2010); Rebecca Pulju, 'Finding a Grand Amour in Marriage in Postwar France', in Kristin Celello and Hanan Kholoussy (eds), *Domestic Tensions, National Anxieties: Global Perspectives on Modern Marriage Crises* (Oxford, 2015); and Sarah Fishman, *From Vichy to the Sexual Revolution: Gender and Family Life in Postwar France* (Oxford, 2017), pp. 126–46. Other works specifically on the history of romantic love take a more cultural and intellectual perspective: see William Reddy, *The Making of Romantic Love: Longing and Sexuality in Europe, South Asia and Japan, 900–1200 CE* (Chicago, 2012) and Luisa Passerini, *Women and Men in Love: European Identities in the Twentieth Century* (New York, 2009).

[4] See Penny Morris, 'A Window on the Private Sphere: Advice Columns, Marriage and the Evolving Family in 1950s Italy', *The Italianist*, 27:2 (2007), pp. 304–32 and 'Feminism and Emotion: Love and the Couple in the Magazine Effe', *Italian Studies*, 68:3 (2013), pp. 378–98; Mark Seymour, 'Epistolary Emotions: Exploring Amorous Hinterlands in 1870s Southern Italy', *Social History*, 35:2 (2010) pp. 148–64 and 'Emotional Arenas: from Provincial Circus to National Courtroom in Late Nineteenth-century Italy', *Rethinking History*, 16:2 (2012), pp. 177–97. See also Martyn Lyons, '"Questo cor che tuo si rese": The Private and the Public in Italian Women's Love Letters in the Long Nineteenth Century', *Modern Italy*, 19:4 (2014), pp. 355–68 and Penny Morris, Francesco Ricatti, and Mark Seymour (eds), *Modern Italy: Special Issue on the Emotions*, 17:2 (2012), pp. 151–285.

sexuality and intimate life.[5] This book builds on this work, and through its use of first-person writing, provides new and original insights into the social history of love, sexuality, and marriage with implications not just for Italy but more broadly for Europe in the same period.

FROM POST-WAR RUIN TO PROSPERITY: THE ITALIAN ECONOMIC MIRACLE

The contrast between the perspectives of Amalia and Livia on love and marriage illustrate the extent of Italy's transformation in the decades following the war. A peasant woman marrying in 1950 and a middle-class woman in 1960s Rome, the two women are divided by place and class but also by time. Italy in the early 1950s was still largely a poor and rural society, recently ravaged by war, socially conservative, and deeply divided. Even as the new Italian Republic sought to distance itself from the recent past, the memory of fascism and the trauma of war were still present in many minds. The men and women at the centre of this book, coming to adulthood in the post-war period, had mostly experienced fascism as children and some as adolescents. Few of the men had been old enough to fight in the war, but they would likely have participated in fascist youth organizations where they imbibed the message of martial masculinity, just as girls received messages about fascist mother-hood: traditional, submissive, and prolific.[6] The reactionary gender politics of fascism ultimately had little demographic impact although it is altogether more difficult to gauge the impression these messages made on young Italians.

The retrenched position of the Catholic Church combined with Cold War politics to make post-war Italy a society that was both conservative and deeply divided.[7] As a legacy of the antifascist resistance, Italy had the largest Communist Party (Partito Comunista Italiano, or PCI) in Western Europe after 1945, creating two strong opposing ideologies with deep roots in society. Communism and Catholicism were not just about politics and religion; each

---

[5] Maria Porzio, *Arrivani gli alleati! Amori e violenze nell'Italia liberata* (Rome, 2011); Anna Tonelli, *Gli irregolari: Amori comunisti al tempo della Guerra Fredda* (Rome, 2014); Enrica Asquer, *Storia intima dei ceti medi: Una capitale e una periferia nell'Italia del miracolo economico* (Rome, 2011).

[6] The literature on gender and fascism is extensive. See especially Sandro Bellassai, 'The Masculine Mystique: Antimodernism and Virility in Fascist Italy', *Journal of Modern Italian Studies*, 10 (2005), pp. 314–35; Paul Ginsborg, *Family Politics: Domestic Life, Devastation and Survival 1900–1950* (New Haven, CT, 2014), pp. 139–225; Victoria De Grazia, *How Fascism Ruled Women* (Berkeley, CA, 2000); and Natasha Chang, *Shaping the New Woman: Body Politics and the New Woman in Fascist Italy* (Toronto, 2015).

[7] See Paul Ginsborg, *A History of Contemporary Italy, 1943–1980* (London, 1990).

one was also a way of life, with social life being organized around the party for PCI members and many millions of Italians belonging to Catholic Action and other Catholic and youth organizations.[8] The Catholic Church of the 1950s continued to fight the battle against both communism and modernity by focusing on gender and sexuality, and the principal target was the purity of girls and young women.[9] Catholicism was especially strong in the north and north-east of Italy, while in the south local tradition also contributed to a social and cultural climate that was deeply conservative in its attitudes towards women. The PCI, strong in the north and central regions, did little in practice to change deeply entrenched ideas about gender roles.[10] In a society that was still predominantly rural, the strongest influence remained that of the family. In the south of Italy, in Sicily and Calabria in particular, the notion of family honour also played an important part in the regulation of women's lives. These attitudes and customs led in extreme cases to crimes of honour, which were regularly in the news, and forced marriages which, with the exception of the 1965 case of Franca Viola, tended to remain private matters.

By the late 1950s and early 1960s, a very different Italy was beginning to emerge. The 'economic miracle' of the industrial north began to take off in the late 1950s, sparking widespread migration to Milan, Turin, and Genoa and more generally from rural to urban Italy. It is estimated that at least nine million and up to twenty-five million Italians (roughly half the entire population) were on the move in these years.[11] Not all of these moved far enough to be properly considered migrants, but it is also certain that the real number of internal migrants was far above the official figures for these years. This unprecedented wave of migration, predominantly from rural to urban Italy, undoubtedly changed Italian society. The rise of prosperity and consumer culture transformed the ordinary lives of millions of Italians both in material terms and in

---

[8] See David Forgacs and Stephen Gundle, *Mass Culture and Italian Society from Fascism to the Cold War* (Bloomington, IN, 2007), pp. 247–68; Sandro Bellasai, *La morale comunista: Pubblico e privato nella rappresentazione del Pci (1947–1956)* (Rome, 2001); and David Kertzer, *Comrades and Christians. Religion and Political Struggle in Communist Italy* (Cambridge, 1980).

[9] Percy Allum, 'Uniformity Undone: Aspects of Catholic Culture in Post-war Italy', in Zygmunt Baranski and Robert Lumley (eds), *Culture and Conflict in post-war Italy: Essays on Mass and Popular Culture*, (London, 1990); Patrick McCarthy, 'The Church in Post War Italy', in Patrick McCarthy (ed.), *Italy since 1945* (Oxford, 2000).

[10] Maria Casalini, *Famiglie comuniste: Ideologie e vita quotidiana nell'Italia degli anni '50* (Bologna, 2010).

[11] Ginsborg reports the figure of just over nine million for intra-regional migration between 1955 and 1971 while Crainz reports a figure of approximately ten million for intra-regional migration: *A History of Contemporary Italy*, p. 219; Guido Crainz, *Storia del miracolo economico: Culture, identità, trasformazioni* (Rome, 2005), p. 108. The disparities and the lack of precise figures can be explained by the fact that a 1939 law designed to limit migration from rural areas—only repealed in 1961—made it very difficult for migrants to establish legal residency in their new town or city. See also Stefano Gallo, *Senza attraversare le frontiere: Le migrazioni interne dall'Unità a oggi* (Rome, 2012).

their values.[12] The rise of mass culture, from cinema and popular illustrated magazines in the early 1950s to television in the late 1950s and 1960s, also transformed identities and perspectives from local to national and transnational. The influence of family and religion on young Italians was giving way to modern secular values, while the popularization of the notion of 'companionate marriage' and the growing commercialization of romantic love in Italy as elsewhere transformed expectations of marriage and increasingly placed the burden of choice on individuals rather than on their families. The opportunities afforded to women were changing too, and new ideas about gender influenced attitudes towards courtship and marriage. Of course, these processes were not as simple or as linear as this narrative might suggest, and this book will explore those complexities.

Those born in the 1940s and coming of age in the mid to late 1960s inherited a very different world to those born during the previous decade. Although they might have (barely) lived through the war as children, theirs was an Italy which quickly left behind the austerity and conservatism of the early 1950s for Italy's 'miraculous' 1960s. This generation was likely to receive a better education than previous generations, with the numbers attending secondary school and university expanding rapidly in these years.[13] By the late 1960s, many of this generation also began to reject the consumerism of the boom years, and the social conformism it fostered, dismissively summarized as the 'three Ms': *'macchina, moglie e mestiere'* (car, wife, and profession).[14] In rejecting the consumerism of the boom years, some also rejected the conventional model of marriage and family, experimenting with new forms of love and commitment. While the Italian '68 is not central to the story of this book, several of the men and women discussed here were involved in the wider movement and had their experiences of love and sexuality shaped by the culture of those years. The Italian feminist movement which grew out of '68 was also crucial to the lives of some of the women, transforming their attitudes to marriage and family, with several women even coming to 1970s feminism in later life as married women. In these cases the encounter was often a catalyst for change, although most memoirs described a gradual shift in outlook rather than a sudden transformation.

In a more general sense, this book aims to tell the story not of activists or of those central to the counterculture of the late 1960s and the social movements of the 1970s but rather of those at the periphery. We will see how the ordinary

---

[12] Emanuela Scarpellini, *Material Nation: A Consumer's History of Italy* (Oxford, 2011), pp. 109–224; Simonetta Piccone Stella, *La prima generazione: Ragazze e ragazzi del miracolo economico italiano* (Turin, 1993).

[13] Robert Lumley, *States of Emergency: Cultures of Revolt in Italy from 1968 to 1978* (London, 1990); Anna Tonelli, *Comizi d'amore: Politica e sentimenti dal '68 ai Papa boys* (Rome, 2007); Anna Bravo, *A colpi di cuore: Storie del sessantotto* (Rome, 2008).

[14] Guido Crainz, *Storia del miracolo italiano*, p. 143.

lives examined in this book reveal a different 1960s to the narrative of liberalization that emerges in popular culture and through a singular focus on '68. Indeed the intention of this book is to complicate and to challenge this narrative. It is not just, as we will see, that expectations did not always match reality and that development was uneven, as was the case particularly in rural Italy and in the south. We must also take account that, as with jealousy, change did not always move in a straightforward, liberal direction. Moreover, it is worth noting that not all experiences are addressed in the book. The absence of homosexuality is a reflection of the strong heteronormativity of the sources, whether those drawn from the media and popular culture or the personal texts. Different sources would have been needed to uncover these hidden experiences; what we see in the diaries and memoirs here examined are the attempts that ordinary people made to place themselves and their experiences in relation to dominant discourses rather than (for the most part) in defiance of them.[15] We can only speculate about what stories might be further hidden. Let us now turn to the personal narratives that are so central to this new story of post-war Italian society.

FIRST-PERSON WRITING: THE NARRATORS

A sample set of 142 first-person texts are used in this book, all drawn from the texts collected in Italy's National Diary Archive, located in Pieve Santo Stefano in Tuscany. While the majority of the texts are memoirs, some are diaries (most of these were adolescent diaries detailing school and university life, although they include one by a woman office worker and one by a male migrant worker in 1950s Germany). The criteria for inclusion in the sample set were broadly defined: all writers born between 1926 and 1946 (and thus growing up and coming of age in the 1950s and 1960s) and where at least some detail of either love, sexuality, courtship, or marriage were included. This amounted to fifty-nine texts by men and eighty-three by women. The texts vary greatly in length and style, and in the level of detail they provide. Some have been used extensively, analysed in terms of language and structure as well as content, while others simply confirmed patterns and trends. Although the sample set

---

[15] Scholars have recently devoted much attention to uncovering the history of Italian homosexuality in the late nineteenth and early twentieth centuries, although more needs to be done for the late twentieth century. These works include Chiara Beccalosi, 'The Origin of Italian Sexological Studies: Female Sexual Inversion *c.* 1870–1900', *Journal of the History of Sexuality*, 18:1 (2009), pp. 103–20; Lorenzo Benadusi, *The Enemy of the New Man: Homosexuality in Fascist Italy* (Wisconsin, 2012); Charlotte Ross, *Eccentricity and Sameness: Discourses on Lesbianism and Desire Between Women in Italy, 1960s to 1930s* (Oxford, 2015); and Valeria Babini, Chiara Beccalosi, and Lucy Riall (eds), *Italian Sexualities Uncovered, 1789–1914* (London, 2015).

happens to have a slightly higher representation of women than men, that is not to suggest that men did not consider love, courtship, and sexuality important to their lives. Many of the men considered in these pages actually wrote in huge detail and with great intensity about these aspects of their lives. At the same time, men were also more likely to write a diary or memoir of work, career, or politics, compartmentalizing their experiences of intimacy or family. In terms of geographical spread, the twenty Italian regions were fairly equally represented (see Figure I.1). The male writers were very evenly spread across Italy, with twenty-two from northern Italy, twenty from the central regions, and twenty from the south, including Sicily and Sardinia. The women were

Figure I.1. Map of Italy, showing the regional provenance of the diarists and memoirists as per Appendix 1.

<http://www.geocurrents.info/cartography/customizable-base-maps-of-italy>.

more likely to be from northern Italy (thirty-nine), with twenty coming from central Italy and twenty-three from the south. Urban, provincial, and rural backgrounds were also all strongly represented. The cultural position of women in the south of Italy, which often meant a more secluded life and lower levels of education and participation in the workforce, may explain the lower number of southern women writers as well as the relative silence on certain topics.[16]

Class is difficult to gauge precisely from the texts. The diarists are over-whelmingly middle and upper class, while the backgrounds of the memoirists are much more diverse. Although less than half of the authors gave definite information on their class or family background, the partial information given suggests that class is fairly evenly represented (see Appendix 1). At least eleven men and sixteen women memoirists came from peasant backgrounds, while the regions were also fairly evenly represented in the rural memoirs.[17] Although the majority of the Italian population was rural until the onset of the economic miracle, the experiences of peasants are difficult for historians to access, beyond regionally specific works such as Nuto Revelli's extremely valuable oral histories of Piedmont.[18] These texts thus represent the enormous value of the National Diary Archive.[19] The strong representation of working-class and peasant memoirists can perhaps be explained by the Italian tradition of popular testimony, which was linked to post-war left-wing political traditions and cultivated in particular by the Diary Archive.

The writers were more likely to disclose their own educational achievement than their family background, and on the subject of education we see a strong gender disparity (see Appendix 2). Although the typical pattern for peasant families up to the 1950s was for boys to attend school until 10 or 11, the male memoirists from peasant backgrounds were often atypical in that they had completed middle school or gone on to further education.[20] Very few of them

---

[16] See Perry Willson, *Women in Twentieth Century Italy* (London, 2009), pp. 71–3 and 117–18 and Simonetta Piccone Stella, *Ragazze del sud: Famiglie, figlie, studentesse in una città meridionale* (Rome, 1979).

[17] Of the ten men from peasant backgrounds, one was from northern Italy, four from the south (including Sicily and Sardinia), and five from the central provinces. The women were spread more evenly: five were from northern Italy, four from the south, and six from central Italy.

[18] Nuto Revelli, *Il mondo dei vinti: Testimonianze di vita contadina* (Turin, 1977) and Nuto Revelli, *L'anello forte. La donna: storie di vita contadina* (Turin, 1985).

[19] Peasant or 'contadino' is generally used to refer to both small farmers and landless rural labourers in Italy. Rudolph M. Bell states that he uses the term 'to refer to all agricultural manual labourer categories noted above (smallholders, landless and ambiguous) and specifically to exclude substantial landholders and agricultural capitalists and middlemen'. Quoted in '"What is a Peasant?"', in Rudolph M. Bell, *Fate, Honor, Family and Village: Demographic and Cultural Change in Rural Italy Since 1800* (Chicago, 1979).

[20] Compulsory secondary school education until the age of 14 was only made legal in 1962: see Ginsborg, *A History of Contemporary Italy*, p. 298.

remained peasants, moving away from the land by means of education, vocational training, or simply migration. In this sense they were typical of their time. The women peasant memoirists were more likely to complete only three years of elementary school, leaving school at 8 or 9. Some remained on the land while others migrated after marriage. Three of them went back to education in later life, typically completing middle school after their children were raised. This later experience of education equipped them with the tools and perhaps the motivation to write their memoirs. While Italian women in general were more restricted in their access to education, those writers with university degrees were disproportionately women. Women graduates were an elite group in 1950s and 1960s Italy and it was perhaps their status as unusual women that prompted the decision to write their memoir or submit an adolescent diary to the archive.

FIRST-PERSON WRITING: NARRATIVE, MEMORY, EMOTION, AND LANGUAGE

The analysis of such a set of personal testimonies, and particularly memoirs, presents both challenges and possibilities for the historian. As the oral historian Alessandro Portelli comments, such sources 'tell us less about events than about their meaning'.[21] They do not so much tell us about people's life experiences, as about how they understood their own lives. For the historian interested in individual experience, attitude, and feeling, the worth of such sources lies precisely in their subjectivity. Memoirs, as carefully constructed written documents, also present their own particular challenges for the historian. Here they will be discussed in terms of narrative, memory, and language.

Rather than forming a simple record of experience, a memoir, as with an oral testimony, always presents a narrative of the self.[22] Mary Evans has argued that autobiography is impossible, since the need for narrative coherence erases any true sense of self or real experience.[23] While her focus was on literary autobiography, Evans was concerned to draw attention to the 'increasingly problematic negotiation of the boundaries between the public and the private', and how this might lead an author to construct a self that was acceptable both

---

[21] Alessandro Portelli, 'The Peculiarities of Oral History', *History Workshop Journal*, 12:2 (1981), pp. 96–107; p. 99.

[22] On oral testimony as narrative of the self, see also Simon Szreter and Kate Fisher, *Sex Before the Sexual Revolution: Intimate Life in England 1918–1963* (Cambridge, 2010), p. 51 and Luisa Passerini, *Autobiography of a Generation: Italy, 1968* (Middletown, CT, 1996), pp. 22–36.

[23] Mary Evans, *Missing Persons: The Impossibility of Auto/biography* (London, 1999).

to the author and to society.[24] The authors examined in this book sometimes gave their reasons for writing; usually along the lines of 'to make a record of the past' or 'to write my story for my family'. While the texts were usually not written explicitly for publication, they were all deposited in a national archive and thus intended in some form for public consumption.[25] As such, they straddle the boundary between public and private. Naturally the authors made choices about how to present themselves in selecting which details to include or emphasize and which to leave out, how to order events, and in what tone to describe them. Politics, religion, nostalgia, or defining events such as an unhappy childhood or marriage might also provide a narrative framework to give shape and meaning to the life story.

None of this devalues these sources for the historian; far from it. Rather it means that careful and close reading that pays attention to the shape of the text as well as the material it presents, and looks closely for gaps and silences, can yield further clues about how we relate ordinary lives to the wider historical picture.[26] Honour crime and kidnap marriage, although practised in Sicily at least until the early 1970s, rarely cropped up in the first-person texts, except sometimes as background or family history. The one memoir dealing with a personal experience of kidnap marriage was excluded from the book on the author's request, indicating that even in the present day some issues remain difficult to discuss openly. Homosexuality is almost never mentioned in the texts, and was indeed absent from public discourse before the 1970s. Even for those writing their memoirs from the 1980s to the 2000s, their formative years were lived at a time when such matters were not for public discussion.[27] Indeed, with the exception of those who 'converted' to a new outlook or ideology such as feminism in later life, formative experience was key.

At the same time, the texts were often surprisingly candid about other matters of sexuality and emotions. The men sometimes gave detailed accounts of pre-marital sexuality, as well as jealous and controlling behaviour in romantic relationships. Women tended to be more reticent about pre-marital

---

[24] Evans, *Missing Persons*, p. 12.

[25] The archive now holds more than 6,500 autobiographical texts: see <http://www.archiviodiari.org>. It is also increasingly exploited by historians of modern Italy. Christopher Duggan's *Fascist Voices: An Intimate History of Mussolini's Italy* (London, 2012) for instance drew extensively on the archive's diary holdings. Perry Willson also drew on the archive's correspondence and memoir holdings in her article, 'The Nation in Uniform? Fascist Italy 1919–1943', *Past and Present*, 221 (2013), pp. 239–72. Some have been published by the archive itself; an annual competition, the *Premio Pieve*, is held by the archive, with publication as the prize. At the same time, those who deposit their texts retain the right of refusal to any public usage.

[26] For further discussion, see Szreter and Fisher, *Sex Before the Sexual Revolution*, pp. 1–19, 51.

[27] See Sandro Bellassai, *La mascolinità contemporanea* (Milan, 2004).

sexuality, but a surprising number disclosed negative feelings about marriage, while remaining married to their spouse. In a memoir written primarily for his family, one man gave a frank and detailed account of his marital infidelity. It seems that infidelity was not in conflict with certain constructions of Italian masculinity, while we can assume that homosexual behaviour was much more threatening. With many of these men growing up during fascism with the hyper-masculine fascist 'new man' as official role model—with virility prized and homosexuality silenced and persecuted as unmanly—the internalized notion of what was and was not manly behaviour is perhaps not surprising.[28] At the same time it could be said that the regime simply amplified and gave official credence to pre-existing attitudes, and the book will explore both continuities and moments of rupture.

When examining a memoir as opposed to a diary, written at some distance from the events described, we must take into account the two kinds of temporality that are at play; the time of the events described and the time of writing.[29] Carolyn Steedman was very much aware of this when recalling her working-class childhood in her memoir. Although she knew as an adult that aspects of her upbringing were unusual, she insisted that 'I don't *remember* the oddness; it's a reconstruction'.[30] We might also take into account what Mary Jo Maynes described as 'the interplay between norms and experiences', when, in a rapidly changing society such as Italy during the boom, the promise of expanding opportunity and affluence created greater discontent about people's own circumstances.[31] We can see this acutely in the contrast between the memoirs of those who came of age in the late 1940s and early 1950s, and those who reached adulthood at the onset of the economic miracle, as is evident in the contrast between the narration of the stories of Amalia and Livia. It is in this complex interaction between what might be termed historical and personal time that we may begin to understand how individuals understand their own lives in times of rapid social change.

---

[28] On fascism and virility, see Sandro Bellasai, 'The Masculine Mystique: Antimodernism and Virility in Fascist Italy', *Journal of Modern Italian Studies*, 10:3 (2005), pp. 314–35; Silvana Patriarca, *Italian Vices: Nation and Character from the Risorgimento to the Republic* (Cambridge, 2010), pp. 133–60; and Martina Salvante, 'Less Than a Bootrag: Procreation, Paternity and the Masculine Ideal in Fascist Italy', in Pablo Dominguez Anderson and Simon Wendt (eds), *Masculinities and the Nation in the Modern World* (London, 2015), pp. 93–112. On fascism and homosexuality, see Lorenzo Benadusi, *The Enemy of the New Man: Homosexuality in Fascist Italy* (Madison, WI, 2012).

[29] Mary Jo Maynes et al., *Telling Stories: The Use of Personal Narratives in the Social Sciences and History* (Ithaca, NY, 2008), p. 3.

[30] Carolyn Steedman, *Landscape for a Good Woman: A Story of Two Lives* (London, 1986), p. 44.

[31] Mary Jo Maynes, *Taking the Hard Road: Life Course in French and German Workers' Autobiographies in the Era of Industrialisation* (Chapel Hill, 1995), p. 12.

Psychology and neuroscience also offer us ways of thinking about time and memory as they are organized by the human mind rather than the calendar.[32] Nancy Chodorow suggests that when an experience evokes strong emotions, it cannot be confined to one moment in time, but may be relived in the telling.[33] Oral historians have also described how interviewees often become caught up in the moment they are recollecting.[34] Detailed descriptions of the rituals surrounding the wedding, and especially its material aspects, such as food, clothing, and the trousseau, often indicated the personal and social significance of these events for men and women. I also came across several instances of traumatic events—particularly women's accounts of sexual violence—being recorded in crisp, clear detail in the memoirs. Amalia's wedding day was recalled with equal clarity. The level of detail and the clarity of recollection signals the importance of these events in the life story.

Some of the memoirs, especially those written by people from peasant backgrounds, tend to resemble oral testimonies rather than more carefully constructed written documents, in their meandering styles and their tendency to jump back and forth across time.[35] It has been suggested that this is also a particular feature of how women write about their lives.[36] Digressions were frequent in such narratives, with the structure of the text illustrating the meandering quality of memory, which had the ability to forge new links across time and space, triggered by a single thought, sound, smell, or taste. In general I found that men tended to be open and direct about their life experiences, while women were often more careful, guarded, and ambivalent, since to admit unhappiness in marriage, particularly for those older women who grew up before the miracle, was barely thinkable. These memoirs required some detective work in order to 'read' the feelings and attitudes they encoded.[37] The memoir of rural woman Laura Massini (Tuscany, 1930) for example, was meandering and episodic, although a closer look revealed that digression also served a more serious purpose, filling silences and diverting attention from uncomfortable subjects. The grammar, filled with qualifiers and the passive voice, also betrayed an ambivalence that could not be directly articulated.[38]

---

[32] William M. Reddy, *The Navigation of Feeling: A Framework for the History of the Emotions* (Cambridge, 2001), pp. 3–33.

[33] Nancy Chodorow, *The Power of Feelings* (New Haven, CT, 1999).

[34] Alessandro Portelli, 'The Peculiarities of Oral History', pp. 99–100; also referenced in Mary Jo Maynes et al., *Telling Stories*, pp. 73–4.

[35] One testimony was actually a recorded oral testimony: MP/85, ADN.

[36] Sidonie Smith and Julia Watson (eds), *Women, Autobiography, Theory: A Reader* (Madison, WI, 1998), pp. 9–10.

[37] Barbara Rosenwein reminds us to tease out emotions from less obvious and hidden places: Jan Plamper, 'The History of the Emotions: An Interview with William Reddy, Barbara Rosenwein, and Peter Stearns', *History and Theory*, 49:2 (2010), pp. 237–65, 250.

[38] Laura Massini, 'Domani è un altro giorno', MP/91, ADN. For further discussion see Chapter 1.

THINKING ABOUT EMOTIONS IN POST-WAR ITALY

Even in autobiographical writings dealing with personal, emotive topics, we can still struggle to pin down the relationship between words and feelings. Yet historians have been thinking carefully about how to uncover and examine emotions in the past. William Reddy's concept of *emotives* is used to describe utterances about feelings. He has defined them as 'at once managerial and exploratory', since they serve the double purpose of evoking and naming the feeling at the same time.[39] They are essentially the imperfect translation of feeling into language and as such Reddy offers a way of thinking beyond Peter Stearns' *emotionology*, defined as the language surrounding emotional norms and standards which for him was always separate to actual emotional experience.[40] By drawing attention to the way in which language necessarily structures thought and feeling in both the availability and absence of suitable words, Reddy does not negate the relationship between words and real emotions.

Language is not the only way we communicate emotions though.[41] For Monique Scheer, emotions are things people do rather than simply feel. They are both always embodied and, drawing on Pierre Bourdieu, always grounded in their social context.[42] Scheer thus offers another way of thinking beyond the distinction that Stearns drew between real emotions and the emotional standards of a society at a particular point in time. Love, hate, or jealousy can be encouraged or shaped by the world people live in, but that does not mean that the emotions are not deeply felt at a personal level. It is simply not up to the historian to distinguish or to judge which emotion, as named or recounted in a diary or memoir, is 'real' (whatever that means) and which is not. Thinking about emotions as both embodied practices and as always embedded in a social habitus is a useful way of thinking about how and why people drew on certain vocabularies rather than others, or even failed to articulate what one might expect at a certain point in time. Bourdieu's concept of the habitus draws our attention to the largely invisible social workings of power—what Scheer terms 'the politics of emotion'—and the unequal power relationships to which people often unconsciously subscribe, whether in terms of gender, class, regional, or ethnic difference.[43]

---

[39] Plamper, 'The History of the Emotions', p. 240; Reddy, *The Navigation of Feeling*.

[40] Plamper, 'The History of the Emotions', pp. 261–5. The term emotionology was originally coined by Peter and Carol Stearns in their article, 'Emotionology: Clarifying the History of Emotions and Emotional Standards', *American Historical Review*, 90:4 (1980), pp. 813–36.

[41] Jan Plamper has criticized Reddy for neglecting other forms of emotional expression in 'The History of the Emotions', pp. 241–2. Monique Scheer, 'Are Emotions a Kind of Practice (And is that What Makes Them Have a History)? A Bourdieuian Approach to Understanding Emotions', *History and Theory*, 51:2 (2012), pp. 193–220.

[42] Monique Scheer, 'Are Emotions a Kind of Practice?', pp. 204–7.

[43] Scheer, 'Are Emotions a Kind of Practice?', p. 208.

If emotions are also embodied, then the historian must pay attention to their physical expression as well as the language of emotions. The first-person texts—and indeed the magazine features, stories, and advice columns used in this book—did sometimes describe bodily expressions of emotion. Amalia described her experience of what seemed like a migraine headache on her wedding day, apparently brought on by the extreme anxiety and fear of her impending marriage. In both personal testimony and mass media sources, jealousy was the emotion most often described in physical terms, often even as an illness. Even emotions which were very much embedded within the social and cultural context of the time—as this book will argue was the case for jealousy in post-war Italy—were inscribed quite firmly on the body.

Neither are emotions merely individual experiences. The fact that there were shared vocabularies of the emotions in post-war Italy indicates that emotions also have a collective, social meaning, and examining them in this context is a key concern of this book. Close attention is paid to the interplay between the personal and the wider socio-cultural context, paying particular attention to popular magazines and film. Livia Colasanti's memoir illustrates how, as a young woman coming of age in early 1960s Rome, ideas and expectations of romantic partnership were in part shaped by popular music and film. Values, habits, and lexicons of feeling are of course shared by families, peer groups, and communities as well as religious, political, or even national groups. Emotions undoubtedly change over time, falling in and out of use according to the needs, values, and conventions of a society.

The example of honour which Ute Frevert argues can be considered as an emotion, is a particularly vivid example of an emotion only given shape by the values of a particular social group.[44] Up until the early twentieth century, upper-class men in the European and US traditions were prepared to kill and die to defend their intangible but deeply felt sense of masculine honour. Without the duel to give ritual shape to these feelings, honour is no longer sincerely and intensely felt among Western European men.[45] In Italy and across the Mediterranean, a different sort of honour connected to both masculinity and family, and measured by the sexual chastity of wives, sisters, and daughters, was gradually falling out of use in the 1960s as it had in earlier decades elsewhere in Europe.[46] As we will see, these feelings may have taken a different form rather than disappearing altogether. At the same time it is certain that the protracted public demise of honour in the post-war decades, as

---

[44] Ute Frevert, *Emotions in History: Lost and Found* (Budapest, 2011), pp. 39–41.

[45] Frevert, *Emotions Lost and Found*, pp. 40–65. See also Kevin McAleer, *Dueling: The Cult of Honor in Fin-de-Siècle Germany* (Princeton, NJ, 1997).

[46] Ruth Harris's work on crime in nineteenth-century Paris argues that while honour and passion were recognized as mitigating factors in crimes, there was also an increasing medicalization of such behaviour, with female crime in particular linked to hysteria. See Ruth Harris, *Murders and Madness: Medicine, Law and Society in the Fin de Siècle* (Oxford, 1989).

played out in politics and the media, revealed much about both gender politics and the dynamics between national and regional identity. The decline of honour in post-war Italy therefore provides valuable insight into the connections between emotions and social context, particularly during a period of rapid change.

Historians of the emotions have come up with several ways of making sense of the social and collective life of emotions, conceptualizing emotional 'regimes', 'communities', and 'styles' in history.[47] While Reddy's expression 'emotional regimes' is rather rigid and schematic, Rosenwein's 'emotional communities' as 'social communities' who share 'systems of feeling' seems more appropriate here.[48] Conceptualized in the plural, people might belong to multiple 'emotional communities' and move between them, moving for example between the public worlds of work, school, or university and the intimate spaces of the home. While Rosenwein coined the term for the medieval world, it also seems particularly suited to a democratic and pluralist society. Italy in the 1950s was rapidly becoming such a place; with the rise of migration and the mass media, Italians had to negotiate different influences throughout their day-to-day lives. For a young Italian coming of age in the late 1950s and moving between the sphere of home and family, the weekly ritual of Sunday mass, and peer gatherings at the beach or the piazza, the idea of slipping between or negotiating different overlapping 'emotional communities', each with its own shared values, interests, and emotional styles, seems particularly apt.

We will also see how religion and politics could create their own 'emotional communities', with different values and attitudes to those of mainstream society. Benno Gammerl's idea of 'emotional style' is useful in encouraging us to pay attention to how space and place shape how we experience and express emotions, with different displays of emotion considered appropriate to the home, the courtroom, the workplace, or the piazza.[49] Moving beyond the obvious contrast between the intimate world of home and the public spaces of work and leisure, the economic miracle was also creating new spaces of intimacy and leisure, such as the beach and the car, which according to many sources seemed almost to suggest or permit new behaviour. While the principal focus of this book is on the intimate sphere, Chapters 3 and 4 will also make some suggestions regarding how we might relate 'emotional community' to the nation and indeed to national identity. In the exploration of

---

[47] On 'emotional regimes', see Reddy, *The Navigation of Feeling*; Plamper, 'The History of the Emotions', pp. 242–5. On 'emotional communities', see Barbara H. Rosenwein, 'Worrying About Emotions in History', *American Historical Review*, 107:3 (2002), pp. 821–45 and on emotional styles, see Benno Gammerl, 'Emotional Styles: Concepts and Challenges', *Rethinking History: Special Issue on Emotional Styles*, 16:2 (2012), pp. 161–75.

[48] Barbara H. Rosenwein, 'Worrying about Emotions in History', p. 842.

[49] Benno Gammerl, 'Emotional Styles: Concepts and Challenges'.

jealousy we see how an emotion could give shape and expression to anxieties about gender relations and social change in these years. In this way we might consider the history of the emotions not just as a method for the historian to access private experiences and attitudes but recognize that emotions could sometimes themselves be a crucial element of social and cultural change. There is certainly no doubt that they were key to public conversations about progress, modernity, and nation.

CHAPTER OUTLINE

Chapter 1 will explore how young Italians met and chose their marriage partners, drawing primarily on the evidence from diaries and memoirs. One of the key themes of this chapter is how and why men and women remembered courtship, love, and marriage differently. Men tended to describe strong, open, and definite feelings of love in courtship, while women were much more likely to recount doubt, hesitation, ambivalence, or indifference. Reaching adulthood in post-war Italy had very different meanings for men and women, with men typically leaving home for military service and migration while women were more likely to remain with their families until their wedding. Love, marriage, home, and family thus had different meanings in their lives. While arranged marriages were becoming less common in these decades, the strong role played by family in courtship meant that it was often difficult to distinguish an arranged marriage from one that was not. With the rise of mass culture, men and women also began to measure their own experiences against romantic ideals, often to see them falling short. Experience of illness and disability marked many courtships, especially in the late 1940s and early 1950s, when malaria, tuberculosis, and pneumonia were common. In some cases this proved to be a barrier to marriage, although attitudes were beginning to change in the late 1950s. Class was also crucial in determining suitability, although it was undoubtedly family that was the ultimate arbiter.

Chapter 2 explores intimacy and sexuality in courtship. The ordinary experiences of the diaries and memoirs are set against the (somewhat) differing codes of morality dictated by the Catholic Church, the PCI, and mass culture, so that we can see how people often measured their choices and experiences against their ideas of how a model man or woman should behave. We will also see how the rituals, rules, and surveillance common in upper- and middle-class courtships in the 1950s often left little room for intimacy. Meanwhile, the piazza, a common site of courtship in most towns and cities, was all too often about display rather than real communication. By the late 1950s, the economic boom was beginning to open up new spaces of leisure and intimacy for young Italians, particularly the beach and the car. As couples began to spend more time out of the home together, courtship was becoming both more public and more private, with these new spaces providing more space for intimacy and sexuality, as well as for shared leisure and communication between the sexes.

Chapter 3 is an exploration of southern customs of love, courtship, and marriage. The notion of honour, strong in the southern regions and particularly in Sicily and Calabria at least up to the late 1960s, strongly shaped courtship and marriage. Since family honour was measured by the sexual purity of unmarried daughters, young women's lives were often tightly controlled. Honour crime, elopement, and kidnap marriage were the outward and most extreme signs of these customs and attitudes. In exploring these themes, the second part of the chapter moves away from the diary and memoirs because of the difficulty in finding sources that both write openly about such experiences, and are willing to be published. Film was a medium that was increasingly used to draw attention to such customs, although crime reportage and the courtroom are the real arena of this chapter. The well-known but seldom explored case of Franca Viola forms the core of the chapter's second part. Kidnapped in 1965 with the aim of forcing her into marriage, Franca Viola was the first Sicilian woman to refuse to marry her kidnapper and by implication to have him prosecuted. The trial of Filippo Melodia and his accomplices in 1966 saw competing definitions of love and honour on trial in the Sicilian courtroom, each connected to different ideas of what it meant to be Italian, Sicilian, and modern. Although the trial was a great public victory for Sicilian women, with Melodia found guilty and sentenced to prison, a closer look at the sources suggests that, in private, attitudes were slower to change.

While honour was never directly named in the diaries and memoirs, men and women often spoke of jealousy. Chapter 4 explores how the behaviour and attitudes associated with honour were made more acceptable in the late twentieth century by being repackaged in the emotional language of jealousy, as couples increasingly married for love rather than family reasons. When we widen the lens to look for jealousy rather than honour, we see that in contrast to the media picture, the masculine controlling behaviour associated with jealousy and honour was widespread everywhere in Italy and not just in the south. Indeed, when we turn to the mass media—magazines and film in particular—we get the impression of what might be termed a jealousy epidemic in Italy. This chapter uses a diverse range of sources—from films, magazines, and crime reportage to diaries and memoirs—to trace how people thought about jealousy and how they experienced it in these years. We will see how it was often represented as illness or madness and could also be experienced as such. Indeed, much more than love, jealousy was likely to be described as an intense bodily experience. It was also something that many Italians were keen to distance themselves from and to combat, whether in society at large or in themselves.

Chapter 5 charts experiences of marriage breakdown and attitudes towards separation from the late 1940s to the 1970s. Although divorce was not legal until 1970, legal separations were permitted. This chapter thus makes use of evidence from a case study of legal separations in late 1940s and 1950s Turin and from a smaller sample of diaries and memoirs which provide a broader geographical picture. While many of these writers separated in the 1970s, 1980s, and later, this chapter argues that the roots of breakdown can often be found in the economic miracle years, when the growing media focus on romantic love often did not match up to the reality of married life. Just as women were more likely to be ambivalent about their wedding, they were much more likely than men to ask for a separation or divorce. What we see also in these years is perhaps not simply greater dissatisfaction in marriage, but new languages to comprehend and give shape to it. The idea of marriage for love was key to the divorce campaigns, although the reality was that it was still very difficult for a woman to leave her marriage even up to the 1970s. While we see alternative narratives about love, marriage, and commitment developing from the unofficial culture around the post-war PCI to 1968, this chapter shows how work and feminism often gave women the tools they needed to leave their marriages.

At the heart of the book are intimate experiences and ordinary lives. The evidence amassed, especially in Chapters 3–5, also tells us a little and perhaps even a lot about how Italians were coming to view themselves as a nation. By the 1960s, Italy had cast off the shadow of fascism and begun to project itself as a self-confident, modern country. The Conclusion offers some thoughts on how love, honour, and jealousy were not just personal experiences but part of the national stories that Italians told about themselves, in the effort to forge a modern identity to suit the new Italy of the economic miracle. On the surface the national story was a simple one, connecting the abandonment of honour to the freedom to marry for love and to modernity in general, a quality which would trickle down from the north and the cities to envelop the rural south. A closer look at the connection between love and jealousy reveals the complexities and contradictions in this process, and exposes the regional prejudices implicit in this national story about Italy's path to modernity, this elusive quality which so gripped the public mind in the post-war decades.

1

'Who to Choose?' Finding a Suitable Marriage Partner

I am being fought over by two young men, one 24 years old (and a goldsmith) and the other 22 [...]. The 24 year old is a nice looking boy, and very much in love with me, the other is a labourer and often doesn't even have the price of a cinema ticket. But we love each other very much and couldn't live without seeing each other. What should I do? Who to choose?[1]

This pressing dilemma was described in a letter to 'Francis', the agony aunt of *Grand Hotel* magazine, in July 1955. The gently mocking response was 'the labourer, naturally... or do you want to choose the goldsmith and die?' What is curious though is that while choosing love over financial security seemed like the obvious choice to Francis as it likely does to the twenty-first-century reader, it was by no means so obvious or clear-cut to the anonymous female reader. For a young woman, particularly in rural and provincial Italy prior to the onset of the economic boom, marriage was far too important a decision to be put down to love alone. This chapter is an exploration of how men and women coming of age between the 1950s and the 1970s met and married their partners. Popular culture in the 1950s and 1960s was saturated with romance, from the illustrated *fotoromanzo* (photoromance) magazines like *Grand Hotel* and *Sogno* to the romantic comedies of Dino Comencini and Dino Risi in the cinema. The ideal of the companionate marriage, with its emphasis on companionship, care, and respect, was becoming more accepted in the post-war world. At the same time, although it was changing by the 1960s, marriage was still largely understood as being about beginning a new household and a family, and as such was inevitably shaped by practical and financial considerations as well as by family obligations and pressures. Despite the music they listened to and the films they watched, most young Italians were aware that they needed a lot more than love to make a marriage work.

[1] 'A.C.T', letter to *Grand Hotel*, 23 July 1955.

At the same time, as mass culture became increasingly influential in the 1960s, with rising incomes and consumer spending transforming lifestyles, the disjuncture between romantic ideas and the often mundane reality of how marriages were made was noted in memoirs, particularly those of women. In a world where it was not broadly accepted for women to work outside the household except out of real financial necessity, marriage was not just about romance but about a future home, family, and as a housewife even a 'career' of sorts. In contrast to popular assumptions both then and in the twenty-first century, it was the men who could afford to be the true romantics, and these gendered differences will be a key focus of this chapter.

At the same time the above letter, with its light-hearted yet dramatic tone, probably misrepresents how most Italians thought about love and experienced courtship and marriage. For many couples, love and pragmatism were not at all in opposition; those of similar backgrounds were likely to meet and court, while family approval might even prompt deeper feelings. For most it was not a case of having to choose between feelings and financial security, but of love itself being shaped by the considerations of the wider world that couples inhabited. Many would have experienced no obvious dilemma about whether or not to 'choose love' in marriage, but it is through the detailed picture of courtship and marriage preparation built up in the memoirs that we can see calculations and hesitations informing the complex web of feelings described. The language used to describe love itself was indeed shaped by gender, class, and regional tradition, while decisions about marriage were coloured by the concerns of family, local custom, class, wealth, and health.

In addition, a new marriage was not just about the couple's own feelings. It was a public and social event, involving a wedding celebration as well as the setting up of a new household. The couple's families were usually involved and numerous details, large and small, had to be negotiated and agreed upon. There was often the exchange of a dowry or trousseau, while a new home had to be furnished. An exploration of how couples and their families dealt with and agreed on all of these practical details reveals much about how Italians viewed marriage and family, and how customs and attitudes changed over time. In the midst of so many practical and ritual considerations, the wedding day itself did not always receive much attention in the memoirs and diaries. In the late 1940s and 1950s, and for longer outside the major cities, weddings were usually simple affairs with few guests, and brides were more likely to wear a skirt suit or a simple, colourful dress than to wear a purpose-made white 'wedding dress'. Although women's magazines, from *Grand Hotel* to *Famiglia Cristiana*, carried countless images of the elaborate, white wedding dress that was becoming the ideal in the US and Western Europe, the reality was that most could not have afforded a dress made to be worn on only one occasion. Indeed, the emphasis in many accounts was not so much on the wedding day as on the practical and emotional work of setting up a new household.

Given the emphasis placed on a wedding marking the foundation of a new household and family, there were also some situations when love was not considered enough to sustain an 'unsuitable' courtship. In the late 1940s and 1950s, illness and disability were often considered obstacles to marriage and carried great shame and anxiety for those who considered themselves affected. This was beginning to change by the late 1950s and 1960s as the war became more distant and nutrition improved, although in some regions the stigma of disability was slower to disappear. Even when not an insurmountable obstacle to marriage, serious illness and convalescence were experiences that often shaped relationships in the 1950s and had to be negotiated by the young couple. While family seemed to dominate how young Italians made their choices, broader considerations of class, background, and wealth were important. The ways in which Italians dealt with these obstacles also reveal specific regional patterns. Underpinning all of these factors though are the very different ways in which men and women approached courtship and marriage, and it is to the question of gender that the chapter first turns.

MASCULINITY, COMING OF AGE, AND EMOTION

Writing about their experiences of youth, coming of age, courtship, and marriage, Italian men and women had strikingly different ways of describing how they met and married their partners. While not all men who wrote their memoirs chose to mention marriage, those who did tended to devote ample space to describing both the first meeting with their future wife and the courtship. Declarations of love were frequent, open, and definite in the pages of these memoirs. Walter Ferrarini's simple statement that 'one day I met love, real love', was typical. Born in Modena in 1929, Walter married in 1959.[2] According to his memoir, he met his wife one day while helping to build a new family home. 'One Sunday, I found a girl at my side, she started to help me with my work.—Why are you here? Today is a holiday, you are young, why don't you go dancing? She answered me with a smile—I want to be with you! And so after a year or thereabouts we married.' In Walter's narrative, and in his memory, love was instantly recognizable and the path to marriage easy

---

[2] For example Lido Testi (Arezzo, 1939) wrote of his first impressions of his wife that 'I confess that she gave me sleepless nights' and 'it seemed like the woman had bewitched me, she disrupted my ordinary life so much': 'Una vita tutta sbagliata', MP/02, ADN. Mario Bertini (Florence, 1933) wrote the following, about meeting his future wife: 'And so it was that 1956 arrived, I was 23 and I finally met Her: a pronoun that I write with a capital "I" not as a typing error but as a prelude to the most important name of my life.' Of their first meeting, he wrote 'a real love had sprouted, but what am I saying, *the* love!': 'Oltre la fame "diario d'una vita in quattro stagioni"', MP/02, ADN.

and natural. Women's memoirs tended to be more reticent in their admissions of love, emphasizing instead ambivalence, hesitation, indifference, and sometimes even anxiety and fear in their accounts of courtship and the lead up to the wedding, even when the marriage itself was happy. In contrast to the open and definite statements of many men's memoirs, reading the women's texts often necessitated interpreting gaps, silences, and digressions. Men and women clearly both remembered and constructed very different narratives of love, courtship, and marriage. This chapter explores the reasons why this was so, uncovering the roots of these gendered narratives in both the sharply differing experiences of coming of age in post-war Italy and the ways in which society, the media, and popular culture represented love and marriage.

Italian men are not unique in describing stronger and more definite feelings of love in courtship; Claire Langhamer noted similar disparities between men's and women's accounts of courtship in her work on twentieth-century Britain, as did Simon Szreter and Kate Fisher in their oral histories of English couples who married before the 1960s.[3] These strongly gendered patterns are worthy of attention. It seems particularly noteworthy that the men's narratives of courtship are filled with much stronger declarations of love, when the vast majority of popular romantic fiction and advice literature of the time was directed at women. Curiously, a survey conducted by Catholic sociologists on young people between the ages of 15 and 25 living in and around Milan in the early 1960s drew quite different answers when asking young men and women about their ideal partners.[4] When asked about their future spouse and family, both men and women said that they hoped to marry and have children. The men described their ideal future wife in terms of moral and practical qualities—someone who would be a good wife and mother—and made little mention of either romantic love or physical attraction. The women in contrast generally thought about their ideal relationship in terms of emotions and romantic love; a model much more in keeping with the post-war narrative of the rise of the companionate marriage. The girls were also much more positive about the idea of relationships developing through companionship and mixed gender friendships than were the boys. While we should be cautious about taking such a survey at face value, it is still worth noting that when young people were asked about their aspirations rather than experiences, the gender disparities seemed to be reversed. Women's ideals seemed likely not to match up to the reality of their courtship experiences, while in the case of the men, they became much more romantic when remembering real experiences.

[3] Claire Langhamer, 'Love and Courtship in Mid-twentieth Century England', *Historical Journal*, 50:1 (2007), pp. 173–96; Simon Szreter and Kate Fisher, *Sex Before the Sexual Revolution: Intimate Life in England 1918–1963* (Cambridge, 2010).

[4] Guido Baglioni, *I giovani nella società industriale: Ricerca sociologica condotta in una zona dell'Italia del nord* (Milan, 1962), pp. 93–132.

The ways in which men and women came of age and experienced their young adulthood may offer some answers as to why this was the case. Women tended to marry much younger than men: the average marriage age of the men who wrote diaries or memoirs was 29, whereas for the women it was 23. This disparity reflects the broader national pattern: the average age at first marriage for women dropped from 25 to 24 between 1953 and 1970 while the national average for men fell from 28.9 in 1949 to 28.5 in 1960.[5] It also mattered where one lived in Italy, at least for women: in Sicily and the south the average marriage age for women was closer to 23, while it was higher in the northern regions of Piedmont, Lombardy, Liguria, and the Veneto (between 24 and 26). Bell also shows how the trend for older men to marry younger women was more marked in rural Sicily than in the rural north or the provincial south.[6] It was diminishing with time as individual choice began to play a greater role in marriage. Class, too, was a factor: men of property or status were more likely to marry at an older age but their wives could be much younger women. Nevertheless, the disparities in ages at first marriage do reflect the different experiences of young men and women in upbringing and opportunity in young adulthood, particularly in the 1950s.

Mandatory military service continued under the Italian Republic until 1977, with a minimum period of eighteen months to two years generally being served from the age of 17 or 18. This formed an important life stage for young men; for many it was the first and possibly only opportunity to travel outside their local area. Universal military service was not of course new—it had been introduced at a national level following Italian unification in 1861—however, coupled with migration which did increase after the war, it shaped the typical male coming of age experience as one of leaving home. Before Italy's economic miracle took hold in the late 1950s, seasonal and temporary migration to northern Europe was very common for young men in rural Italy.[7] Migration was generally to Germany, Switzerland, and Belgium. Unlike the later wave of migration to northern Italy, seasonal migration in the 1950s was a movement of young men only. As with military service, it involved living in male only environments for periods of months or years; migrants working in Germany commonly lived in dormitory-style accommodation.[8] There were of

---

[5] *Annuario Statistico Italiano*, 1950–70.

[6] Rudolph M. Bell, *Fate, Honour, Family and Village: Demographic and Cultural Change in Rural Italy Since 1800* (Chicago, 1979), pp. 78–99.

[7] See Paul Ginsborg, *A History of Contemporary Italy: Society and Politics, 1943–1988* (London, 2003), pp. 218–29 and Guido Crainz, *Storia del miracolo economico: Culture, identità, transformazioni* (Rome, 2003), pp. 87–8.

[8] Ulrich Herbert and Karin Hunn, 'Guest Workers and Policy on Guest Workers in the Federal Republic: from the Beginning of Recruitment in 1955 Until Its Halt in 1973', in Hanna Schissler (ed.), *The Miracle Years: A Cultural History of West Germany, 1949–1968* (Princeton, 2001), pp. 187–218.

course some courtships and sexual encounters with local women, but the lack of integration with the local population, including the language barrier, meant that they did not often become lasting relationships.[9] Alvaro, a Tuscan migrant worker in Switzerland in the late 1950s, described in his diary how he felt awkward and ashamed of his rough peasant looks when briefly dancing to a jukebox song with a Swiss girl.[10]

Courtship and love often began to acquire very specific meanings in these contexts, whether deferred or performed by distance and letter. In the memoirs and diaries I examined, love was generally associated with home, nostalgia, and longing, and with the idea of family and community. Alvaro wrote in his diary soon after he arrived that every Sunday afternoon, when he was unsure what to do with his free time, he would experience a profound melancholy, bound up in part with his feelings of nostalgia for home: friends, family, and village.[11] Love might be further connected to the idea of stability during a period of rootlessness. Angelo Pettinari (born 1926, province of Brescia) who spent two years apart from his future wife, first for military service and then a year spent working in Luxembourg, described his reaction to receiving her first letter:

> The steady thought of Piera made her feel so near to me. I still nourished the hope that she returned my love. One day I received her letter. Inside the envelope was a photograph of her in a bathing costume. Faced with such beauty, my eyes began to blur.[12]

He had felt obliged to migrate since work was so difficult to come by at home, and described feeling like a 'stray dog who doesn't know where to go or what to do'. However, their love sustained him through the difficult year in Luxembourg: 'Although life was very hard, the thought of Piera gave me the strength to go on.'[13]

Many of the men's accounts also focused on the visual impact of the first meeting with their future wife. Some, like Vittorio Romani (born 1935, provincial Tuscany and married 1960) focused on the woman's childlike qualities; her innocence and virtue: 'Graziella was a little flower. Slender, with a marvellously clean little face, well mannered, sweet, she seemed like a child to me.'[14] Giobatta Rossi (1926, rural Tuscany) was old enough to serve in the war, describing his sexual adventures in the army as well as his unsettled, itinerant existence in the years immediately afterwards.[15] In 1950, he returned

---

[9] There are at least no examples in any of the memoirs or diaries I examined. Histories of this migration wave also emphasize a lack of integration: see Herbert and Hunn, 'Guest Workers'.
[10] DP/93, ADN. [11] DDP/93, ADN.
[12] Angelo Pettinari, 'Autobiografia', MP/Adn2, ADN.
[13] Angelo Pettinari, 'Autobiografia'.
[14] Vittorio Romani, 'Il racconto della mia vita', MP/00, ADN.
[15] Giobatta Rossi, 'I miei ricordi', MP/Adn2, ADN.

to Tuscany and met his future wife Ines at a dance. He was 24 and she was 18. Of their first meetings, he wrote, 'that little girl of 18 interested me, I had to tutor her, to get to know her better'.[16] These tropes fitted well with the custom for a man to return older and more experienced from his time in military service or working abroad, to marry a younger woman. The custom in much of rural Italy—although this varied by region and class—was also for a man to marry a local woman known to him through family networks or from childhood. Bell's work shows how this was particularly the case in the rural south and Sicily, although it was changing.[17] In the late 1950s in particular, the economic miracle began to transform society and provide new ways for young Italians to meet and interact with each other. Increased access to secondary school education was leading to more mixed gender friendships, while the rise of mass leisure and particularly the beach was providing new opportunities for couples to meet and court.[18] However, even as courtship was changing, older ways of describing attraction and courtship continued to colour the memoirs and diaries of men. Mario Bertini met his future wife in 1956, before he departed for military service.[19] He was 23 and she was 21. Their meeting and courtship seemed to fit with changing patterns; they met through friends on the beach, the site of so many youthful romantic encounters during the boom years. Nevertheless, he described her in childlike terms: 'She was the smallest of the group. She was 21 even though she seemed like a teenager.' He also made reference to her 'eternally childlike smile', further infantilizing her in his memory.[20] Older ways of thinking thus permeated new patterns of courtship and gender relations.

Increasingly, as courtships were formed through meetings in the village piazza and on the beach, the description of the first meeting also focused on physical attraction. Francesco first laid eyes on his future wife in the central piazza of his southern village, after returning from a period of working in the north of Italy in the 1950s.[21] The first encounter with her made a vivid impression on him, retaining in his memory the precise details of how she looked that day, while she was initially hesitant.[22] In 1960s Catania, another memoirist also named Francesco described meeting his wife for the first time on the beach, when he was 32 and she was 18. He was strongly attracted to her although she was reluctant to commit at first.[23] Eventually she relented and they married two years later. These descriptions of first meetings or encounters all describe moments of intense male physical attraction and love,

---

[16] Rossi, 'I miei ricordi'.   [17] Bell, *Fate, Honour, Family and Village*, pp. 89–99.
[18] On secondary school education in the 1950s and 1960s, see Robert Lumley, *States of Emergency: Cultures of Revolt in Italy, 1968–78* (London, 1990), pp. 49–62.
[19] Mario Bertini, 'Oltre la fame: Diario d'una vita in quattro stagioni', MP/02, ADN.
[20] Mario Bertini, 'Oltre la fame'.   [21] MP/02, ADN.   [22] MP/06, ADN.
[23] MP/02. Another very physical description of the author's first meeting with his wife is that of Franco: MP/03, ADN.

concentrated in visual impressions and one decisive instant of knowing. The woman's reluctance or hesitation is a recurring theme in these narratives, whether accurately remembered or moulded to fit cultural assumptions about gendered behaviour. Szreter and Fisher suggest that men more often described strong feelings of love and physical attraction because they were more likely to actively choose their partner, while society expected women to appear reluctant initially in order to be 'won over' and to prove their virtue.[24] This was undoubtedly true in the case of post-war Italian courtship. However, differences between rural and urban Italy as well as between class and region suggest that there may also be deeper Mediterranean cultural traditions of gender, courtship, and romantic love structuring these accounts.

WOMEN'S EXPERIENCES OF COURTSHIP: BETWEEN SELF AND FAMILY

Laura Massini was born in 1930 in the village of Castiglione della Pescaia on the Tuscan coast. She married a local man, celebrating her wedding in 1950. Her courtship blended modernity and tradition in a way that was typical of rural Italian society. She met her future husband through a friend and the three used to go out dancing together. Inspired by film stars and beauty contests, she and her friend took great care to arrange their hair and dress in the latest styles, usually sewing their outfits themselves. From this perspective the courtship was quite a modern one, Laura having freely chosen her suitor. However, Laura's family, and especially her father, also loomed large in her memoir. What follows is her description of her first courtship at the age of 17:

> And I too fell in love with a young man whom I won't name, as I desired to start a family myself since my parents told me that at my age it was time to get settled; since here in my village it would be much more difficult to marry by the age of 20.[25]

The ambivalence she felt is clear from the way her long sentences are structured, each clause being a statement that needed qualification. Laura used similar language when describing the wedding day itself (as shown in Figure 1.1), indicating the strong role that familial obligation played in her decisions:

> You can imagine the happiness as with all the marriages in the world, I awaited that day with pleasure not least so that I could give my parents some relief from

---

[24] Szreter and Fisher, *Sex Before the Sexual Revolution*, p. 183.
[25] Laura Massini, 'Domani è un altro giorno', MP/91, ADN, p. 25.

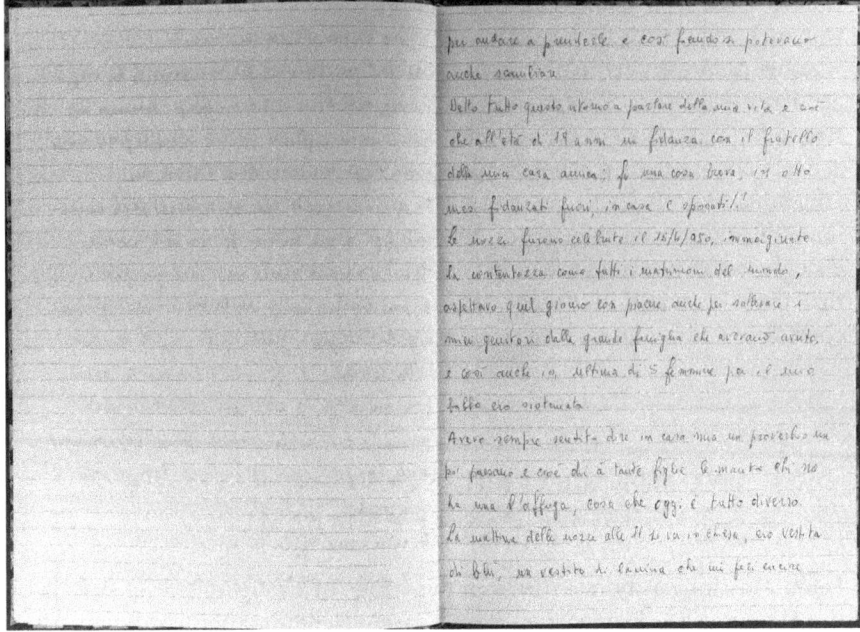

Figure 1.1. Page from memoir of Laura Massini, describing her wedding.
Archivio Diaristico Nazionale.

their large family, and so it was that I the last of five children, was settled as far
as my father was concerned. I always heard this country proverb at home: that
is that whoever had many daughters should have them married and whoever
was left with no husband should be drowned, something that is completely
different today.[26]

Despite the fact that Laura chose her husband and courted him on the dance
floor rather than in the home, it is her sense of obligation towards family and
her father's relief at her marriage that dominate her description of the wedding. Laura lived in rural Tuscany, one of Italy's traditional sharecropping
regions, where a strong patriarchal family structure was prevalent.[27] The
importance of father and family in guiding such life decisions could reflect
these regional family patterns.

It was also difficult in both social and economic terms to be an unmarried
woman anywhere in post-war Italy but especially in rural society. A survey

---

[26] Laura Massini, 'Domani è un altro giorno', p. 31.
[27] On the social and family structure of the *mezzdria* system, see Perry Wilson, *Peasant
Women and Politics in Fascist Italy: The Massaie Rurali* (London, 2002), pp. 7–29; Ginsborg,
History of Contemporary Italy, pp. 23–8; and Leo Goretti, '"Un posto che gl'andava a morire":
Genere e generazioni nella fine della mezzadria in Toscana', *Zapruder*, 26 (2011), pp. 44–58.

carried out by a team of sociologists in and around Milan in the 1960s, found that while the idea of marrying for convenience rather than love was becoming much less acceptable to young women, there was still a slightly higher tolerance for such arrangements in the smaller towns around Milan than in the city itself.[28] In rural Italy, there were fewer partners to choose from and work opportunities for women were more scarce, usually leaving marriage as the only 'career option'. Therefore, as the survey suggested, women could not always afford to be idealistic about marriage. Fear of spinsterhood was strong. The advice columns of the popular magazines from the period tell a similar story although the reactions of agony aunts did differ. Signora Quickly, the fictional persona of *Grazia*'s agony aunt, advised her largely urban and middle-class women readers that when in doubt, they should always choose marriage; for an unmarried woman, any husband was better than none.[29] Letters from women entering into or considering marriages at very young ages frequently appeared in the pages of *Grand Hotel* magazine, famed for its illustrated love stories and circulated more widely in rural Italy, and the pressure these young women described to marry young in order not to be regarded as spinsters seemed quite real.[30] Generally these readers were advised not to marry in haste for fear that they might regret it afterwards. Agony aunt Wanda's reply to 'sad Mari' in August 1955 expressed outrage that at 20 she would be considered a spinster in her village, and reassurance that outside her village this age was not considered old.[31] Seventeen-year-old Laura Massini evidently perceived and internalized a similar pressure from both her family and community, despite the fact that hers had the outward appearance of a modern courtship based on friendship and feeling.

This sense of pressure and the uneasiness Laura must have felt was never put directly into words, but expressed in the underlying structure of the text. The courtship was described in a short, factual sentence; engaged at 19, Laura was married eight months later. A long digression in the text followed before Laura described her wedding day. Details of the wedding itself were scant, but were followed by an extremely rich and detailed picture of the practical work of setting up home as newly-weds. The bride and groom both wore blue in a simple church ceremony. There were no flowers or photographs, and the only

---

[28] Guido Baglioni, *I giovani nella societa industriale.* pp. 116–18.

[29] Penny Morris, 'A Window on the Private Sphere: Advice Columns, Marriage, and the Evolving Family in 1950s Italy', *The Italianist*, 27:2 (2007), pp. 304–32. On the interwar origins of *Grazia* see also Patrizia de Landi, '"La rivista ideale della donna italiana": I primi passi di "Grazia" tra innovazione e informazone', in Raffaelle de Berti and Irene Piazzoni (eds), *Forme e modelli del rotocalco italiano tra fascismo e guerra* (Milan, 2009), pp. 235–303.

[30] Anna Bravo, *Il fotoromanzo* (Bologna, 2003); Niamh Cullen, 'Changing Landscapes of the Emotions? *Grand Hotel* and Representations of Love and Courtship', *Cultural and Social History*, 11:2 (2014), pp. 285–306.

[31] Reply to 'Mari triste', *Grand Hotel*, 20 August 1955.

guests present were the witnesses and family; a simple lunch was served afterwards at her family home. There were no attempts to describe her feelings for her husband or their relationship as newly-weds. The gaps and the silences in Laura's text—as well as the curious way in which she saw her own happiness only in terms of her parents' relief—point to her possible ambivalence at the way in which the marriage came about. She also repeatedly referred to 'sistemazione', which could mean 'convenience' or 'being settled' in marriage, although it did not directly imply that her own was a marriage of convenience. Neither is there any suggestion that she did marry freely or out of love; nothing in her account directly alludes to this possibility. Although there are scant details of their courtship, Laura did make reference to the love that she and her husband shared in the course of their marriage. The doll that her husband (who is never named) bought as a birthday present in their first year of marriage was an indication that 'from the first moment he understood me', and she was persuaded to migrate with him temporarily in 1955, leaving their daughter behind, because her 'love for [her] husband was strong'.[32] Indeed, it seems anachronistic to attempt to judge whether Laura married for love or out of obligation; her memoir shows that she understood marriage in different terms, and that both elements could complement rather than contradict each other. Claire Langhamer's work on courtship in mid-century England indicates that marriage was usually not a clear-cut choice between pragmatism or love; rather, 'suitability' could itself suggest and encourage stronger emotions.[33] However, Laura's memoir of her courtship and marriage does suggest that women, even entering into marriage freely and out of love, might experience and approach it differently under such strong family and community pressures to marry and 'settle down'.

The way in which Laura described her courtship and marriage fits with the memoirs of other rural women marrying in the early 1950s, before the onset of the economic boom and the deep social changes it brought. She did not directly express any dissatisfaction or unhappiness and wrote freely of her love for her husband. However, the gaps, silences, hesitations, and qualifications in her text convey an ambivalence and perhaps a feeling of a lack of agency that she did not articulate openly either at the time or even decades later when writing her memoir at the age of 58. The other memoirs share a sense of ambivalence towards their marriage that was never directly named. As with Laura's memoir, any ambivalence was firmly qualified by their love for their husbands, but only in the context of marriage. They did not remember or describe the giddy certainty or excitement of 'falling in love' during their courtship. Amalia Molinelli (born 1928, province of Piacenza) was a rural

---

[32] Laura Massini, 'Domani è un altro giorno', p. 29 and p. 44.
[33] Langhamer, *The English in Love*, pp. 61–90. Similar findings are described in Szreter and Fisher, *Sex Before the Sexual Revolution*, pp. 165–95.

woman who, as we saw in the Introduction, wrote candidly of her great fear of going to live with her husband's family who were sharecropping farmers. Despite her professed love for her husband, this fear entirely overshadowed her wedding day. It was traditional in sharecropping communities of northern and central Italy for the extended family to live together and for the daughters-in-law to join her husband's household.[34] Strife between mother and daughter-in-law was familiar and frequent enough to make it a common trope in local folk culture.[35] Amalia's memoir points to the significance of marriage in the life of a young rural woman; it was not just about choosing a partner but a new family, home, and household. Typically the daughter-in-law would also contribute her work to farm and household; in this way her marriage might determine her lifelong occupation.[36] Her love for her husband might therefore be balanced with a very real apprehension about her future life.

Marriage as a way of escaping from parents and family was also a common theme in the women's memoirs. In rural Italy up to the 1950s it was common for girls to leave school at 8 or 9, while their male counterparts typically graduated at 10 or 11; even attending middle school was the preserve of the few. While in the north and centre of Italy rural girls might have left home to work in domestic service, this was seen as a temporary phase and undertaken to save up for marriage. In Sicily and Calabria, poorer women might go into domestic service in order to save up for their trousseau. At the same time any family who could afford the luxury of it confined their unmarried daughters to the home out of concern for their modesty, the cloistered female life becoming a mark of class distinction.[37] Single women did not generally migrate alone and it was considered shameful for a woman to spend time away from the family home or even to go out very much alone.[38] Particularly in middle-class families, such as that of Sicilian Maria Lamonica who struggled to attend secondary school against her parents' wishes, it could be considered a mark of social status for a woman not to work, become educated, or learn a trade.[39] The letters page of *Grand Hotel* highlighted this issue in 1955, carrying letters from two young rural women who desperately wanted to find work despite

---

[34] Perry Willson, *Peasant Women and Politics*, pp. 7–29; Agopik Manoukian, 'La familia dei contadina', in Piero Melograni (ed.), *La famiglia italiana dall'ottocento a oggi* (Rome, 1988), pp. 3–6, 49–51.

[35] See Roberto Leydi, *Canti popolari italiani* (Milan, 1984).

[36] Agopik Manoukian, 'La familia dei contadina', pp. 51–3.

[37] Jane and Peter Schneider, *Festival of the Poor: Fertility Decline and the Ideology of Class in Sicily 1860–1980* (Tucson, AZ, 1996), pp. 106–8.

[38] Simonetta Piccone Stella, *Ragazze del sud: Famiglie, flglie, studentesse in una città meridionale* (Rome, 1979); Charlotte Gower Chapman, *Milocca: A Sicilian Village* (London, 1973); Linda Reeder, *Widows in White: Migration and the Transformation of Rural Italian Women, Sicily, 1880–1920* (Toronto, 2003).

[39] Maria Lamonica, 'In un piccolo centro di provincia', ADN MP/03.

having few marketable skills.[40] Their situations prompted agony aunt Wanda Bontà to reflect on the dangers of insisting that girls leave school early to be cared for at home until marriage; should they not marry, how would they get by after their parents' deaths?

Even for those who attained a secondary school or university education, career options could be extremely limited. In such circumstances, marriage might be seen as the best or even the only viable option for leaving the family home and establishing an independent adult life. Sara Martinelli (born 1930, Florence) was married in 1953 to Gabriello, a man from the town of Arezzo, whom she had met while she was evacuated there as a child during the war.[41] In her memoir she recounted that Gabriello had pursued her and although she hesitated, reluctant to be tied down, she agreed to become engaged to him.

> That morning I woke up very confused; I had gone out on a whim, never imagining the consequences and I found myself *fidanzato* [engaged] the next morning to a boy who was seven years older than me, and whom I barely knew. I felt like I was too deeply involved, almost oppressed, and I understood that this was something that weighed down on me, despite the distance and the need to get to know each other.[42]

Although she resolved almost immediately to call off the engagement, even writing a letter to Gabriello, her mother talked her out of sending it and the relationship endured. Describing the courtship she continually referred to his love for her and her inability to end their engagement due to family and social pressure. Taking into account all his good qualities, 'it was difficult not to feel almost obliged to love him'.[43] However, as her parents' marital problems worsened, the difficult circumstances at home led her to accept the impending marriage as a way of escaping her family and beginning an independent adult life. Writing in the 1990s, Sara described their marriage as a happy one, although she still spoke in terms of her husband's enduring love for her rather than her feelings for him. In all of these memoirs of marriage in the early 1950s, the writers were careful to put references to family pressures, fears about marriage, or even wishing to marry to escape family life, in the context of love and a happy marriage. For them, marriage was for life; therefore love and contentment had to be an intrinsic part of the narrative.

---

[40] Letters from 'Giuseppina' and 'Lonely soul' to Wanda Bontà, *Grand Hotel*, September 1955.

[41] Sara Martinelli Polvani, 'Io, Sara', MP/02, ADN. See also the memoir of Vilma Prarizzi, who married at 21. Although later in the text she professed her love for her husband, the wedding was described simply as what people did then, and the only way to escape parental control: 'Diario di Vilma', MP/06, ADN. *Fidanzato* corresponds roughly to the English term fiancé although the formality of the relationship it describes can also depend on context and region. It generally implies that the relationship is serious and marriage expected, although there does not always have to be an official agreement.

[42] Sara Martinelli Polvani, 'Io, Sara'.   [43] Sara Martinelli Polvani, 'Io, Sara'.

Those who married later in the decade, or in the 1960s, were in contrast more likely to openly describe discontent, coercion, or indifference in their accounts of courtship, engagement, and the decision to marry. Birgitte Søland, in her large-scale study of working-class women's autobiography in Denmark, found that the texts written by women born in the late nineteenth century in conditions of poverty and hardship were unlikely to express regret or discontent about the way their lives had turned out.[44] Those born from the early twentieth century onwards, as living standards were beginning to improve, were more gloomy in contrast, focusing on constraints and missed opportunities. As conditions improved, the women writers were more aware of the opportunities they might have had and resentful when their own circumstances did not match. A similar pattern can be detected in the Italian women's memoirs of courtship and marriage: as the economic miracle began to transform society through popular culture and the media as well as new spaces of leisure, education, and work, the memoirists were more aware of how their own lives did not measure up to the ideal they now expected.

Marriage as a means of escaping parents and the family home was a continued theme in the memoirs. However, unlike in earlier texts, those marrying in the late 1950s and 1960s did not feel the need to soften this admission by stressing love or subsequent happiness. Lidia Musso (born 1934, Savona) married her childhood sweetheart, Lino.[45] Theirs was love at first sight, according to the memoir: they met when she was 16 and a secondary school student and she described their early courtship in terms of physical attraction and romantic love. He was referred to in these early passages simply as '*Amore*' with a capital A. However, as time went on, Lidia was less attracted to Lino and began to see her relationship with him at least in retrospect as closing down opportunities that she might have taken in life. Describing the chances that she did not take, Lidia repeated the word 'mistakenly'. The couple married when Lidia was 21, and in her memoir it was described as inevitable. Considering they had been together for so long, marriage was the natural next step in their lives. Her motivation to marry was framed more in terms of her eagerness to begin her adult life than in terms of her feelings for Lino: 'We were tired, especially me, of living like this [apart, and she with her family] and after so many years of being *fidanzati* we wanted to be together completely.'[46]

---

[44] Birgitte Søland, 'Employment and Enjoyment: Female Coming-of-age Experience in Denmark, 1880s to 1930s', in Mary Jo Maynes, Birgitte Soland, and Christina Benningham (eds), *Secret Gardens, Satanic Mills: Placing Girls in European History, 1750–1950* (Bloomington, IN, 2005), pp. 254–68.

[45] Lidia Musso, 'Il mio diario 1934–1955', MP/10, ADN. Germana also entered into an unhappy marriage at 18, motivated by the desire to escape her parents, and ending in divorce: MP/88, ADN.

[46] Lidia Musso, 'Il mio diario 1934–1955', MP/10, ADN.

Adriana Libutti Pedacci (born 1937, province of Livorno) met her husband Roberto at the age of 21.[47] She was by then a university student in Rome living with her parents, and resented the fact that she had not been not allowed to leave home to study elsewhere. Describing her decision to marry Roberto, she stressed that she did not love him and neither was his proposal a romantic one. The decision to marry was based rather on the fact that they both had similar goals and desires for their lives. According to her memoir, Adriana was also strongly motivated by a desire to get away from her mother. By marrying so young, and not finishing her university degree, Adriana was also making a gesture of rebellion against her parents. She acknowledged that even at the time she was aware that she was probably making a mistake.

In contrast, several memoirs describe marriages that were much more clearly arranged by the family and in the family interest; the women described themselves as unwilling in their memoirs although they may not all have articulated this at the time. Lauretta Cavinato (born 1938, province of Padania) was coerced into getting engaged to the brother of her sister's husband. He was apparently very taken with her and considered a good prospect by her family since he had a job at FIAT in Turin.[48] Her memoir described how she was set against marrying him, although it is unclear whether she voiced her feelings fully at the time. She had other boyfriends previously and she also 'had her own idea of her ideal man'. This man 'was not her type but was a serious man, the type whom mothers liked. It was not that he was a bad person I saw him as a man and I was still a girl even though at my age I was also full of dreams and hopes of finding a man I liked.'[49] They carried out a long-distance relationship for three years, corresponding with each other even though Lauretta only saw it as a way of 'expressing [herself] and knowing that there was someone else who was thinking of her'. They did not see each other very frequently during that time and she 'understood that he wasn't important to her, but she couldn't find a way of ending the relationship'.[50] When she tried to leave him by letter it only hastened the marriage preparations, and even though she 'prayed to the Madonna to give her the strength not to go through with it', everything went according to plan.[51] What seems particularly evident from her words is that she had an idea of how marriage and romantic love would be linked and thus resented the reality of how her marriage happened. It also appears that she never felt able to openly articulate her feelings and instead actively continued the courtship through her

[47] Adriana Libutti Pedacci, 'Diario di Tania', MP/99, ADN.
[48] Lauretta Cavinato, 'Cocco e il fratello', ADN MP/02. Assunta Papalia (1943, Reggio Calabria) also described being coerced into marriage with her deceased sister's fiancé. She described herself as being indifferent towards him although they did marry after several years, when Assunta was 18. See 'Diario di piccolo ricordi', MP/09, ADN.
[49] Lauretta Cavinato, 'Cocco e il fratello'.   [50] Lauretta Cavinato, 'Cocco e il fratello'.
[51] Lauretta Cavinato, 'Cocco e il fratello'.

correspondence with her husband. Her experience complicates the definition of an arranged or forced marriage.

Amalia Molinelli's fear of married life in rural Italy was probably not given voice until she compiled her memoir decades later. As it turned out, she and her husband only lived with his family for several more years before moving to Milan in the late 1950s, where they started their own family. By that time, the idea that a woman would refuse to marry a peasant so as to ensure a better life for herself away from the land, was one that was firmly anchored in the popular imagination. A young rural man remarked on Italian television in 1963: 'The girls aren't interested in peasants. They go to the factory, they put on some lipstick and they're gone.'[52] By this stage the notion was so commonplace that the interviewer used it as a leading question to elicit comments like the one above. It is also one that has been repeated many times in academic texts as well as in popular culture; from the sociologies of the early 1960s to more recent histories of rural Italy, women, migration, and social change, without much questioning of the original source.[53] There is little evidence, apart from quotations from local rural men mainly in Piedmont and Tuscany, to support these claims. Nuto Revelli was convinced from his oral histories of rural Piedmont that it was local women who were driving migration to the cities, encouraged by their mothers and grandmothers who wanted them to live different lives to theirs. The problem was such that a matchmaking service had begun to arrange marriages between northern peasants and rural southern women because of the lack of marriageable local women.[54] However, even the details of this scheme raise questions about the simple conclusion that 'girls didn't want to marry peasants'; it was mainly older bachelors rather than young men who availed of the scheme, so it may not tell us much about courtship in the 1950s.

In 1956, the bestselling Catholic magazine *Famiglia Cristiana* published a letter in its advice column from a reader with the pseudonym 'country girl'.[55] A sub-heading asked the question, 'Is it right that the country girl is humiliated and valued less than the others?' The letter outlined the position of the 'humble country girl who works the land' who felt mocked and humiliated by 'those who go to work in the city'. 'They tell me that nowadays it is not the good and honest girls who do well, but the ones who know how to enjoy

---

[52] Quoted in Elisa Danese, 'Costumi sessuali e genere femminile nell'Italia degli anni sessanta: Inchieste cinematografiche e televisive', *Storia e futuro*, 13 (2007), p. 13.

[53] For contemporary mentions, see Guido Baglioni, *I giovani nella società industriale*; Don Lorenzo Milani, *Esperienze pastorali*, (Florence, 1957), as well as the countless letters on this subject and short stories warning of the dangers of women and the city in *Grand Hotel*. For recent academic texts that repeat this notion, see Perry Willson, *Women in Twentieth Century Italy* (London, 2009); Stefano Gallo, *Senza attraversare le frontiere: Le migrazioni interne dall'Unità a oggi* (Rome, 2012).

[54] Nuto Revelli, *L'anello forte: La donna: storie di vita contadina* (Turin, 1985), pp. xxxvii–xl.

[55] Letter from 'La ragazza di campagna' to Padre Atanasio, *Famiglia Cristiana*, 22 July 1956.

themselves, deceive and be modern.'[56] Although she wanted to stay on the land, she was unsure what to do as her beloved rural way of life was so undervalued in a changing Italy. Followed by a lengthy response defending her position and reminding readers that 'life on the land is commonly regarded as the most healthy both morally and physically', the letter reads now as a fairly obvious fabrication.[57] Responding to the same perception that there was an exodus of young women from the land in search of a 'modern' and morally unsound life in the city, it was a reminder to young readers of the Church's position on migration for women in particular. These endlessly repeated assumptions—and coded warnings—that women were driving migration because they did not want to marry peasants tell us as much about marriage and migration as do the leading questions of television presenters and the melodramatic stories in *Grand Hotel* warning readers about the dangers of the city for young women. They provide some insight into popular anxieties about the ways that migration and the boom were changing Italy, particularly when it came to gender roles and relations. However, the memoirs show that women's own motivations, emotions, decisions, and experiences were more complex than this and were more closely bound to local and familial concerns—and sometimes strategies—than to any overarching desire to leave the land for an urban life of leisure and consumption.

The women's descriptions of courtship and marriage also give some insights into the reasons why romantic feelings were not always centre stage when they thought about courtship and made decisions about marriage. Of course there were some who did write openly and in detail about love in their courtship. Neither, as we have seen particularly in the memoirs of marriages beginning in the early 1950s, were pragmatic concerns in any way incompatible with love, affection, or companionship. However, the hesitation and reluctance articulated both openly and in coded terms, as well as the indifference and dissatisfaction described by others, points to the reality for women that despite what they might read in magazines or see in films, marriage in the 1950s and 1960s was about much more than love. It was almost always bound up with the concerns of family, whether the burden of supporting an unmarried adult daughter, the desire to strengthen family or community bonds, or to improve the family's social status through marriage. Family and community pressure could encourage the growth of love as in the earlier memoirs. However, as society began to change in the late 1950s, the popular culture promise of romantic love could also work against such local and familial interests, with varying social and psychological consequences. Dissatisfaction or indifference did not always lead a woman to directly oppose her family's wishes, as many of the memoirs demonstrate. Particularly in the 1950s and early 1960s, such

---

[56] Letter from 'La ragazza di campagna'.
[57] Padre Atanasio response to 'La Ragazza di campagna', *Famiglia Cristiana*, 22 July 1956.

feelings might be internalized at the time of the marriage and expressed only years later. Lauretta Cavinato summarized her courtship with the words 'marriage in 1960 because everyone has to get settled'.[58] This note of resignation reflects the general acceptance that marriage was not just about the couple; it was ultimately about setting up a new household and beginning a family. For women these concerns were particularly important since they were expected to depend on their husbands for financial security; they were aware that romantic love alone would not be enough. Economic and practical considerations were a part of every courtship, whether stated directly or merely implied, and no matter how strong the couple's feelings for each other.

THE ECONOMICS OF MARRIAGE: DOWRY, TROUSSEAU, AND THE NEW HOUSEHOLD

If the wedding was just the first, decisive step towards establishing a new household and family unit, what kind of practical and financial responsibilities were involved and for whom? Dowries were on the decline in post-war Italy, and seldom mentioned in the memoirs and diaries. In the memoir of Alda Maria Dei (born 1930 to a middle-class Florentine family), the dowry was only notable by its absence.[59] In her boyfriend's first meeting with her father to formalize their engagement, she noted that since there was no dowry to speak of, they discussed regulations for when the couple were allowed to see each other. Here the dowry was mentioned in an offhand manner; its absence was no real issue but the idea was present nevertheless. Sometimes it could still be a very real point of contention.

Anna Maria (born in the early 1930s in Bergamo to a Neapolitan family) recounted in her memoir that her first love, whom she met while they were both secondary school students, left her because she did not have a dowry.[60] Even though they had an immediate connection, pragmatic concerns meant that it was not to be. Unusually in this case, it was the couple themselves who discussed Anna Maria's lack of a dowry together and the relationship petered out over the following months.[61] Sixteen-year-old Graziella Pezzino (born Catania, 1943) was much more indignant about being courted, or not, only for her dowry. Writing in her diary in 1959, she reflected on how she had been courted by a young army lieutenant.[62] The couple went out dancing several times and Graziella was beginning to develop feelings for him.

> I liked him well enough and to hurry things along I said that I would say yes to him if he spoke to my parents first. First he went to speak to an acquaintance of

---

[58] Lauretta Cavinato, 'Cocco e il fratello'. [59] Alda Maria Dei, 'Graffitti', MP/03, ADN.
[60] MP/88, ADN. [61] MP/88, ADN. [62] Graziella Pezzino, 'Il mio diario', DP/86.

ours telling him that he liked me and asking if my father would have given me a
house in dowry when I married. Luckily we do not actually own any property so
it's better that he stays away because I would never marry anyone who only
wanted me for a house.[63]

On the cusp of the 1960s and as marriage became associated with romantic
love and with equal partnership, the dowry seemed increasingly out of place in
Sicilian society.

Even in the wealthy and mostly southern families where dowries were still
exchanged, they were coming to be viewed in more negative terms.[64] The diary
of Giovanna Cavallo (born 1931, Calabria) noted that her Tuscan fiancé was
indignant at her father's offer of a dowry, since it was not his intention to
marry her for money. In his letter to her he wrote that, 'all of these things smell
of the market and are ruining the beauty and poetry of marriage for me'.[65]
Giovanna had to explain to him that in Calabria it was a matter of family
honour and pride to provide a dowry and that a refusal would offend her
family. Here the differing views on dowries were not just an indication of
changing social norms but also of clashing regional styles. We might note at
the same time that the examples from the diaries and memoirs all bring up the
dowry as a point of contention. If the dowry was only noted in these terms, it
might have actually have been in much more frequent use, but such a normal
part of the wedding rituals that it was not usually worthy of remark. This may
have been true for wealthy families in particular, although overall it certainly
seems as though customs and attitudes were changing.

More widespread than the dowry was the *corredo*, which corresponds best
with the trousseau; this was a collection of mainly household linens that the
bride brought with her to set up a household with her new husband. It was
mentioned in passing or in detail by many more couples. It seems that while
the dowry was on the decline, the *corredo* was still central to marriage in many
Italian regions up to the 1960s. What it contained and how it was assembled
varied by region and class. Donald Pitkin observed that in 1950s south-central
Italy, sheets formed the traditional core of the *corredo*, while it was also
expected by then that the bride would provide furniture, kitchen items, and

---

[63] Graziella Pezzino, 'Il mio diario'.

[64] Twenty per cent of couples who married in one Sicilian town in 1880 and 26 per cent of
those who married in 1890 registered the dowry with a local notary. See Jane Schneider,
'Trousseau As Treasure: Some Contradictions of Late Nineteenth Century Change in Sicily', in
Eric B. Ross (ed.), *Beyond the Myths of Culture: Essays in Cultural Materialism* (New York,
1980), pp. 323–56, 326–7. They usually consisted of either a house or a small piece of land.
The work of John Davis suggests that the dowry was still exchanged by many couples in the
town of Pisticci, in Basilicata, up to the 1960s: *Land and Family in Pisticci* (London, 1973),
pp. 39–41 and 87–90.

[65] Giovanna Cavallo, *Ho sognato i suoi occhi* (Milan, 1996), p. 321. A copy is the diary is also
conserved at the ADN.

sometimes a dining set.[66] From his fieldwork in Lazio, he found that the absolute minimum *corredo* was six sheets and their supporting linens, while most brides brought twelve and wealthy families might bring fifty or even up to a hundred. The average cost of a *corredo* was, he estimated, a little more than the annual income of an agricultural worker. The amount of time it took to assemble all the necessary items often determined the length of a couple's engagement.[67] In poorer peasant families it was not uncommon for the bride herself to work as a domestic servant in order to earn enough for her *corredo*. Indeed, the letter of a 'poor girl' from a large family who wrote to *Oggi* magazine seeking the help of readers since she lacked the resources to assemble her *corredo* herself, indicates just how important the *corredo* was to marriage in the 1950s (see Figure 1.2). While appealing to a magazine for help was certainly an inventive strategy, it was altogether more usual for the family to pitch together in order to provide a girl with the necessary materials for marriage.[68] While mother and daughter did the sewing work, father and brothers laboured to buy the consumer goods and linens. In nineteenth-century rural Sicily, and perhaps also more widely, it was usual for sons not to marry until the daughters had celebrated their weddings.[69]

Pitkin maintains that it was not possible to separate dowry neatly from *corredo*, as by the 1950s the *corredo* included expensive furniture items if not property. Schneider argues in a similar vein that in Sicily the trousseau of richly embroidered linens increased in both symbolic and material value in the mid-nineteenth century, just as a dowry consisting of property was becoming more rare and confined to wealthy families.[70] Up to the 1950s and 1960s—when commercially available goods gradually began to replace them—the Sicilian trousseau consisted of a 'letto' or bed: an elaborate display of embroidered linen bed coverings. While the core items of the 'letto' were sheets and pillowcases, it might typically include lingerie, tablecloths, napkins, and towels.[71] Both Pitkin and Schneider report that a trousseau of some form was necessary for marriage at least up to the 1950s; no woman married 'with nothing'.[72] Local religious charities often took on the responsibility of 'dowering' poor girls so that they could marry, again indicating the absolute necessity of bringing some form of *corredo* to the marriage.[73]

[66] Donald Pitkin, 'Marital Property Considerations Among Peasants: An Italian Example', *Anthropological Quarterly*, 33:1 (1961), pp. 33–9; p. 36.

[67] Pitkin, 'Marital Property Considerations Among Peasants', pp. 35–7.

[68] Jane and Peter Schneider, *Festival of the Poor*, pp. 106–8.

[69] Schneider, 'Trousseau as Treasure', p. 325.

[70] See Schneider, 'Trousseau as Treasure'.

[71] Schneider, 'Trousseau as Treasure', p. 123.

[72] Pitkin, 'Marital Property Considerations Among Peasants', p. 36; Jane and Peter Schneider, *Festival of the Poor*, p. 107.

[73] Jane and Peter Schneider, *Festival of the Poor*, pp. 133–4.

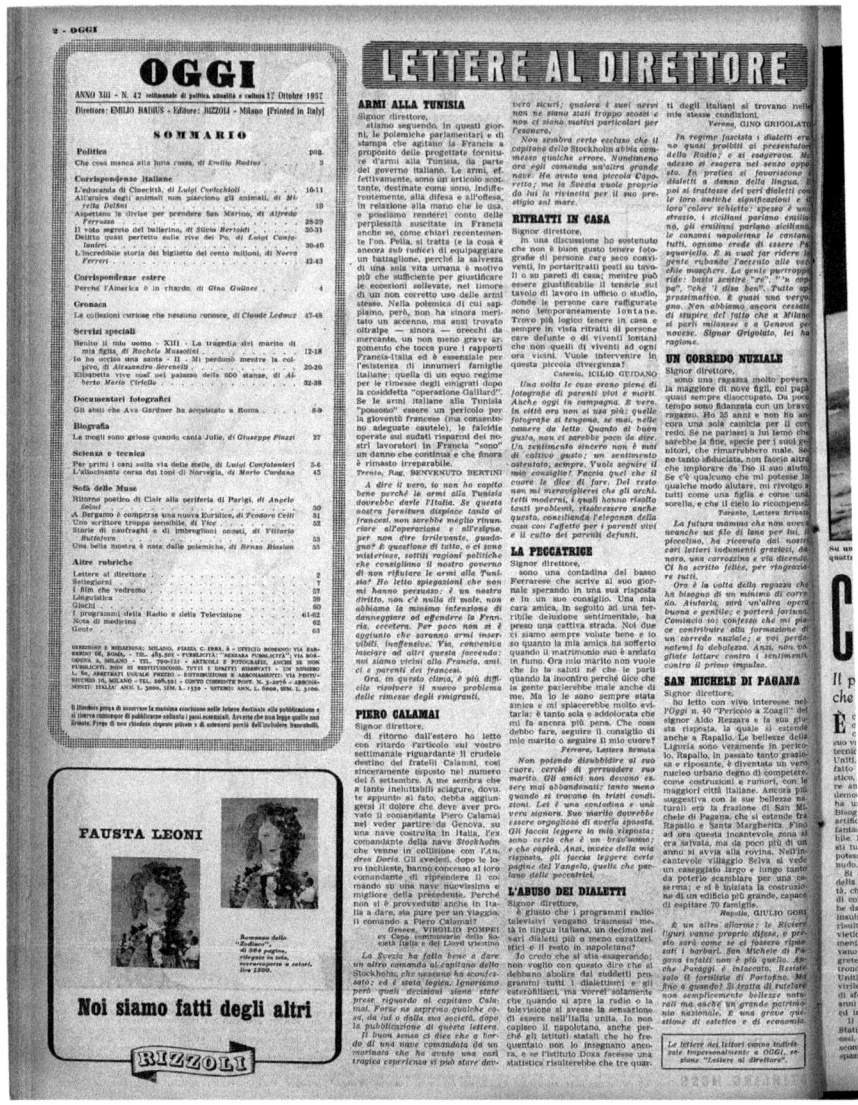

Figure 1.2. The importance of the *corredo* in getting married. A letter from a 'poor girl' who lacked the resources to put together her *corredo*, asking the readers of *Oggi* magazine for their help.

Oggi, 17 October 1957. Biblioteca Nazionale Centrale di Roma.

In Lazio, the trousseau was gathered and displayed at the bride's house in the week leading up to the wedding, while in Sicily it was traditional for each item to be valued and priced by an appraiser on the eve of the ceremony.[74] A record of the contents of the trousseau—itemized and valued, and sometimes notarized—would typically be retained by both families.[75] These rituals further reinforce the social place of the trousseau; a certain minimum was necessary for marriage while extra consumer items such as a dinner set, a collection of particularly fine linens, or very elaborate embroidery work were a further mark of social worth. While the embroidered linen trousseaus of Sicily seemed like a time-honoured tradition, Schneider suggests the custom was only widely adopted from the mid-nineteenth century, when it became a mark of status and upward mobility to keep mothers and daughters out of agricultural or domestic work, thus leaving them with the time to dedicate to elaborate and laborious needlework.[76] In middle-class southern families, it was often seen as the mother's responsibility to provide her daughter with her trousseau. Schneider describes how the mothers of upwardly mobile peasant families dedicated their energies to embroidering their daughters' trousseaus, seeing it as a matter of family pride and social competition.[77] Indeed, Maria Lamonica, born in Sicily to a provincial middle-class family in 1942 and growing up in the late 1950s, recalled how she was not allowed to help with the work of her own *corredo* as her mother considered it her duty to provide it.[78] The preparation of the *corredo* was clearly the province of the women of the family, and the skills of needlework and crochet was a form of knowledge passed between mothers and daughters across the generations, so that the linens must have had an emotional as well as a material significance.

The *corredo* was not just a southern practice, nor a rural tradition; a diarist from the Veneto mentioned working on her *corredo* in the early 1950s, while several Tuscan diarists and memoirists also referred to it. Neither was there any class distinction about whether the bride herself or her family should prepare the *corredo*, outside the south. Luisa Rebecca (born 1933 to a wealthy family in the Veneto) asked her father to provide her with the necessary linens so that she could embroider them herself; Alda Maria Dei (born 1930 to a lower-middle-class family in Florence) also wrote of working on her *corredo*.[79] In addition, it seems to have been the custom for a young woman to work on the *corredo* as a matter of course, even before she seriously

---

[74] Schneider, 'Trousseau as Treasure', pp. 327–8.

[75] See 'Nota di corredo, 1925', in Anna Maria Restaino and Noemi Montagnoli, 'Il Corredo della sposa. Valore e tradizione', *Basilicata Regione Notizie*, 123–4 (2010), pp. 116–33, 130.

[76] Schneider, 'Trousseau as Treasure'.

[77] Jane and Peter Schneider, *Festival of the Poor*, p. 104.

[78] Maria Lamonica, 'In un piccolo centro di provincia'.

[79] Luisa Rebecca, '29 Aprile, giovedì', DP/96, ADN; Alda Maria Dei, 'Graffitti'.

considered becoming engaged.[80] In 1950s Lazio, Settimio knew that his future wife was responsible and industrious because she worked on her *corredo* every evening.[81] Laura Massini, who married in 1950 in rural Tuscany, listed in meticulous detail the *corredo* that she brought to her marriage; a blue cotton bed cover, four sheets, four pillowcases, one dishcloth, six towels, two night-dresses, and twelve nappies.[82] A bed, along with some other furniture, was ordered from the nearby town by Laura's husband to complete the furnishing of their first one-room home. She too is likely to have assembled the *corredo* herself. She and her husband did not have a home of their own directly following the wedding since he was unemployed and forced to migrate soon afterwards. Her unusually detailed catalogue of what she brought to the marriage thus gives us some sense of the minimum material costs of setting up home in post-war rural Tuscany.

Even when the dowry and *corredo* were not mentioned, it is clear that families often played an important role in supporting the couple in their new life. Some of the women's memoirs mentioned parents arranging the wedding celebration, in both practical and financial details. There was a strong regional and class dimension to this practice; both Maria Prinzivalli and Carmela were from middle-class southern families and passively accepted marriages that seemed to be arranged in every sense of the word.[83] Some couples expected and depended on some form of parental assistance. In Lidia Musso's case (born 1934, to a middle-class Ligurian family), her parents paid for the wedding and her mother-in-law promised to pay half the cost of the couple's new home, although in the end this never happened.[84] Her parents also paid to furnish the kitchen and bedroom of their apartment, while the couple furnished the rest of the home themselves over time. From Lidia's account, there was a clear expectation that both sets of parents should have been assisting the couple in establishing their new married life. Sara Polvani Martinelli's parents were unable to pay for her wedding, and as a result it took place in her husband's hometown of Arezzo, rather than in Florence where her family lived.[85] This was noted in her memoir because it was unusual, as was the fact that the financial assistance promised by Lidia Musso's mother-in-law never actually arrived. We might assume from this that it was common for the couple to receive help from either or both sets of parents for the cost of the wedding and setting up home, but in most cases not remark-able enough to be noted. Class may also have played a part; in both cases where the expectation of assistance was mentioned, the women came from relatively comfortable middle-class families. Other memoirs stressed the need

---

[80] Pitkin, 'Marital Property Considerations Among Peasants', p. 36.   [81] ADN MP/90.
[82] Laura Massini, 'Domani è un altro giorno'.
[83] Maria Prinzivalli, 'Come vapori al sole…', MP/01; Carmela, MP/98, ADN.
[84] Lidia Musso, 'Il mio diario dal 1934–1955'.   [85] Sara Polvani Martinelli, 'Io Sara'.

to save or make personal sacrifices in order to marry as they could not rely on parental support.[86]

The question of where to live as a newly married couple was equally pressing. The advice columns of popular magazines were filled with letters addressing the question of whether the couple should live with their parents or asking for advice on conflict, particularly between mother and daughter-in-law.[87] These letters were always answered with the firm advice that the couple should live in a home of their own and not with the extended family, as such arrangements inevitably led to conflict. The magazines treated the issue as one of changing norms regarding family and marriage in the 1950s and 1960s, ignoring the regional dimension to such living arrangements. Although it seems as if middle-class southern women were more likely to have their parents arrange all the details of the wedding for them, including the *corredo*, the dowry if there was one, and potentially even the husband, it was northern and central Italians who were more likely to live with their in-laws as a married couple. This fits with the traditional settlement patterns of sharecropping families in the rural northern and central regions, where it was usual for the extended family to live together in one household and to work the land, with married sons bringing their wives to live in the parental home. In the rural south it was more typical for each nuclear family to have a separate house, with the extended family living nearby. In traditional folk music from the northern sharecropping regions, the relationship between mother and daughter-in-law was a recurring theme, with some songs being sung to ward against any potential conflict between the older and younger woman who would now live under the same roof, indicating how it was a normal part of rural life, if not one without tension.[88] In the case of Maria Guerrini (born 1934 in rural Tuscany), this was accepted as the natural course of events following her marriage in 1962.[89] Even in the case of urban couples in Tuscany and Emilia-Romagna, married life with the in-laws was happily accepted. Franco brought his wife to live in the family home in Bologna after their marriage in 1957.[90] However, the house was adapted so that each couple had their own independent living spaces, perhaps as a nod to changing notions of marriage and family. In this case as in others, the decision to live with the husband's family was framed in terms of the need to care for ageing parents.

---

[86] Giobatta Rossi, 'I miei ricordi', MP/Adn2; Francesco Baldassi, 'Il ritorno', MP/04, ADN.

[87] For example, a 30-year-old woman wrote to *Grand Hotel* asking for advice about conflict with her father-in-law over listening to the radio, 17 June 1950. *Grazia* featured a letter from 'Alba' who had received an annulment because of her mother-in-law's insufferable behaviour, 27 May 1950. Letters describing similar conflicts both major and minor were frequent in both magazines.

[88] Roberto Leydi, *Canti popolari italiani* (Milan, 1973).

[89] Maria Guerrini, *I miei ricordi—6 gennaio 1999*, MP/T2, ADN.

[90] ADN MP/03. See also Alda Maria Dei, 'Graffitti'.

However, the fact that most examples are found in the sharecropping regions of the centre-north indicates that traditional rural patterns of family life were also being mapped on to a changing urban society.

Living with the in-laws did in some cases lead to real tension. Lauretta Cavinato (born 1938, Veneto) went to live with her in-laws in Turin following her marriage in 1960, but tensions between the younger and older couples meant that the arrangement did not last.[91] Both Lauretta and her husband worked, and when her parents-in-law demanded that she give her full salary to them, the couple decided to find a place to live by themselves. Although rural living patterns did persist in urban society, Lauretta's case shows how changing gender roles, as well as changing attitudes to work, leisure, and family, were putting pressure on them. However, her story is also an example of the rural family's adaptability in changing circumstances. We saw how Lauretta's marriage was strongly encouraged by her parents because of her fiancé's solid employment prospects. The rural family was clearly not just being prised apart by migration, but was able to use the changing society of the miracle years to serve the interests of its members, securing a marriage that promised both security and social status.

STRUGGLING WITH OBSTACLES TO LOVE

Mothers and fathers were strangely absent from the story of Patrizia and Roberto, but their situation is yet another indication of how love might be perceived not to be enough when it came to setting up a new household and starting a family. Patrizia met Roberto, a film director, when he was shooting on location near her home outside Rome. They fell in love and the relationship quickly intensified, until Patrizia realized that she had a brain lesion which would almost certainly drive her mad and eventually kill her. Determined to keep the illness a secret from Roberto so that he would not feel obliged to marry and care for her, she fled Rome with no warning. Roberto continued to search for her for months afterwards until the couple were finally reunited. This melodramatic story of tragic, thwarted love was serialized over many months in *Grand Hotel* in 1955.[92] It is just one example of a very popular plot line in the magazine in the late 1940s and early 1950s; illness, disability, or disfigurement as a potential barrier to true love. Sometimes these plot lines might be linked to the war, as in the story of Paolo who was so disfigured as a result of war injury that he begged his friend Guido to tell his fiancée that he

---

[91] Lauretta Cavinato, 'Cocco e il fratello'.
[92] 'Ai Confini dell'amore', *Grand Hotel*, 1955.

had died in combat.[93] In other 1950s plot lines it might be a scar or other disfigurement acquired as the result of a childhood accident, or simply a vague, unnamed illness.[94] Such a plot device neatly suited the magazine's need for heightened emotions, the course of true love derailed by tragic misunderstanding, while protecting the protagonists' purity of intentions. However, it also reflected quite real concerns and experiences in Italy between the war and the onset of the economic miracle.

The letters pages in *Grand Hotel* alone indicated as much. Letters from young men and women who were either terrified to tell their boyfriend or girlfriend about an illness or disability for fear that it would end the courtship, were worried that they would never find a partner, or were afraid to commit so as not to be a burden, were very frequent in the late 1940s and the first half of the 1950s. It is not surprising that in a society so recently ravaged by war— both the fascist colonial wars and the Nazi occupation and civil war—that disability and disfigurement should have been common concerns when it came to courtship.[95] Illness too—especially in childhood—was common in both peasant and working-class society where, until the economic miracle began to bring better living conditions in the late 1950s, malnutrition was frequent as were diseases such as pneumonia, malaria, and tuberculosis.[96] The agony aunts generally called for openness and understanding when it came to illness and disability, indicating a shift in attitudes. 'Melancholic Mimma' was advised in April 1947 by *Grand Hotel*'s 'Francis' to believe her fiancé (presumably when he told her he would stay with her despite her unnamed disability) and to behave as if she was physically normal, since she had already overcome her 'physical defect'.[97] It seems, though, that in keeping with the tone of the magazine's melodramatic fiction, many still chose to deal with such issues through secrecy and personal sacrifice, renouncing love in order not to be a burden.

Letters and plot lines about disability and illness were on the wane in the late 1950s and had almost disappeared by the 1960s, indicating that as living conditions improved and war became more distant, such concerns were no longer as common as they had been. Perhaps as they became less pressing issues, prejudice against illness and disability also lessened and there was no longer such a need for concern and secrecy. Whether disability was accepted or not in a marriage partner may also be an indication of the changing purpose

[93] 'L'escluso', *Grand Hotel*, 5 April 1947.

[94] 'Vicenda vissuta', *Grand Hotel*, 25 November 1950; 'L'Adorabile sconosciuta', *Grand Hotel*, 2 April 1955.

[95] The parliamentary inquiry into poverty begun in 1951 highlighted the difficult conditions of life in post-war Italy for much of the population. See Paolo Braghin (ed.), *Inchiesta sulla miseria in Italia* (Turin, 1978).

[96] On childhood mortality in rural Italy see Bell, *Fate, Honour, Family*, pp. 54–65.

[97] *Grand Hotel*, 5 April 1947.

of marriage. In the context of marriage being about a household and a family as much as the couple, with the husband as economic provider and the wife as child bearer, disability might well be a concern for the couple or their families. However, if as *Grand Hotel* argued, it was simply about romantic love, then should love not conquer all?

Memoirs provide further insight into how people dealt with illness and disability as part of a couple. Several women described the difficulties of being married to a war veteran in 1950s rural Tuscany, their husbands unable to work or to find employment due to illness or disability.[98] Yet others described how courtship might be punctuated by a long illness. Both Sara Polvani Martinelli (Florence, 1930) and Lidia Musso (Savona, 1934) mentioned that their fiancés were very ill and had to spend long periods of time away recuperating.[99] Lidia Musso found that the several years her fiancé spent away recovering from an unnamed illness changed her attitude towards him, intensifying her feelings towards him at first but eventually creating a distance between them. The distance was never fully repaired even when they married.[100] Sara Polvani Martinelli's fiancé Gabriello became ill with pneumonia and had to spend a long period away convalescing before their marriage in 1950.[101] In two years she rarely saw Gabriello, who was first working in another nearby town and then in a convalescent home. While he was ill, she was only able to communicate with him by writing and sending magazines. In the meantime she herself was working as a skilled dressmaker in Florence. In both of these cases, illness did not seem to pose any real barrier to marriage although it shaped the way in which courtship was experienced, forcing the couple to articulate their feelings at a distance and through letters.

However, in other cases the prejudices and fears that were hinted at in the pages of *Grand Hotel* were reflected in individual experiences. Vittorio Marianini (1933, province of Pisa) was in love with a local girl at the age of 16 but her family disapproved of the relationship partly because of his ill health. As a result, they stopped seeing each other.[102] In the case of Amato Varini and Stefano, it was they themselves who saw their illness as a barrier to love.[103] Stefano suffered from chronic illness in his early adulthood and was exempted from military service because of poor health. Born into a Tuscan peasant family, he was working in Florence in the late 1940s when he was hospitalized for appendicitis and spent many months afterwards recuperating. During that time he was corresponding with a girl from his home village and hoped there might be something deeper than just friendship between them. He dared not tell her about his feelings though, since he was afraid that he was

[98] Laura Massini, 'Domani è un altro giorno' and Livrearia Soldi, 'Diario', MP/85, ADN.
[99] Sara Polvani Martinelli, 'Io, Sara'; Lidia Musso, 'Il mio diario'.
[100] Lidia Musso, 'Il mio diario'.   [101] Sara Polvani Martinelli, 'Io, Sara'.
[102] MP/92, ADN.   [103] Amato Varini, 'La storia di uno di noi', MP/07; MG/Adn2, ADN.

gravely ill and might not be able to work again.[104] Amato Varini (Modena, 1936) described in his memoir how he decided to break up with his girlfriend, despite the fact that they both loved each other, because of both his ill health and the class difference between them. He spent four months at home gravely ill with influenza during the Asian flu pandemic of 1956, and during that time was in dread of not being able to work again to support his family. He communicated with his girlfriend through weekly letters, ashamed of allowing her to visit his humble family home, and when he recovered he met her one final time to tell her of his decision to end the courtship. The illness in this case seems to have deepened Amato Varini's feelings of shame about his family's lower social status and his belief that he could not make her happy, leading him, in his view, to sacrifice his own happiness for hers. Both Varini's and Stefano's reservations about marriage were related to work. The urge to sacrifice their own happiness so as not to burden their loved one may also have been predominantly a male experience since men were expected to be the main economic providers in a marriage.

In several of these examples, considerations of class intersected with shame or prejudice regarding illness. They point to the fact that marriage was not just about family but about community, and that class considerations were both deeply rooted and sharply defined in rural Italy. Laura Massini's first relationship had ended after sixteen months together because of class differences. Her boyfriend was a bank clerk and his parents didn't want him to marry a peasant.[105] Aware of her low social status as a peasant in post-war Italy, Laura's response was one of resignation. 'And so I had no doubts: I knew that sooner or later it would all be finished and it was, therefore my life had to begin all over again.'[106] In 1950s Tuscany, Mario told his girlfriend that he could not marry her as he was of a lower social class than she and had nothing to offer her.[107] Although her family was also opposed to the marriage, it was Mario who made the decision to end the courtship.

Amato Varini, whose illness had brought the class differences between himself and his girlfriend into sharper focus, described his decision to end the courtship in similar terms. He was acutely aware of the difference in status between his peasant background and her family's more elevated artisan status. During the months of illness and convalescence, his girlfriend continually asked to visit him. He refused, ashamed to let her see him so physically reduced and in his humble, disordered family home; an attic apartment in a working-class district. Her family in contrast were wealthy artisans, the first to build a villa after the war. His reduced earnings and the dependency caused by

---

[104] MG/Adn2, ADN.   [105] Laura Massini, 'Domani è un altro giorno', p. 25.
[106] Massini, 'Domani è un altro giorno', p. 25. See also Maria Blengino, 'I Santarè', MP/07, ADN.
[107] MP/99; see also Lido Testi, 'Una vita tutta sbagliata', MP/02, ADN.

his illness accentuated fears about being able to provide properly for her. Neighbourhood gossip thus confirmed his own anxiety:

> Through relatives of mine who lived in the same town, I came to know that my fiancée's parents were not happy about our relationship, because given my financial situation I would never be able to make her happy and therefore it would be better if I left her.[108]

The way in which both he and his fiancée responded to the finality of his decision is perhaps equally telling:

> When I told her that because of my family situation I would never be able to make her happy because I really was a poor wretch and her parents were right to tell her these things, she at this point burst into tears, I on the other hand felt such anguish that I was sure my chest would burst from the pain, we embraced each other and exchanged many long passionate kisses, when the train came we separated with sorrow and a goodbye.[109]

Even though the couple clearly felt great sadness at their parting, neither of them resisted it in any way. Once the decision was made, family and economic security were recognized as insurmountable barriers to marriage. Both sadly accepted that love was simply not enough. In fact, in each of the cases described, there is no mention of any challenge to the notion of class as a barrier to marriage; resignation rather than resistance was rather the dominant theme in each narrative. The narrators were also open and definite in naming class as the barrier between the couple. These findings fit with other studies; Claire Langhamer in her work on courtship in mid-century Britain described a similar sense of resignation and acceptance of class differences as an obstacle to marriage.[110]

This was one area in which the differences in emotional codes and vocabularies between the north and centre and the south of Italy became much clearer. With the exception of Amato Varini, who lived in Campania, all of the above examples were drawn from northern and central Italy, where society offered no way of accepting such relationships. However, in Sicily and Calabria there were distinct codes and traditions for speaking about or acting in matters of romantic love. The concept of honour also allowed for a couple to flee together to force the families to accept the marriage; once the woman's reputation had been destroyed by spending time alone with the man, the families had no choice but to accept the situation and bless the marriage.[111] These extreme solutions were not always, or even often, employed; however, their very existence points towards a different way of shaping vocabularies and

---

[108] Amato Varini, 'Storia di uno di noi'.   [109] Amato Varini, 'Storia di uno di noi'.
[110] Langhamer, *English in Love*, pp. 74–87.
[111] Bell, *Fate, Honour, Family*, pp. 91–2; Chapman, *Milocca*, pp. 94–6.

narratives of love. In some cases the 'elopement' also masked coercion. The complex entanglement of love and honour and the darker forces with which they often blended, will be the subject of Chapter 3.

The memoir of Carmela shows how even when an elopement was not mentioned or employed, it could shape the way in which love was experienced and felt. Carmela, born in rural Sicily in 1930, centred her memoir around the great love affair of her adolescence whom her parents forced apart.[112] A school companion of hers, she described the boy in heightened terms as her great love, blessed and beautiful. She married another man in the late 1950s, from whom she later separated. The marriage was arranged by Carmela's family and she described it in terms of a forced marriage; her whole memoir was structured by what she termed the tragedy of her marriage.[113] The end result in this situation was similar to that of many of the northern and central Italians who were parted because of class differences, but the language that described the emotions surrounding it was very different. The language of romantic love in this case offered a way of framing the situation; however, it was a much older Sicilian tradition that Carmela was drawing on rather than the modern ideal of companionate marriage.

Southern folk culture offers some further insights into how people coped with thwarted love or being forced to accept a loveless marriage. Since the custom of forced and arranged marriages took longer to die out in the southern provinces than elsewhere in Italy, this was likely a pressing issue for many men and women. Ethnologist Ernesto De Martino carried out extensive research on what he described as southern magical culture in the 1950s. Examining magical practices and magical beliefs within their social context, he surmised that magic gave people a way of living with the negative aspects of their lives that could not be controlled.[114] Magic allowed them to act out through ritual, feelings that were suppressed in ordinary life, offering an outlet for expression when actual circumstances could not be changed. Women were more likely to use magic rituals and potions to attract a man because they had less social power in matters of courtship than men. Magic also had a very powerful role in dealing with thwarted or forbidden love. A woman who destroyed her wedding dress while in a sleepwalking state or *fascinazione*, which might translate as a spell or possession, was acting out her feelings of opposition to the marriage in a—marginally—socially acceptable manner.[115] The *fascinazione* allowed her to make a symbolic protest without refusing the marriage; the social order was thus maintained.

De Martino also linked the *taranto*—a ritualized dance that simulated hysterical and sometimes sexual behaviour—to the repression of women's

[112] MP/88, ADN.   [113] MP/88, ADN.
[114] Ernesto De Martino, *Sud e magia* (Milan, 2012), first edition 1959.
[115] De Martino, *Sud e magia*, p. 21–7.

sexuality in southern Catholic and patriarchal culture.[116] Performed only in the Salento region at Italy's south-eastern tip and linked to the local cult of St Paul, the dance was performed by women on certain feast days. It consisted of what seemed like uncontrolled, hysterical movement leading into what could be several days of energetic dancing. The dancing of the *taranto* had often been linked to frustrated adolescent love, the dance offering the women a channel for the expression of repressed feelings.[117] The case of Maria was a classic illustration; De Martino reconstructed her story through interviews with both Maria herself and her family. She fell in love at 18 but the man's family opposed the marriage because she was poor; sometime after this she became a *tarantata*. She was then obliged to marry another man against her wishes, and described how St Paul visited her and 'forced her to dance for nine days'.[118] While she accepted the marriage, she repeated the ritual dance regularly throughout the year. It seemed that magic belief and ritual could provide a socially acceptable outlet for repressed emotions. Yet despite the appearance of inhibition and erotic charge, such rituals actually reinforced the highly restrictive gender codes of the rural south. Chapter 3 will show how in a somewhat similar manner, the notion of a courtship developed through fleeting, meaningful glances in southern communities where men and women could not easily get to know each other, allowed exaggerated or semi-imagined emotions to be codified as love. This southern tradition of love, with its heightened passions, dependence on both the male gaze and woman's virtuous distance, and the ever-present threat of elopement or kidnap, constitute a distinct regional understanding of courtship and emotion. Unlike magic and ritual dance, the trope of the 'love through glances' did sometimes allow couples to break free of these constraints by means of an elopement, although the initiative and the power still tended to rest firmly with men.

CONCLUSION

Renate Siebert in her sociology of Calabrian women remarked that the women born in the 1930s were on the threshold between 'choice and obligation' when they married in the 1950s.[119] This is an observation that could apply to almost all of the women, and indeed the men, whose texts are mentioned above. It is

---

[116] De Martino, *La terra del rimorso* (Milan, 1961). For a discussion of De Martino's work on the *taranto* see also David Forgacs, *Italy's Margins: Social Exclusion and Nation Formation since 1861* (Cambridge, 2013), pp. 173–90.

[117] Forgacs, *Italy's Margins*, p. 197.   [118] Forgacs, *Italy's Margins*, pp. 180.

[119] Renate Siebert, *È femmina però è bella: Tre generazioni di donne al sud* (Turin, 1991), p. 85.

in the interplay between obligation and agency, emotion and restraint, whether in the narrative recounted or even in the structure of the texts themselves, that we can see how choices, possibilities, responsibilities, and roles were negotiated in the memoirs of courtship. Above all we see that family played a crucial role in women's experiences of courtship and coming of age in particular throughout this period, although the women's responses to family pressure did change over time.

The women's coming of age was almost always experienced above all in the home, while for men it was structured by the act of leaving home. This goes some way towards explaining the different ways in which gender structured emotion in the first-person texts; men might associate love with a longing for home or even the idea of family and stability if their lives were marked by transience. For them, courtship was usually very much bound up with highly visual first impressions of their future wife, and with strong emotional declarations. Intense expressions of love tended to be rare in the women's accounts. In contrast they were more likely to be concerned with the practical details of courtship and the new home; whether fears about living with the in-laws, details of the *corredo* and the new home, or the need to escape the parental home. The details given in some diaries and memoirs about dowries, the *corredo*, and the living arrangements of the newly-wed couple give some further insight into the pragmatic, economic, and familial concerns that surrounded each courtship and wedding, whether or not the marriage was one of individual choice and love.

However, the fact that some memoirs and diaries emphasized feelings such as fear or anxiety, or practical details over emotions, did not necessarily signal an absence of love in a marriage. Instead, love was understood in different ways and had different meanings in the lives of many of the narrators. While the men's accounts emphasized love and passion in courtship, the women's accounts of the early 1950s tended to speak of love or at least contentment in the context of the marriage that followed. As the decade wore on, women began to measure their marriages up more closely to the idea of romantic love and sometimes found that they did not match. The texts that mention illness also chart how attitudes towards disability as well as love were changing over the course of the post-war period.

However, it is through a closer study of class differences and parental opposition in courtship, that we can see a pattern of different regional understandings of love emerge. Here it becomes clear that the southern tradition of a secret love cultivated through glances was very different in character to the modern ideal of a companionate marriage based on romantic love, even though the two were often conflated in popular culture, whether film or romantic magazines such as *Grand Hotel*. The fact that it is still strong in memoirs of courtship written in much later years as well as in nationally available magazines such as *Grand Hotel* raises further questions: how did these regional understandings of love inform national ideas about love in Italy and about 'Italian lovers', particularly when migration was bringing Italy into ever greater contact with the south in the 1960s? This thread will be picked up again in Chapter 3 in order to examine the darker side of these regional traditions of passionate love and elopement. But first, Chapter 2 will turn to the experiences of courting couples, examining how they negotiated intimacy, sexuality, communication, and love before the wedding took place.

2

'Forgive Me, Love…It Was Stronger than I am': Negotiating Intimacy and Sexuality

> Formerly, I could choose whether to be with you of an afternoon, or not. Now, on the other hand, I have felt that in these months I could not choose anymore, that I had to come to you without any escape, there to your home, because I had jolly well made my choice, once and for all. I had to do what everyone was expecting of me, what you along with the others expected of me. So, I have taken to driving my thoughts underground.[1]

This speech which Tommaso made to Elsa—the protagonists of Natalia Ginzburg's 1961 novella *The Voices in the Evening*—marked the end to their short engagement. The novella was a short and savage critique of the mores and marriage customs of middle- and upper-class provincial northern society. Elsa, a 27-year-old university graduate, lived with her parents and secretly saw her boyfriend Tommaso, the son of a wealthy local industrial family, twice weekly in the nearby city. There, free from the stultifying atmosphere of the village and the prying eyes of the community, they conducted an intimate relationship of companionship and sex, going for coffee and visiting the library while also spending time privately together in a rented room. It was when they made the decision to become formally engaged and involve their families, setting in motion the complex set of bourgeois marriage rituals from the exchange of rings and wedding preparations to the trousseau and furnishing the new home, that their intimacy and companionship became suffocated. Time that was previously spent freely together was now formally regulated by the rules of respectable courtship, with regular visits in Elsa's family home under the silent, watchful eye of her unmarried aunt. Their love for each other drowned under the weight of family and convention, the couple eventually decided not to marry after all. Ginzburg's presentation of provincial courtship is particularly bleak, but it chimes in some respects

[1] Natalia Ginzburg, *Voices in the Evening* (London, 1963), p. 155, Italian edition 1961.

with memoirs of the 1950s, when class snobbery might combine with family obligations, rules, and conventions to make courtship a stultifying rather than a joyful experience.

These patterns of course varied greatly depending on region and class, and society in the 1950s was never quite as static or as conventional as it is usually portrayed. Although the 1960s brought the greatest and most lasting changes, the war had already disrupted traditional codes of gender, sexuality, and courtship. Many memoirs mention interruptions to courtship in the mid to late 1940s, whether through active military service, displacement, or separation from family. The presence of partisans and both German and Allied occupiers also brought about disruptions to sexual and gender norms. Those who were not old enough to experience the war for themselves often recounted particular episodes or rumours absorbed in childhood. Underneath the apparent respectability of the 1950s lurked the shadow of the sexual violence and the disruption of war. Of course, in Italy as across Europe, the conservative social climate of the 1950s, with its emphasis on family, normality, and respectability, was itself a response to the war which had so starkly exposed the fragility of the family.[2] This pattern was again disrupted during the economic miracle as migration and urbanization diminished family surveillance. Mass culture, in the form of *fotoromanzo* magazines, cinema, and television, also brought new ways of thinking about intimacy and sexuality while often simultaneously reinforcing existing ones. Mass consumption also transformed intimacy; as cars grew more affordable with the arrival of the new FIAT 500 in 1957, they offered new, private spaces for couples away from the eyes of family and community. Moving out of the domestic sphere, courtship became increasingly a 'private act conducted in the public world'.[3] Throughout this time religious codes of morality were certainly present in many people's minds. Communism was also strong at the local level in the northern and central regions, structuring the way in which PCI members may have thought about family, gender, and sexuality, although it was never as much in conflict with Catholic values as it was perceived to be. However, as the 'rules' of courtship became less set, young men and women had to tread a more complex path between informality, sexual liberty, and respectability; reconciling their own values with the new freedoms offered and balancing the expectations of peers with those of family and with their own religious and political values.

---

[2] On the broader European context see Richard Bessell and Dirk Schumann (eds), *Life After Death: Approaches to the Social and Cultural History of Europe during the 1940s and 1950s* (Cambridge, 2003) and Dagmar Herzog, *Sex After Fascism: Memory and Morality in Twentieth Century Germany* (Princeton, NJ, 2007).

[3] Beth Bailey, *From Front Porch to Back Seat: Courtship in Twentieth Century America* (Baltimore, MD, 1988), p. 3.

FAMILY, *FIDANZATI*, AND THE 'RULES OF ENGAGEMENT'

The memoirs of middle-class courtship in the 1950s were those most likely to describe the kind of rigid template for engagement against which Tommaso revolted. Once the engagement was made official, the *fidanzati* or engaged couple would be allowed to see each other several times a week according to a strict timetable. This might include dinner with their families, or an evening at home under the watchful eye of older relatives, but there was often also a place for trips to the cinema, the dance hall, or a *passeggiata* (afternoon stroll), where the local community replaced family surveillance. It was the family who set the tone and pace for the couple's engagement, although over the course of the decade this pattern was changing.

The 'declaration of love' is a good illustration of how the level of formality in courtship was changing from the early 1950s to the years of the economic miracle. The declaration was traditionally an important part of the courtship ritual, whereby the young man officially declared his love for his intended and asked her to become his *fidanzata* or fiancée. This usually happened before he spoke to her family in order to formalize their engagement, and in regions where unmarried men and women were not meant to meet and socialize, the declaration was often supposed to be secret. However, by the 1950s, the declaration was increasingly seen as outdated and unnecessary. In a roundtable interview with a group of Milanese teenagers published in *Tempo* magazine in 1959, the question was posed whether a woman could declare herself to a man or whether it always had to be the man who took the initiative.[4] The answers from the group in fact dismissed the notion of the declaration altogether, broadly agreeing that neither partner needed to make his or her intentions formally known. Instead the relationship should simply evolve at its own pace. However, a look at the advice columns of the 1950s reveals that not everyone found these changes in expressing and understanding romantic love quite so easy to grasp. A *Grazia* reader wrote a letter in 1955 under the pseudonym of 'Laura who waits', describing how she waited expectantly for a declaration from the 'indecisive lover' with whom she flirted in mass.[5] In 1955 'Anxious Maura' kissed a boy and then treated him coldly as he did not make the formal declaration of love that she expected; *Grand Hotel*'s agony aunts told her she was being unreasonable to expect this and should simply tell him her feelings.[6] 'Rondinella' was, however, given very different advice in the same magazine that autumn. Indignant that her boyfriend had left her, the response given by agony aunt

---

[4] Dino Origlia, 'I giovani e l'amore', *Tempo*, 23 June 1959.
[5] 'L'innamorato indeciso (Laura che attende)', *Grazia*, 15 June 1955.
[6] Letter from 'Maura ansiosa', 12 March 1955.

'Francis' (Mario Macciò) was that the seriousness of the man's actions all depended on whether he had already made the formal declaration of love to her.[7] If he had not done so, then the relationship had not yet become serious and he was within his rights to leave her for somebody else. No wonder young Italians might have been confused. The declaration gave the man a chance to vocalize his feelings of love in a ritual, formalized manner, while it was also a statement of his intentions towards the woman, setting in motion the steps to make a formal engagement leading to marriage. As emotions and intimacies became increasingly disentangled from the formal rituals of engagement, rigid gender roles began to ease and courtship became more informal and liberated, especially for women, but these changes also brought uncertainty. The declaration made expectations very clear: it was up to the man to make it while the woman simply waited and then decided whether or not to accept. The path from that point onwards was also clearly laid out. As these rituals were abandoned, the codes of expectation were becoming more difficult to read.

The diaries and memoirs which mention making or receiving a declaration all date from the 1950s, indicating that it was falling into disuse by the 1960s. In 1950s Campania, Francesco did make a formal declaration on first meeting his future wife. In their case the declaration, which they kept secret from their families for quite some time, served the important function of allowing their long relationship to begin.[8] This seemed particularly important in southern society where gender roles were more rigid and courtship more formal. Vittorio Romani (Arezzo, Tuscany, 1932), who began his relationship with Carla in 1952, described how they dated openly for some time and were known locally as a couple before the question of the declaration arose. Content to kiss at first, Romani began to want more sexually from Carla. She told him:

'Steady on, first you have to ask me to be your fiancée and then we'll see.' My world fell down around me. 'But how come, are we not already *fidanzati*? Hold on!'

You have to understand these were different times. I was obliged to make a true and proper declaration of love, with the ritual formula 'Would you like to be my fiancée?'

The response was yes, but not straight away. Such a strategy was necessary in love as in war and Carla was a master of it.[9]

In this case, the declaration could be used as a negotiating tool; formal commitment in exchange for greater sexual intimacy. Even though the declaration could only be made by a man, it could be requested by the woman, giving her some power over him. However, in contrast to Francesco's experience, it was not required to begin the relationship. Romani himself

---

[7] Letter from 'Rondinella pellegrina', 27 August 1955.   [8] MP/06, ADN.
[9] Vittorio Romani, *Viaggio nella memoria*, MP/00, ADN.

evidently thought it unnecessary and somewhat archaic; he saw the words he pronounced to Carla as formulaic and outdated and did not feel that the ritual did much to change the reality of their relationship. Both men were courting in the 1950s and came from middle-class professional backgrounds; the primary difference in their understanding of the declaration seems to be regional.

A minor character in Ginsburg's *Voices in the Evening* made a declaration of love, followed by a hasty marriage 'for fear of changing his mind', showing that by the early 1960s the declaration was often seen in ironic terms, a perform-ance intended to will certain feelings into being, rather than to give expression to them.[10] Several diaries and memoirs mentioned the declaration in similarly playful or less serious tones. Aldo Mariotti (province of Siena, 1932) made the declaration to several girls in his teens, but never meant it seriously. He did it, in his own words, 'to try it' and 'to try out the emotion'.[11] The sentiment of the declaration was intended to be so formal and serious, that it could be 'tried on' at will; a performance more than an expression of feeling. We see something similar happening in the teenage diary of Anna Soprani (Forlì, Romagna, 1939), who described her correspondence with Antonio, a soldier stationed overseas, from 1953 to 1954 during her early teens.[12] In January 1953 she received quite a formal and heartfelt letter from Antonio, and hoped a declaration would follow. Her diary was full of musings on how she did not want to marry too soon, simply to avoid being a 'spinster'. She also had very particular ideas about her future husband and how he should treat her. When Antonio sent her gifts of money she immediately replied that it was too much, and when he wrote that October asking to marry her she protested that she was too young. The correspondence ended some time afterwards. Playing with the idea of love and engagement in her exchanges with Antonio, Anna had hoped for a declaration but was in no sense prepared for the reality of an engagement. The declaration was there to give shape to a relationship; it might allow it to begin or act as a pathway to greater intimacy, but its formality and ritual nature meant that it could also be toyed with and performed. Even in the 1950s it hinted at obligation and tradition rather than sincere emotion.

While formal rituals were not essential to every relationship leading to marriage, they were seen as important and natural steps in most middle- and upper-class courtships. The exchange of rings was a ritual that typically bound the couple together and formalized the promise of marriage, particu-larly among those of certain means.[13] It was not a necessary part of the engagement though, and the most important and common ritual was simply

---

[10] Natalia Ginzburg, *Voices in the Evening*, p. 60.
[11] Aldo Mariotti, 'Il prete rosso', MP/02, ADN.
[12] Anna Soprani, 'Diario personale', DP/08, ADN.
[13] It is mentioned in the memoirs of Aerre, 'Esisto anch'io', MP/05, Anna Maria (MP/03) and Luisa Rebecca, 'La bambina e il camionista', DP/96, ADN.

bringing the man home to meet his future wife's family, or the presentation of the couple to both families. The term 'engagement' or 'official engagement' was in fact often used interchangeably with *fidanzato/a in casa* or 'engaged at home'. This step was especially prominent for couples who met and married in the late 1940s and 1950s. Alda Maria Dei (Florence, 1930) gave a fairly detailed account of how she came to be officially engaged to her future husband Silvano.[14] The couple met when she was 17 and married in 1954 after a seven-year relationship. Alda Maria's parents—a dressmaker and a gardener—were artisans but in her description were always at pains to give the appearance of middle-class respectability. She met Silvano, an engineering student, at a dance for university students. When they began to court, each made it clear to the other that they did not want a serious relationship leading to marriage. Alda Maria was not allowed to go out alone with a man and thus they had to meet in secret. Silvano was allowed to see women, but his mother grew gradually more wary of the relationship as it became more serious and exclusive and eventually forbade her son from seeing Alda Maria. Meanwhile it became known in her community and among her extended family that she had a *fidanzato*, and once her parents became aware of this she was obliged to introduce him to them. By this stage Silvano was ready to meet her parents and make the engagement official. Although Alda Maria would have preferred to wait, there was no other option once the relationship was in the open. The meeting between her father and Silvano formalizing the engagement was fairly conventional, apart from the fact that it took place in a café rather than at home:

> Silvano wanted to speak with my father [...] even if, because of a certain anti-conformism, he didn't want to come to my home. They met in a café in Piazza Vittorio, in the centre. Not being able to discuss dowry (which there wasn't) or salary (still to come), nor date of marriage (distant and as yet unplanned) they spoke of timetables. My father was concerned about Silvano's studies and about my reputation: it was therefore decided that we could see each other one evening after dinner at my home—not going out—from nine to eleven; Saturday afternoon, with permission to go out; Sunday at midday Silvano would have lunch with us, and then we were free to go out until eight.[15]

Maria Vanzi (Empoli, Tuscany, 1931) also met her future husband at a dance in 1947.[16] Her parents were not in favour of the relationship, but when they finally consented to an official engagement the terms were similar. The pair were allowed to go out alone during the day but in the evenings they could only see each other in Maria's home, from nine to eleven. During this time

[14] Alda Maria Dei, 'Graffitti', MP/03, ADN.   [15] Alda Maria Dei, 'Graffitti'.
[16] Maria Vanzi, 'La mia vita. Flash di ricordi', MP/Adn2, ADN.

they were also supervised by Maria's mother who would sit in the corner of the room reading while the couple whispered their private conversation.

Aldo Mariotti described the formal engagement from a masculine perspective, writing his memoir in the third person. Born in the province of Siena, Aldo was educated to middle school although he came from a peasant background. He met his future wife Adriana at the age of 23 at a dance held at the local *Casa del Popolo*, the social hub of the local Communist Party branch. A card-carrying member, Mariotti's politics were no barrier to a conventional courtship and engagement. The couple were together for just a week before they were officially engaged.

> One evening, after having been to the cinema together in Torrenieri [Adriana's village], he [Aldo] walked her home, stopping at the foot of the entrance steps, soon after that her father arrived home from the village too, after making the introductions he invited them to come in. At that point the two doves liked each other very much. They had already decided to get engaged.[17]

Aldo and Adriana were engaged for four years before they married in 1959. Although Aldo's account stressed that the couple had already decided to get engaged, he did also give the impression that the meeting with Adriana's father hastened the plans somewhat. Once Aldo had met her parents, their relationship had to be made official. The process is nevertheless described as a natural one, understood and welcomed by both the couple and Adriana's father.

These couples were all from similar backgrounds and lived locally to each other. While none of the families were acquainted before their children met, it was clear that being from the same city or locality meant that they understood each other easily and shared courtship rituals. Before the onset of the economic miracle, migration was already beginning to change these local webs of custom and understanding, diminishing the role of the family and giving more autonomy to the couple themselves. While the war had already disrupted courtship by separating young men from their families, it was really the migration waves of the 1950s to Northern Europe that displayed initial signs of more lasting changes. Angelo Pettinari (born 1926, province of Brescia) whom we met in Chapter 1 was in the first of these migration waves. After competing military service he found himself unemployed and migrated to Luxembourg as an agricultural worker.[18] He remained in correspondence with his future wife Piera, who was from the same village as him and working as a waitress in Milan. The couple decided they would marry on Angelo's return to Italy. On a visit home, Aldo told his family over lunch that when he next returned, he would bring his wife. His mother was upset at the news, but his

---

[17] Aldo Mariotti, 'Il prete rosso'.
[18] Angelo Pettinari, 'I miei primi 78 anni', MP/Adn2, ADN.

father and brothers told him that 'for them, it was all right'. When Angelo asked Piera to marry him, she answered 'Angelo for me it is a yes but I will have to ask my mother first'.[19] The next day she was able to confirm her acceptance. While family were involved, it was the couple who made the decision about marriage and the family who simply accepted the arrangement. The fact that both had lived and worked away from family likely had some impact on their ability to make the decision more independently. It seems as if both Angelo and Piera had earned the majority of the funds needed to set up home themselves, due to their experiences as migrant workers. Angelo came from a working-class family and had to leave education after completing primary school; Piera's background was probably similar. Although family was clearly very important to the couple, they may have been less able to support the couple financially to set up home, making the dynamics of the engagement a little different to the earlier examples.

There were a few examples of women carving out completely independent lives for themselves as migrants and coming to marriage later in life with little intervention from family.[20] However, these were the exception and more frequently, migration preserved and even reinforced traditional patterns of courtship and family dynamics. Maria Blengino (province of Cuneo, 1935) migrated to Turin as a young woman to work as a domestic servant where her employers very much saw themselves *in loco parentis*. Her female employer stayed up late worrying about her when Maria came home late after a date, and even phoned Maria's father the next day.[21] Her experience was in the early 1950s, before the economic miracle had really transformed older migratory patterns into the more permanent migration of the 1960s. While migration was beginning to change the dynamics of young Italians and their families in matters of love and marriage in Italy itself, the experience of Calogero (Sicily, 1937) indicates that emigration, in his case to America, could actually reinforce traditional models of courtship as emigrant communities struggled to preserve bonds of family and culture in their new homes.[22]

In 1964 Calogero emigrated from Sicily to New York where he had an aunt already living. Already in his mid-twenties by this stage, his aunt immediately began to seek a wife for him. Since Italian American girls were apparently reluctant to marry new immigrants, his aunt found a suitable candidate in a local girl from the Puerto Rican community, whom he married later that year reproducing a highly traditional Sicilian courtship in 1960s New York with a Puerto Rican woman. The marriage was arranged between the two families and the initial negotiations and investigations carried out between the two

[19] Angelo Pettinari, 'I miei primi 78 anni'.
[20] Sebastiana Tarascio, 'Io mi racconto', MP/87, ADN.
[21] Maria Blengino, *Maria Blengino e Aa. Vv.*, 'I santare', MP/07, ADN.
[22] MP/02, ADN.

older women rather than the couple themselves. Calogero and his future wife barely spoke before they began their courtship and he seems to have decided to marry her based purely on physical attraction, in keeping with the Sicilian tradition of love and courtship 'through glances'. Indeed, it may have been easier to reproduce this traditional pattern with a Puerto Rican rather than an Italian American woman in New York, due to the changing times and the influence of American mass culture. The official engagement was also an interesting blend of the old world and the new. Calogero asked her parents' permission rather than making the decision with her. Then, in a gesture more in tune with 1960s America than Sicily, he sealed the engagement by present-ing her with a diamond ring.

Only very rarely were family completely absent from the picture. In those few cases, it could usually be put down to economic circumstance or class custom. It was not necessarily a symptom of the changing society of the miracle years, since the family proved remarkably adaptable to migration. We saw in Chapter 1 how Amato Varini (Modena, 1936) was ashamed to continue his relationship with his first girlfriend because of class difference. At the same time, when he did meet and marry another woman, Bruna, their courtship was remarkably free of any family considerations.[23] They each came from landless labourer backgrounds and met in 1961 while queuing for unemployment benefit, as they were both seasonal workers who spent some months of each year without work. Their relationship developed as the couple went dancing together each week and they married in 1965. It was described as a relationship remarkably free from family considerations, and very much one of mutual respect and love. The decisions to marry and have children were taken collectively. By the time they married, Amato was 29 and an active member of the PCI. Although age and politics likely had some influence over his outlook and his freedom from family ties, it was also significant that both came from poor landless families who could contribute nothing materially to the marriage. The couple themselves worked and saved to set up home together, their very lack of family appearing crucial to their freedom to take decisions as a couple rather than as son and daughter.

In other cases, family might be absent for reasons of 'morality' rather than class or wealth. Mario Bertini's (Florence, 1933) mother lived in a common law union with his father until his death. She was later institutionalized due to illness and disability until her early death, while Mario grew up between the orphanage and his grandparents. When he met his fiancée Annalisa in 1956, her parents were perplexed that she would want to marry a man with no family and no 'name'. While they did not obstruct the courtship, they did their own very thorough investigations of his background before consenting to an

---

[23] Amato Varini, 'La storia di uno di noi', MP/07, ADN.

'official' engagement, while Mario's parish priest, taking on the role of family for him, did the same.

> There were reciprocal, legitimate information gathering missions on the part of [Annalisa's] mother, who inquired with the priests of the Opera Madonnina del Grappa, and on the part of my mentor Don Nesi, who inquired with Annalisa's parish. These were the obligatory steps that were part of the culture at the time, and had to be undergone before the engagement could be made official.[24]

While the lack of family was not an insurmountable obstacle to a respectable, middle-class courtship, it was certainly something to be noted. In this case Mario's institutional religious upbringing worked in his favour, and the shared Catholic ties of both partners made up for his lack of family. It was evidently not only family wealth that was important to a good marriage, but also the reputation and respectability that a family background conferred.

Once the terms of the engagement had been set, and assuming the family were in agreement with the match, it was up to the couple to create their own spaces of emotional and physical intimacy and to decide what kind of relationship they both wanted to have before the marriage. Apart from the rules and boundaries set by family—close supervision of the couple, rules about when and where they could meet—the individuals themselves had to negotiate their own cultural and social preconceptions about what was correct and what was welcome in a relationship. While these notions varied by region, they were also informed by film, fiction, women's and youth magazines, political convictions, and their Catholic faith. Naturally, gender shaped the manner in which all of these ideas were internalized and how sexuality was experienced.

SEXUAL KNOWLEDGE AND EXPERIENCE

The diary and memoirs vary greatly in the extent to which sexuality is described, with a small minority giving extremely detailed accounts not just of the acts performed, but of how they were negotiated between the couple, and how the other partner responded. Very many others give barely any details at all. Generally the men's texts tended to include more explicit and detailed references to sexuality. The women's texts tended to use more euphemistic language to refer to sexual experiences, or to discuss general attitudes towards sexuality rather than to give details of their own physical intimacy. None of this is especially surprising and is in keeping with the society of the time, which expected men to be experienced in sexual matters

---

[24] Mario Bertini, 'Oltre la fame: diario di una vita in quattro stagioni', MP/02, ADN.

and women to be virgins upon marriage. While these tropes no doubt did not completely shape the reality of the sexual lives of Italians, what we likely see in diaries and memoirs are the attempts of ordinary people to fit their own lives, ideas, and attitudes into the narratives of gender roles and gender identity that were available to them.

The acquisition of sexual knowledge and experience in the context of coming of age is a recurring theme in many of the texts. At least five of the men describe very early sexual encounters with prostitutes; an experience entirely in keeping with a culture that expected men to be sexually experienced upon marriage to a virgin bride. State-regulated brothels were legal until 1958 and the prostitute a familiar figure in film and fiction, from Pratolini's *Tale of Poor Lovers* and Moravia's *The Woman of Rome* to *Adua and Friends*.[25] Indeed, the prostitute became a focal point for anxieties about gender and morality in an unstable society as Italy made the transition from war and occupation to economic recovery and growth.[26] The long and difficult passage into law of Senator Angelina Merlin's bill for the outlawing of state brothels revealed just how deeply rooted the notion of regulated prostitution was in Italian society.[27] Of the five men who described such first sexual experiences with a prostitute, two were Sicilian, one from Puglia, one Lombard, and one Tuscan, indicating that this rite of passage had national rather than regional roots. Two described visiting the brothel in terms of the familiar coming of age ritual which was viewed with such nostalgia and even national affection in the surveys and media discussions in the late 1950s on the eve of the closing of the state brothels.[28] One further memoirist referred to the need to practise with a prostitute before becoming sexual with his girlfriend.[29] We might note at the same time that, when set against the media conversation of the 1950s, the numbers describing this ritual are actually relatively few, adding weight to Tambor's argument that the media storm was concerned more with 'ideas more than reality'.[30] Indeed, evidence suggests that the brothels were already dying out in the post-war period, as the post-war years wrought changes in gender relations and courtship.[31]

[25] Vasco Pratolini, *Cronache di poveri amanti* (Florence, 1946); Alberto Moravia, *La Romana* (Milan, 1947); Antonio Pietrangeli, *Adua e le compagne* (1960). Both novels were also made into films in 1954.

[26] Danielle Hipkins, *Italy's Other Women: Gender and Prostitution in Italian Cinema, 1940–1965* (Oxford, 2016).

[27] Molly Tambor, *The Lost Wave: Women and Democracy in Postwar Italy* (Oxford, 2014), pp. 108–40. See also Molly Tambor, 'Prostitutes and Politicians: The Women's Rights Movement in the Legge Merlin Debates', in Penelope Morris (ed.), *Women in Italy 1945–1960: An Interdisciplinary Study* (London, 2006), pp. 131–45.

[28] Giovanni described how at the age of 23 his friends organized a visit to a prostitute as a surprise, but he declined the offer: MP/96, ADN.

[29] Vittorio Romani, 'Il racconti della mia vita'.   [30] Tambor, *Lost Wave*, p. 138.

[31] Tambor, *Lost Wave*, p. 138.

Aside from prostitution, sexual knowledge in childhood and early adolescence varied widely by class and gender. Several of the men memoirists described sexual experimentation in their childhood and early adolescence, although this was not a frequently occurring theme.[32] The backgrounds of these ranged from working class and southern to middle-class provincial Tuscan, so such experiences clearly crossed class boundaries. For those born to working-class and peasant families where family members often lived and slept in close proximity to each other, a certain knowledge of sexual matters was inevitable. Sicilian Calogero described being able to hear the sounds of his aunt's wedding night in the family home, although the lack of electric light meant that he could not see anything.[33] His memories were not unusual, and indeed others in crowded living conditions reported a similar familiarity with the sexual sphere indicating that class was clearly important to sexual knowledge.

However, sexual education—which happened entirely within the family— was highly gendered too. Women were much more likely to describe the lack of any instruction in this regard. Lieta Harrison's popular sociology of Italian adolescent girls, published in 1966, found that few girls received any education about sexual matters from their parents. The mothers interviewed openly admitted their reluctance to provide their daughters with this knowledge, with only eighteen out of 265 parents surveyed giving their daughters any sort of sexual education, which in any case was usually limited to an explanation of menstruation.[34] While Harrison's sampling methods are not explained, thus leaving the evidence somewhat anecdotal, her findings fit with the partial and patchy evidence of the first-person texts. Ignorance of their own sexuality was a familiar trope, particularly in the middle-class texts. Luisa Puliti (Florence, 1931) described how her mother did not tell her about periods at all, and it was the dressmaker who noticed it on her weekly visit, and explained matters.[35] There was not necessarily much change by the early 1960s either; Giuliana's mother (Piedmont, 1945) also told her daughters very little about sexual matters, despite being consumed by the fear that Giuliana, the most extroverted of her daughters, would lose her virginity before marriage.[36]

As we saw in Chapter 1, men were also more likely to have a period of living away from family and home, either by design or necessity, while women were much more likely to be confined to the family sphere until marriage. Even those peasant women who worked away from home as domestic servants still

---

[32] Pasquale and Mauro: MP/01, ADN.   [33] MP/02, ADN.
[34] Lieta Harrison, *L'Iniziazione: Come le adolescenti diventano donne* (Milan, 1966), pp. 42–3.
[35] Luisa Puliti, *È nato un bambino di sesso femminile* (Viterbo, 1994), p. 16. A copy is also conserved at the ADN.
[36] MP/87, ADN.

lived within a family environment. Some middle-class women diarists did attend boarding school in the 1950s but those who attended university all did so while still living in the family home. The few texts describing the experience of living away from home as a female university student all date from the 1960s.[37] In contrast the rootlessness that many men experienced in the post-war years and the 1950s might have brought sexual adventures. At the age of 18, Giobatta Rossi (Anghiari, 1926) was posted to Ivrea as a soldier of the Republic of Salò where he had various romantic adventures, including with Ines, with whom he corresponded for some years afterwards, along with other brief sexual encounters before marrying a younger woman in his late twenties.[38] The trope of male sexual experience and female innocence was one created in part by cultural expectations about gender and in part by social conditions.

NEGOTIATING PHYSICAL INTIMACY

Even if one partner was more experienced, physical and sexual intimacy still had to be negotiated between the couples themselves, once they began to court or became engaged. One of the primary spaces of courtship, as we have seen, was the family home. In arranged marriages, particularly in the south or among families from the south, physical contact was extremely limited. It was usually the men who reflected on the physical restrictions that local custom placed on courtship, while women from similar backgrounds tended to focus on their lack of freedom or autonomy. Sicilian Calogero described how he stole a kiss from his Puerto Rican fiancée after courting her at home for two weeks, and one of the reasons he wanted to hasten the marriage was so that they could kiss without fear.[39] Giovanni Frasca (Ragusa, 1931) had migrated to Genoa but returned to Sicily to become engaged to a local woman in a match arranged by their families.[40] When the engagement was formalized he wanted to kiss his fiancée but, mindful of local traditions, limited himself to a handshake.

Many sources indicate that displays of physical affection were not acceptable in rural Italy before the economic miracle and the incursion of mass culture. In Natalia Ginzburg's *Voices in the Evening*, the protagonist's mother

---

[37] Giuliana and Carla both attended university in Milan from the very late 1950s to the late 1960s, describing their experience of leaving the family home in provincial Lombardy to live alone in the city, MP/87 and MP/08, ADN.

[38] Giobatta Rossi, 'I miei ricordi', DP/99, ADN.   [39] MP/02.

[40] Giovanni Frasca, 'Il mio diario', MP/10, ADN.

could not believe that her daughter was in a relationship with a local man, as it was 'impossible' to imagine that her 27-year-old daughter would 'let her hands be held by a man in public'.[41] Piedmontese Maria Paola spent some time in London at the age of 22 and was struck by the sight of a couple kissing openly in Hyde Park.[42] In the 1950s, this would have been unacceptable in her hometown. As part of a survey carried out by sociologist Lidia De Rita in 1957 on the impact of television in rural Basilicata, an elderly man was asked about the best thing he had seen on television. His reply: 'The kiss, kissing in public... because you can see that it's not a sin, you can do it.'[43]

Commercial magazines such as the *fotoromanzi* also played their part in both expanding and delimiting the boundaries of acceptability. Even though the visual representation of romantic love was the very currency of these magazines, editors were extremely careful about what level of physical intimacy was portrayed. While in the mid-1950s couples were usually only depicted sitting close to each other, they were gradually allowed to move closer, first being portrayed in close embrace and then about to kiss, until by 1959 stories began to show couples kissing (see Figure 2.1)[44] Such illustrations always showed the couple carefully posed with hands on each others' shoulders to underline the chaste nature of the kisses. The arrival of mass culture and especially television, despite the limitations on what could be depicted, clearly did much to open rural Italy up to new ways of acting and feeling.[45]

However, even in the late 1960s, women in particular might be wary of showing too much affection in smaller towns and villages. Mauro met his wife in provincial Tuscany in 1967, when she was 16 and he was 21.[46] During their four-year engagement, the couple used to argue because she was wary of showing too much physical affection in public. Although the mass media may have played a role in opening up new conversations about intimacy, it was the new spaces of private and public leisure that really transformed the intimate lives of young Italians. The beach was a space that offered new ways for younger generations to interact as it combined leisure with display of the body (see Figure 2.2).[47] Popular culture points to the beach being considered a space apart from 'respectable' mainstream culture even in the inter-war years; in the 1933 film *Treno Popolare* (*Tourist Train*) Carlo and Lina had just met that day when they capsized in a rowing boat and had to change their clothes. When Lina objected that she could not undress in the presence of a man, Carlo

---

[41] Ginzburg, *Voices in the Evening*, p. 144.   [42] Maria Paola, MP/05, ADN.
[43] Quoted in Guido Crainz, *Storia del miracolo*. Translation by this author.
[44] See for example the illustrations for 'Mio amore sconosciuto' and 'Giuramento d'amore', both serialized in *Grand Hotel* in 1959.
[45] See F. Montoleone, *Storia della radio e della television in Italia* (Venice, 1992).
[46] MP/01, ADN.
[47] Michela De Giorgio *Le Italiane dall'Unità ad oggi* (Rome, 1992), pp. 260–72.

Figure 2.1. The 1959 photo story 'My Unknown Love' was one of the first to depict a couple sharing a full kiss although illustrators were still careful to place the couple's hands on each other's shoulders to underline the limits of their physical intimacy.

Grand Hotel, 17 October 1959. Biblioteca Braidense, Milan.

Figure 2.2. Beach cover image of *Grand Hotel*, illustrating the growing importance of the summer holiday for Italians.

Biblioteca Braidense, Milan, 28 August 1950.

replied, 'pretend we're at the sea [. . .] it's easy'.[48] The numbers of holiday-makers naturally exploded during the boom years.[49] The anxiety about how the beach was transforming how young Italians thought about their bodies and interacted with each other is clear from the letters page of bestselling Catholic magazine *Famiglia Cristiana*, among other sources.[50] The 1955 editorial 'The Tragedy of the Two-piece', written in response to readers' letters about revealing swimming costumes, railed at how modern fashion and consumer culture violated the modesty of young women with their new styles.[51] Many sources, including diaries and memoirs, attest to the beach being a space apart from the usual norms of physical display, intimacy, and

---

[48] David Forgacs and Stephen Gundle, *Mass Culture and Italian Society from Fascism to the Cold War* (Bloomington, IN, 2007), p. 84.

[49] Crainz, *Storia del miracolo*, p. 144.

[50] Niamh Cullen, 'Morals, Modern Identities and the Catholic Woman: Fashion in *Famiglia Cristiana*, 1954–1968', *Journal of Modern Italian Studies*, 18:1 (2013), pp. 33–52, 43–6.

[51] Padre Atanasio, 'La tragedia del due pezzi', *Famiglia Cristiana*, 13 February 1955.

gendered interaction. When Francesco met his future wife on the beach near Catania in the early 1960s, the pair kissed that same day.[52] The rest of their courtship took place under the watchful eye of both Castiglione's family and her family friend, standing in for her absent family. The kiss on the beach stands out as an anomaly in an otherwise traditional and chaste courtship.

However, if the beach was a space where the rules of public display and intimacy were suspended, physical intimacy still required some measure of privacy. While the darkness of the commercial cinema offered courting couples some opportunities for amorous contact, it was not until the advent of mass car ownership that many couples had access to intimate spaces that were fully their own. This was a theme common to courtship in the 1950s and 1960s everywhere and its impact was particularly marked in rural and provincial settings.[53] There were many passing references, both in the memoir material and in magazine advice columns, to the necessity for a young man to own a car in order to attract women's interest, and equally of the dangers of getting into cars with boys.[54] However important it was as a status symbol, the car also crucially meant freedom and privacy. The question of how much intimacy was acceptable was one on which the couple ultimately decided. These 'negotiations' were often long and protracted, continued across many days and evenings of courtship. Inevitably in the memoir material, the pattern was usually that of the man wearing down the defences of his 'beloved'. One memoir described such a 'negotiation' from the masculine perspective: the author planned the encounter by driving his fiancée to a secluded spot while claiming afterwards that his passions had overcome him.[55]

Any number of popular culture sources, from magazine fiction and advice columns to film, make it clear that there was an expectation that men should— or an acceptance that they would—push for pre-marital sex, while it was the woman's role to resist. This model of masculinity was often associated with the south of Italy but sometimes also took on national connotations feeding into the familiar image of the 'Latin lover', being developed through film as a national brand in these years. Vittorio Brancati's 1949 novel *Il bell'Antonio*, followed by the 1960 film starring Marcello Mastroianni, parodied this notion of the suave, virile Latin lover, while highlighting the cultural expectations

---

[52] MP/02, ADN.

[53] The car played an important role in courtship in post-war America: see Beth Bailey, *From Front Porch to Back Seat*. Catriona Clear similarly describes how car ownership transformed courtship in rural and small-town Ireland: *Women's Voices in Ireland: Women's Magazines in the 1950s and 1960s* (London, 2016), p. 85.

[54] For example a letter to *Grazia*'s agony aunt, in the column, 'Ditelo pure a me', 11 October 1955, was from a girl who had lost her virginity after taking a car trip with a boy. A letter to *Grand Hotel*'s letter page from 'Gamba L, Bolzanetto' (3 January 1959) described going on regular car trips with a group of boys who behaved respectfully towards them, rejecting the obviously commonplace notion of the car as a site of sexual danger for young women.

[55] MP/06.

such rigid gender norms placed on men.[56] It was a familiar trope of letters to the *fotoromanzo* agony aunts that a man would ask his *fidanzata* for the 'test of love' and that it was her duty as a woman to resist.[57] Lieta Harrison, in her 1966 study of adolescent girls, indicates that girls too might collude in this performance of masculinity. When questioned as to what they would think of a man who 'respected' a woman so much than he only wanted to kiss her, they all answered that such a man was not for them, with one answering that such a man was 'abnormal' and another that he was likely a 'fag' (*checca*).[58] Lieta Harrison's study seems intended to shock, although this gendered double standard was present to some extent almost everywhere. Beth Bailey and Claire Langhamer both acknowledge its presence in English and American courtship, but their focus is on the economics of the dating game, whereby sexual favours are 'bought' by men in exchange for dates.[59] Italian society was not as affluent as the US or Britain until the 1960s when Italian consumer culture began to catch up, and this may partly explain why this kind of thinking is not so strong a feature of the Italian sources. Rather the power seems to lie in strong regional and national codes of masculinity. The letters compiled in Gabriella Parca's anthology *Italian Women Confess*, come from young women all over Italy, uncertain how to navigate this thorny issue, with the women strongly socially conditioned not to 'give in' just as men were expected to push the boundaries. The experience of one young woman from Emilia was fairly typical.

> Taking advantage of our solitude, he asked for the famous test of love and hearing my refusal, he got angry, he wouldn't speak to me anymore and before he left he told me that if I was going to be like this, he didn't love me anymore, that he had already waited long enough [...]. I didn't give in, I don't feel ready to take this step, I wouldn't have the courage to look my mother in the face. [...] Now what do I do, I'm desperate. It's eight days since I've heard from him, I can't take it anymore. [...] I love him so much, I don't want to lose him as it would finish me. Help me![60]

The letters pages were also full of warnings from women who had given their boyfriend 'the proof of love' that he had begged for and now found that he was

---

[56] Vittorio Brancati, *Il bell'Antonio* (Mondadori: Milan, 1949); Mauro Bolognini, *Bell'Antonio* (film) (1960). For a closer analysis of the film and its portrayal of masculinity, see Jacqueline Reich, *Beyond the Latin Lover: Marcello Mastroianni, Masculinity and Italian Cinema* (Bloomington, IN, 2004), pp. 56–66.

[57] While such letters were published regularly in *Grand Hotel*, they also featured heavily in Gabriella Parca (ed.), *Le Italiane si confessano* (Florence, 1959) where a whole section was devoted to 'la famosa prova'.

[58] Lieta Harrison, *L'Iniziazione*, pp. 58–9.

[59] Beth Bailey, *Front Porch to Back Seat* and Claire Langhamer, *The English in Love: The Intimate Story of an Emotional Revolution* (Oxford, 2013), pp. 125–45.

[60] Gabriella Parca (ed.), *Le italiane si confessano*.

no longer interested—or claimed that it was not her first time—leaving their marriage prospects damaged by the loss of their virginity. In such letters emotions often ran to baroque heights of intensity and exaggeration; they are useful not so much as real case studies but as illustrations of a certain mentality about men, women, and their sexuality that was omnipresent in post-war popular culture.[61] By the late 1960s such attitudes could be parodied in popular culture, but in the 1950s we still see them being absorbed unquestioned into narratives of love and courtship, coercion blending uncomfortably with romance in some personal texts.[62]

A 1955 short story published in *Grand Hotel* also mirrors very closely the tropes seen in the letters and some memoirs, although the flowery language was intended to strike a more romantic tone. In the story 'Closed Envelope', young diplomat Giulio slept with peasant girl Nora and she became pregnant. Unusually the story actually alluded directly to the sexual act in the following passage:

> Giulio held her tightly and started kissing her passionately. For a while, Nora didn't understand what was happening, and had the impression that all the stars were raining down on her in splendour. Love—Giulio whispered—forgive me. It was stronger than I am [...] Nora didn't know what to think, she felt sad and lost. [...]—What have we done?[63]

Nora was completely passive, too innocent to realize what was happening until it was too late. These were the qualities that saved her; while the women in such stories were generally demonized for their sexuality, she appeared virtuous even when she had sinned. There was no hint of her desires either; it was simply a matter of 'giving in' to Giulio's sexual appetite. As in the earlier memoir, Giulio could claim that he was simply overcome by desire. If there was some pleasure in the experience for her, it was presented in a romantic rather than a sexual vein. Afterwards it would only be justified to the woman, either by the man or to herself, as an act of love.

Of course, not all men and women conformed this closely to the exaggerated expectations of male predators and passive, innocent women that we see in popular culture. Such detailed descriptions of sexual experiences are relatively unusual in the diaries and memoirs, although many men and women did reflect on their general attitude to sexuality. Some proudly discussed how they waited until marriage for sexual intercourse and such admissions tended to fit with the person's set of values and broad outlook. Here there were some quite interesting divergences from the gendered cultural expectations of virginity and sexual morality. Whereas a number of the men mentioned their

---

[61] This is particularly true those collected in Gabriella Parca's *Le italiane si confessano*.
[62] For example in the film *Girl with a Gun* (Mario Monicelli, 1968).
[63] Cecilia Palau, 'A busta chiusa', 15 January 1955.

decision to wait until marriage to have sexual intercourse, very few of the women did. For two of the men, this decision was strongly informed by their Christian faith: Lucio Bartolomeo (Genoa, 1930) was a committed Catholic and an active member of Catholic Action who described his faith in fairly progressive terms; and Vincenzo Rotundi (Foggia, 1927) was a trainee priest and teacher when he met his wife Gioy in Rome.[64] Vincenzo explicitly described the love that he and Gioy shared as grounded in their Catholic faith. The couple also had some quite abstract, intellectual discussions about love, sex, and marriage, reflecting on the need to balance emotion and 'animal' passions in their marriage. Mario Bertini (Florence, 1933) described his decision to wait not in terms of religion but in terms of love, and a respect for female chastity. He met his wife Annalisa on the beach on Elba, where they exchanged a chaste kiss. In 'a decision made together, in liberty', they decided to wait until their wedding four years later. He described in his memoir the emotions that his wedding night still stirred in him: 'What I want to fix into the memory of this computer [. . .] is the extraordinary emotion of possessing for the first time, on our wedding night, the complete intimacy of A.'[65]

There were no such declarations of the value of chastity in the women's texts, and considering the enormous cultural pressure on women to remain virgins until marriage this may seem like a curious omission. The pressure on women was coming from all quarters. The canonization of Maria Goretti in 1950—a young peasant girl from the Marche who had died in 1902 while resisting rape—was symptomatic of the Catholic Church's desperate attempts to instil the values of sexual purity and chastity in the new generation of Italian girls growing up in a rapidly modernizing world.[66] While priest and family would have worked to impress such values on Italian girls, popular magazines also reinforced such attitudes. Catholic magazine *Famiglia Cristiana* expounded regularly on the need for chastity and purity among women in particular, while commercial women's magazines from *Grand Hotel* to *Grazia* also emphasized the importance of female purity, although more for reasons of respectability than morality.[67] In the south, the honour code also reinforced such values, linking them again to society, community, and appearance, in contrast to the Catholic emphasis on inner purity as well as outward modesty.

---

[64] Lucio Bartolomeo Galileo Cadenelli, 'Trucioli e freguggie', MP/06, ADN; Vincenzo Rotundi, 'Io e te insieme. Storia di una vita vissuta insieme 1957–1996', MP/99, ADN.

[65] Mario Bertini, 'Oltre la fame: Diario d'una vita in quattro stagioni', MP/02, ADN.

[66] Patrick McCarthy, 'The Church in Post War Italy', in Patrick McCarthy (ed.), *Italy Since 1945* (Oxford, 2000), p. 140; Forgacs and Gundle, *Mass Culture and Italian Society*, pp. 255–6.

[67] See Niamh Cullen, 'Morals, Modern Identities and the Catholic Woman'; Niamh Cullen, 'Changing Emotional Landscapes? Grand Hotel and Representations of Love and Courtship in 1950s Italy', *Cultural and Social History*, 11:2 (2014), pp. 285–306; and Penny Morris, 'A Window on the Private Sphere: Advice Columns, Marriage, and the Evolving Family in 1950s Italy', *The Italianist*, 27:2, pp. 304–32.

It is striking that none of this is strongly evidenced in the first-person texts; there are of course hints of such attitudes in the negotiations between couples over degrees of intimacy, however none of the women discuss it in terms of personal values or piety.

Those who did describe their efforts to wait until marriage framed it in terms of respectability or fear of pregnancy.[68] Cristina Bernhard (province of Bolzano, 1939) was born into a peasant background in the South Tyrol. Her family situation was also unstable, since her mother died young and she was treated cruelly by her stepmother. Remaining a virgin until marriage was described less as a freely made decision to wait, than as an achievement in evading the sexual predations of local men. Neither was her decision informed by religion, of which she was sceptical, but rather by an empowering knowledge of sex and reproduction and a desire to better herself. As an adolescent, she narrowly escaped rape while cleaning out the milking stalls. She also considered herself better informed in matters of sexuality than other girls her age, having found a book explaining sex and pregnancy among her mother's possessions. Forearmed with this knowledge, Cristina 'made a vow of chastity':

> Almost all of the village girls were pregnant or had illegitimate children before they married, they let themselves be deceived by words, that they could get pregnant just by kissing, and so the men had their fun and then abandoned them. Few married them. The old women of the village spoke about me behind my back, when I went off to work [as a domestic servant in Austria and then Milan] saying that I was a pretty girl, to watch that I would come back with a full belly, but they waited in vain.[69]

It was important to Cristina that when she did marry in 1961, her first child was not born until more than a year had passed so that it was clear to all that the wedding had in no way been decided or rushed by a pregnancy.

> They were saying in the village, she must have had to get married because she's pregnant, they were very disappointed [that this was not the case] and they would have been better cleaning their own front doors by explaining to their daughters how babies were born, as this was total taboo, maybe they believed that talking about sex was a sin, although in any case they ended up breaking the sixth commandment with all its consequence.[70]

Cristina evidently took pride in the fact that she had managed to wait until after marriage to start her family, evading the trap of single motherhood apparently so common in her village. Hers was a decision made out of knowledge and the desire to make a better life for herself, rather than one

---

[68] Among others see Wilma Prarizzi, 'Diario di Wilma'.

[69] Cristina Bernhard, 'Infanzia, difficile tra i miei bei monti', MP/08, ADN.

[70] In the Catholic catechism, the sixth commandment refers to adultery.

born from piety or ideas linking love and chastity. The men to whom such values were important perhaps felt the need to distinguish their own attitudes from the mainstream, sexually predatory constructions of masculinity. Conversely, since there was no strong social pressure on men to cultivate the appearance of modesty and sexual purity, those who wished to do so were more free to focus on the inner meaning and personal importance of such values in their own lives.

Even in the case of women who came from more open backgrounds and lived comparatively liberated lifestyles, such messages were often internalized to some extent, and in the life narratives served to qualify, explain, or excuse certain life events and decisions. Anna di Montegnacco Menichetti (Udine, 1931) lived a bohemian lifestyle, growing up with her mother and among extended family in Rome from 1940. She grew up in the midst of the social and political upheaval of wartime and liberated Rome, recalling in her memoir the intense political energy that infused the post-war city. She herself was drawn to Republican, then monarchist circles, and finally to the far Left. She and her mother then lived in a series of squalid shared accommodations, in one case with an ex-model landlady who cohabited with an older, wealthier man and had regular abortions. After finishing secondary school, she worked as an air hostess. Despite this relatively open and unusual upbringing and early adulthood, her attitudes to love and sexuality were more in keeping with the times. She commented in her memoir, writing in 2000, that girls in the 1950s and 1960s were 'anything but free', with the double standard ingrained in society.[71] While she had many boyfriends, sexuality was clearly tricky territory to navigate and such considerations seem to have bled somewhat into her own emotional life. When she fell in love with a Sardinian engineer, the attraction was partly his traditional approach to love. He wrote her 'letters that were beautifully romantic and melancholy', and when they holidayed together it was 'all completely chaste and wonderful'.[72] However, it fell apart when his family arranged a match for him with a distant cousin, leaving Anna heartbroken. She then met her future husband, Gian Carlo, on a flight from Rome to Milan in 1953. Gian Carlo at that stage was already married. Although the couple did go on to cohabit and eventually marry, Anna was careful to balance her courage and boldness in defying convention by describing how rather than choosing to begin a sexual relationship, she fell into one. She 'had no intention to make love but that November, at his place, it happened'. The grammar of her sentence reinforces her sense of diminished responsibility for their sexual relationship; 'it' merely happened to her.[73] Even though her memoir was primarily a story of defying convention, a close reading showed how she was

---

[71] Anna di Montegnacco Menichetti, 'Il fili del destino', MP/07, ADN.
[72] Anna di Montegnacco Menichetti, 'Il fili del destino'.
[73] Anna di Montegnacco Menichetti, 'Il fili del destino'.

still somewhat shaped by the gender norms she critiqued, professing her own passivity as if to soften the impact of her transgression.

A decade later, Elisabetta Battistini (Rome, 1941) experienced similar contradictions in her emotional life as a young single woman working in Rome. Despite having many boyfriends and an emotional life that was always 'active and intense', she was always aware of the limits of her sexual freedom.[74] Before her marriage in 1966 she had an affair with a married man which lasted for two years and, like Anna, she was careful to clarify that she had not meant to enter a sexual relationship. However, the recollection of her unease and his insistence on coming inside her home when nobody was in, gave her account a more predatory tone. Nevertheless, she also mentioned her lack of concern when he did not contact her for some time and her own 'desire to have fun'.[75] It is not easy to read the contradiction and ambivalence of Elisabetta's account, and perhaps even she herself did not have a clear recollection of her own agency in the affair. It is evident that 1960s Rome, despite the reputation for decadence created by *La Dolce Vita*, was not an easy place to be for a single woman, even with 'modern' ideas and an independent income.[76] The lines between liberation, agency, and exploitation were not easy to untangle. Indeed, the realization that the very notion of sexual liberty had its own gendered power dynamics—often expressed simply as unease and rarely openly interrogated at the time—was what lay at the heart of feminist critiques of the sexual revolution of the 1960s.[77]

THE POLITICS OF INTIMACY

That is not to say, however, that there were not many couples who did engage freely and lovingly in pre-marital sex. There are regional patterns to note here as well as class ones; in some of the northern and central regions, pregnancy and cohabitation were quite usual, and this could be a prelude to marriage. This tended to be the case particularly in working-class families and in the Emilia-Romagna region, where anticlericalism was traditionally rife. One of the best known examples is Mussolini himself; a native of Romagna and an

[74] Elisabetta Battistini, 'Del divorzio ovvero massacre di un'identità', MP/96, ADN.

[75] Elisabetta Battistini, 'Del divorzio ovvero massacre di un'identità'.

[76] For an exploration of the seedier side of Rome's film and celebrity culture, see Karen Pinkus, *The Montesi Scandal* (Chicago, 2003) and Stephen Gundle, *Death and the Dolce Vita: The Dark Side of Rome in the 1950s* (Edinburgh, 2011).

[77] On the gendered narratives of Italy's sexual revolution, see Rebecca Clifford's analysis of the oral histories of 1968. 'Emotions and Gender in Oral History: Narrating Italy's 1968', *Modern Italy*, 17:2 (2012), pp. 209–21. For one account of personal disillusionment with the sexual revolution, see Jenny Diski, *The Sixties* (London, 2009) pp. 49–68.

anticlerical socialist, he was in a common law marriage with Rachele Guidi from 1909 and only married her in the Catholic Church in 1925 for reasons of political expediency.[78] Bruna Bignozzi (Bondeno, 1935) came from a working-class background near Ferrara and commented on the relatively liberated working-class culture of her region. In her experience, young men and women mixed freely at dances and it was usual for couples to have babies and even cohabit outside of marriage.[79] There was no great shame in such circumstances or unions for the women, although their children were considered illegitimate unless they subsequently married, and such legal distinctions remained unchanged until the family law reform act of 1975.[80] A number of the memoirs did mention a marriage being hastened by pregnancy although usually in quite a matter of fact tone, as if to suggest that it was not so much a crisis as a confirmation of the union and a spur to bring events to their natural conclusion. As Mauro (Tuscany) described, he and his girlfriend slowly began to talk about marriage after some years together in the late 1960s, after which she became pregnant and they quickly moved from talk to serious planning.[81]

Politics often intersected with regional dynamics, and the regions where pre-marital sexuality and cohabitation were common coincided with those where communism was strongest at grassroots level. In post-war Italy PCI membership and activism could confer a complete identity and a different way of approaching family, gender, and sexuality.[82] Much has been written about the limits of communist culture when it came to changing gender roles and attitudes; from the moral hypocrisy of the party in the 1950s to the expectation that for militants, party would always come before family.[83] Leo Goretti has highlighted how in politically progressive households, there still was reticence about young women assuming greater freedoms, while moving into the 1960s Italian communists remained wary of the notion of sexual freedom, linking it to consumer culture, prostitution, and the 'double standard'.[84] However, it is also true that in many cases there was a sort of politicization of intimacy, where political values and intimate relations coincided. This was the promise

---

[78] Richard Bosworth, *Mussolini: A Biography* (London, 2010), pp. 64–5.

[79] Bruna Bignozzi, 'La mia piccola Calabria', MP/04, ADN.

[80] Diana Vincenzi Amato, 'La famiglia e il diritto', in Piero Melograni (ed.), *La famiglia italiana dall'ottocento ad oggi* (Rome, 1988), pp. 629–700, 685–6.

[81] Mauro, MP/02, ADN.

[82] See Maria Casalini, *Famiglie comuniste: Ideologie e vita quotidiana nell'Italia degli anni cinquanta* (Bologna, 2010) and 'The Family, Sexual Morality and Gender Identity in the Communist Tradition in Italy (1921–1956)', *Modern Italy*, 13:3 (2013), pp. 229–44.

[83] Anna Tonelli, *Gli irregolari: Amori comunisti al tempo della guerra fredda* (Rome, 2014); Maria Casalini, *Famiglie comuniste*, pp. 49–61.

[84] Leo Goretti, 'Irma Bandiera and Maria Goretti: Gender Role Models for Communist Girls in Italy (1945–56)', *Twentieth Century Communism*, 4:4 (2012), pp. 14–37; Mauro Pasqualini, 'Politics of Emotions in the Italian Left: Gender, Consumption and Intimacy in Lorenza Mazzetti's Advice Columns and Novels, 1961–1969', *The Italianist*, 32:3 (2012), pp. 415–36, esp. p. 425.

contained in Marina Sereni's memoir of her marriage to fellow activist Emilio Sereni, which clearly struck a chord with readers on its publication in 1955.[85] While the desperate conditions of clandestine activity and imprisonment under which this ideal activist couple had met were no longer present in the 1950s, the heightened political tensions of the Cold War still made political allegiances a firm foundation on which to build a relationship, just as the lack of such ties could be an obstacle.[86]

Marina Sereni had described herself in her bestselling memoir as 'a girl like any other, without any original ideas or special qualities' who only through her love for Emilio, discovered the communism which gave her life its purpose.[87] Luisa Puliti (Florence, 1931) did not quite see herself in this way; she reflected on how she had not wanted to marry before she met her future husband Paolo, hoping for something more from life than simply the roles of wife and mother. The couple met when Luisa was in her early twenties and Paolo some years older, and it was through him that Luisa became immersed in the world of Italian communism. She joined the party in 1951 and when they married shortly afterwards (*c*.1952) she devoted her life to full-time activism at Paolo's side. Luisa described how, after two years together and some months before the wedding, she and Paolo made love. 'It wasn't easy. I was rigid and it felt painful.'[88] She found out soon afterwards that she was pregnant and in an inversion of the usual imperative to repair the situation through marriage, she had an abortion on her honeymoon.[89] Although in many respects their early relationship resembled that of the classic 'militant couple' of the 1950s, it also had a less conventional side which will be explored in Chapters 4 and 5.

Amato Varini's (Modena, 1936) courtship with his future wife blended left-wing politics with a more traditional idea of family. After his first relationship ended due to illness and class difference, as documented in Chapter 1, Amato met his future wife in 1961. He was at this stage a member of the PCI, while his wife was certainly active in the social world of post-war communism if not a card-carrying member. They went to local PCI dances together and a deep love developed between them. Coming from similar backgrounds, they shared values: in politics, work ethic, and family. He describes how they made the final decision to begin a family together in August 1965:

> We began to make plans together about how to begin our new family and about our wish to have a child even in difficult financial circumstances. In these times

---

[85] Maria Casalini, *Famiglie comuniste*, pp. 21–32.

[86] Letters to *Famiglia Cristiana* often asked for advice on whether it was acceptable for a Catholic girl (it was usually a woman) to marry a PCI member. They were usually advised to steer clear of such unions.

[87] Quoted in Maria Casalini, *Famiglie comuniste*, p. 38.

[88] Luisa Puliti, *È nato un bambino di sesso femminile* (Rome, 1999) p. 37. A copy is also held at the ADN.

[89] Luisa Puliti, *È nato un bambino di sesso femminile*, pp. 37–8.

family values were still very strong, we felt the weight of Catholic tradition and the example of those who had come before us: as we counted the falling stars we talked about how we wished they would be our future children. The evening was so beautiful, the sky full of stars, the marvel of falling stars, the smell of the freshly cut hay and the dew that refreshed your body...it was an atmosphere for making love. And that is what happened, with the precise intention of making our first child.[90]

The wedding happened several months later in October 1965. Curiously, Amato mentioned Catholic tradition in his description of the decision to start their family, even though pre-marital sex was clearly in breach of Catholic values. Even though the Church saw PCI membership and Catholicism as incompatible it is evident that at a personal level, religion and politics could sit reasonably comfortably together, the contradictions between the two world views never fully teased out. Amato Varini's memoir framed the decision to engage in pre-marital sex very much as a natural one, arising simply and clearly from love and from the emotional intimacy of shared values and plans. Physical and emotional intimacy were of course bound up together in most if not all memoirs and diaries. The final section of this chapter thus turns to the terrain of emotional intimacy, teasing out the shifting vocabularies of love that we can see in the first-person sources over the course of 1950s and 1960s.

CORRESPONDENCE TO COMPANIONS: SHIFTING VOCABULARIES OF LOVE

The ways in which couples communicated and understood their emotions— and then narrated these experiences—were of course highly individual and private, but they also drew on broader ideas about gender, family, and marriage. The very mode of communication also shaped the ways in which emotional intimacy was created, and for very many this was likely to be the epistolary form. One of the common threads in the experiences of the 1950s in particular was the need to keep the relationship alive even when the lovers were apart, usually because of military service or migration. Leave was infrequent while travel was very expensive before the tourism boom of the 1960s, leaving written correspondence as the only way of maintaining regular contact. The physical pen and page, and the delays of the postal system, shaped the ways in which men and women could articulate their feelings. Some were comfortable with the written word, drawing on a wide vocabulary and even

---

[90] Amato Varini, 'La storia di uno di noi'.

making literary allusions, while others were ill at ease with the formality of the page, struggling with spelling and grammar.

For some couples, such a separation represented a chance for love to grow and develop, their emotions enriched through the written word as through physical longing, and the distance cementing their feelings for each other. When Francesco Baldassi (Rome, 1938) was parted from his *fidanzata* Gabriella for two months while on military service, he found that her absence only intensified his feelings. He largely retreated to an interior world of imagining and longing, which he poured out in letters to her. 'I wrote her letters and lyrical prose, managing in this way to pass hours and hours reflecting and dreaming, managing in this way to transform real things into objects of free and delicate fantasy.'[91] Baldassi, a university student and subsequently a published writer, was clearly at ease with the written word, perhaps more so than he was in the military. Others found it much more difficult to sustain love and companionship with pen and page; literacy was still not universal in 1950s Italy, while among those who could read and write levels of fluency no doubt varied. The fact that many Italians still spoke a local dialect in their ordinary lives, but had to use standard Italian in their writing, no doubt complicated matters further for many couples. Martyn Lyon's work on the written correspondence of ordinary European couples in the late nineteenth and early twentieth centuries has underlined both the importance of letter writing to relationships and the challenges involved in sustaining a correspondence.[92] He described the efforts that people not ordinarily fluent in writing might go to in order to obtain pen and paper as well as carve out the space and time during busy lives and amid often crowded living spaces in order to communicate with loved ones.[93]

Angelo Pettinari (province of Brescia, 1926) provided some insight into the challenges of keeping a relationship alive through correspondence. Separated from his future wife Piera for several years (as detailed in Chapter 1), first for military service and then as a migrant worker in Luxembourg while Piera worked as a waitress in Milan, their courtship was conducted almost entirely through letters. Angelo had completed the full five years of primary school, meaning that he would have had a basic level of literacy although perhaps not much more.[94] Piera, as a woman from a similar working-class or rural background in provincial Lombardy, would likely have had a similar level of education if not lower. Although gender disparities in education were improving from the 1950s

---

[91] Francesco Baldassi, 'Il Ritorno', MP/04, ADN.

[92] Martyn Lyons, *The Writing Culture of Ordinary People in Europe, c. 1860–1920* (Cambridge, 2013).

[93] Sonia Cancian, *Families, Lovers and their Letters: Italian Postwar Migration to Canada* (Winnipeg, 2010).

[94] This was quite usual for men of working-class and peasant backgrounds up to the 1950s, see Introduction, pp. xx.

to the 1970s, it was still usual enough for girls from peasant backgrounds in the 1950s to leave school after completing three rather than five years of primary education, while boys were more likely to receive the full five years.[95] The fluency of the couple with formal, written Italian could have been fairly rudimentary as they likely spoke dialect as their first language and in conversation with each other.[96] As we saw in Chapter 1, the knowledge of Piera's love sustained Angelo on his travels and the photograph she sent to him was a great comfort. Indeed, Lyons described the importance of receiving regular correspondence for men in particular who were living away from family and loved ones during World War I, letters representing the only real link with home and 'ordinary' life.[97] Angelo, similarly living away from home and most likely in dormitory accommodation in a foreign country, clearly relied on Piera's correspondence for his emotional sustenance. We can see from Angelo's description of the photograph of his beloved that letters might be treasured as material objects as much as written texts.[98] As Sofia Cancian suggests in her study of love letters between post-war Italian migrants to Canada, the photograph might be used to create a symbolic 'bridge' between the two lovers.[99]

Several of Cancian's corresponding couples also remarked in their letters about the limitations of the written word in allowing them to express how they felt.[100] The memoir sources used in this study could be particularly candid in discussing the limitations of letter writing in sustaining an intimate relationship, perhaps because the writers are reflecting on the correspondence and are thus somewhat removed from it. As Angelo wrote:

> A letter from Piera kept my spirits up: she wrote telling me to be patient and to remain strong, that we would soon be back in the village. But it seemed like the time would never pass. And the fear of losing her grew day by day: in two years we had seen each other at the most two or three times. Our love was lived entirely in letters, in which we always wrote the same things, the same words: 'Yours forever Angelo', 'Yours forever Piera'. The day of our return came. Finally we could begin to love each other close together.[101]

Angelo and Piera did marry, clearly deepening their relationship once they managed to spend more time together. It is also clear from Angelo's words that that many couples like them, separated for some time and with limited

---

[95] Perry Willson, *Women in Twentieth Century Italy* (London, 2009), pp. 115–17.

[96] Sebastiana Tarascio (Florida, Sicily, 1935) described how her relationship with her first boyfriend—a local boy who walked her home from school each day—was entirely false as they spoke to each other in Italian rather than in dialect: 'Io mi racconto: Bilancio di una cinquantenne', MP/87, ADN.

[97] Lyons, *Writing Culture of Ordinary People*, pp. 154–69.

[98] See also Lyons, *Writing Culture of Ordinary People*, pp. 37–9.

[99] Cancian, *Families, Lovers and their Letters*, pp. 115–16.

[100] Cancian, *Families, Lovers and their letters*, pp. 137–8.

[101] Angelo Pettinari, 'I miei primi...72 anni'.

capacities for expressing thoughts and feelings in writing, may have been engaged for years without really knowing each other. As we can see from Angelo and Piera's formulaic repetition of the words 'yours forever', ties of commitment and obligation may have taken root without a couple having much chance to know each other, with familiar phrases repeated like a formula or mantra rather than necessarily a reflection of deeply rooted feelings.

While couples such as Angelo and Piera struggled to communicate and to sustain their love for each other across great distances, other courtships were built and developed entirely through letters, barely existing in reality. Elisabetta Battistini (Rome, 1941) was, from the age of 18 to 22, *fidanzata* to a marine officer she had met on holiday in Venice. Since they rarely saw each other after the holiday, the relationship existed entirely through letters, until almost overnight Elisabetta became tired of waiting for him and ended the relationship. She was able to reflect ironically on the experience from the vantage point of her relatively liberated life in 1960s Rome, using inverted commas to refer to their supposed engagement. The teenage Anna Soprani (Forlì, 1939) also carried out a similar relationship by letter with Antonio, an older Italian man posted abroad by the military. As we saw earlier in the chapter, she did not seem to take the correspondence particularly seriously, using it as a way of trying out romantic postures, although Antonio may have seen it differently. Such courtships were not uncommon and would likely have meant much more for a young woman living a relatively isolated provincial or rural life, presumably leading to marriage in many cases.

Such was the experience of Giovanna Cavallo (province of Cosenza, 1931) in early 1950s Calabria. Although Giovanna's early family life was somewhat unconventional, she came from a wealthy background and by her adolescence her father emerged as a traditional southern patriarch in her diary. By 1949 she was corresponding with a man named Carlo, who had been on holiday in the area the previous year. She was also being pressured by her father to accept an arranged marriage but was adamant that she would only marry for love. By love she meant Carlo, and her correspondence with him seemed to be the only way for Giovanna to break out of the path prescribed to her by her father, as the daughter of a provincial southern nobleman. Giovanna's diary entries charted how her feelings for Carlo gradually intensified. Initially, although she wrote of her certain love for him, she did not yet think of marrying him, but rather of refusing marriage (understood as arranged marriage and thus associated in her mind with obligation and family and in opposition to love) because of the depth of her feelings for Carlo.[102] Writing in March 1950 and frustrated that he did not write as often as she expected, she mused over her feelings for him: 'two years ago I knew nothing of him, I couldn't even imagine

---

[102] Giovanna Cavallo, *Ho sognato i suoi occhi* (Milan, 1996); see for example p. 81 and p. 204, 8 December 1949 and 27 November 1950. A copy is also conserved at the ADN.

his existence and now my whole life seems centred on him. Is he the ideal man? The man that I would like? Yes, spiritually and physically. I will wait.'[103] Over the next few years, Giovanna battled her father and finally convinced him to accept her marriage to Carlo, framed as a marriage of love rather than the arranged marriage intended for her. A conversation with her father, in which he told her that arranged marriages were best since love always disappointed, resulted in a long reflection on Giovanna's own poetic and idealized understanding of love.

> Love? Those who really manage to love are few. That which we all call love is nothing but affection mixed with desire. For many that's all it is. Love is a great, sublime thing that people diminish by saying 'I love you' too easily. No, whoever manages to love, loves forever, and if as they say, the love ends and the flame is extinguished, that means it wasn't real love.[104]

In November 1953, Giovanna and Carlo married in a proxy wedding. Carlo was posted abroad to Africa and custom dictated that Giovanna had to be married in order to travel to join him. Carlo's posting thus entitled the couple to a proxy wedding. In Giovanna's case, the relationship with Carlo did seem to develop through correspondence into one of love, and their marriage was a happy one.

It is also clear from Giovanna's diary that the couple did not really know each other until after the wedding, and Giovanna's professions of love seem to be informed as much by her imagination, and her desire to experience freedom and adventure, as by the reality of her relationship with Carlo. Her experiences fitted with what we know of the limited horizons and opportunities afforded to many young women in the 1950s, particularly in middle- and upper-class households and in the south. With few opportunities for meeting men in their daily lives, and with career or migration rarely an option for a single woman, often the only way to escape the family home was through marriage. Stories about young women escaping the boredom of rural life or indeed the grip of family through marriage could be found in the pages of popular magazines like *Grand Hotel* in the 1950s.[105] Indeed, young women have long read and dreamed about romantic love as an escape from the dreariness or hardship of ordinary life, the man himself perhaps secondary to the fantasy of the imagined life as somebody's wife.[106] This was particularly the case up to the 1950s, when women's circumstances still depended very much on the men in their lives. Although Giovanna's

---

[103] Cavallo, *Ho sognato i suoi occhi*, p. 105, 28 February 1950.
[104] Cavallo, *Ho sognato i suoi occhi*, p. 98, 2 February 1950.
[105] L'albero maladetto', *Grand Hotel*, 4 July 1959.
[106] Carol Dyhouse, *Heartthrobs: A History of Women and Desire* (Oxford, 2017).

epistolary courtship did lead to love and marriage, the musings in her diary also fit with the pattern of women dreaming and thinking about love in the abstract. This can be seen particularly in diaries and usually before they had begun a serious relationship. While women often thought and mused about love in adolescence, men tended to reflect more openly and in much more depth on their experience of actual love.

As the notion of companionate marriage gained currency in Italy and indeed across the post-war western world, things were beginning to change.[107] In Italian popular culture as in the personal testimonies we can see also how the rise of friendships between men and women was leading to new ways of characterizing courtship and marriage.[108] Romance, while important, was not everything and there was an increasing recognition in *Grand Hotel* that while the notion of love at first sight might still make a good storyline, it was not enough to sustain a relationship. When 'Bruno in love' (Naples) wrote to *Grand Hotel* in 1955 to say that he was in love with a girl he hadn't spoken to, he was told that this was impossible and to get to know her first.[109] As the economic climate too began to change, the importance and duration of male migration was lessening; correspondence might still be a stage in the romantic life of a couple, but not a prolonged state. Indeed, the heroes and heroines of *Grand Hotel*'s fictional world were changing too; the rich landowners, glamorous film directors, and poor rural women of the early 1950s were yielding to working men and women, and to school and university students in the late 1950s, and their romances were increasingly founded on a more equal basis. Many in the 1950s and 1960s thus also characterized their courtships in terms of friendship, companionship, and shared values, such descriptions sometimes blending seamlessly with romance, and sometimes acting in opposition to it. The gendered pattern we saw in Chapter 1 of men tending to describe open and definite feelings of love in courtship while women were more likely to fantasize about love in their adolescence but emphasize negative feelings in the lead up to marriage, is reflected again in this discussion. Even those women who did include love in their diaries and memoirs of courtship tended to describe it in fairy-tale terms, writing of meeting 'my Prince Charming' rather than describing their feelings in depth.[110] As a consequence, it is still mostly the voices of men that we hear in this section.

Giuseppe Rigoni (province of Vicenza, 1941) began courting his future wife Lilia through correspondence while working as a manual labourer in

---

[107] See Langhamer, *The English in Love*; Marcus Collins, *Modern Love: An Intimate History of Men and Women in Twentieth Century Britain* (London, 2003); Anthony Giddens, *The Transformation of Intimacy: Sexuality, Love and Eroticism in Modern Societies* (London, 1993).
[108] See the roundtable discussion 'I giovani e l'amore', *Tempo*, 23 June 1959.
[109] *Grand Hotel*, 8 January 1955.
[110] One such example is Maria Guerrini, 'I miei ricordi', MP/T2, ADN.

Switzerland, an experience that many others shared in the 1950s.[111] However, the development of the relationship, and Rigoni's reflections on it, had a very different tone to Giovanna Cavallo's epistolary 'great love'. He had been disappointed in love already when his first girlfriend returned to Italy for an arranged marriage, and although the correspondence with Lilia was tempered by Giuseppe's grief over the end of the previous relationship, gradually 'with each letter his feelings for her grew'.[112] The pair met, holidayed together, and became real companions. They spoke together of their plans for the future and the decision to marry was one that they made together. As they got to know each other better, Giuseppe was able to remark that his 'love for her became more solid, less passionate than others I had lived through, but very sincere and intense'.[113] Reflecting on his apprehension and somewhat ambivalent feelings about the wedding, he wrote that 'for her I didn't have a passionate love, such as I had experienced at other times, but I was living a sweet, realistic dream that would last through time and wouldn't disintegrate in the first storm'.[114] Companionship and shared values rather than romance, passion, and physical attraction were the attributes that he treasured.

For other couples, particularly those who met in the 1960s, romantic love, partnership, and companionship were not mutually exclusive and often blended in their accounts of courtship. Gianfranco (Piedmont, 1939) met his wife while they were both working together at the Olivetti factory in the Piedmontese city of Ivrea.[115] Although she made a strong first impression, Gianfranco was careful to add in the memoir that afterwards he had the chance to get to know her better by talking to her and developing a friendship.[116] Olivetti was a progressive company, influenced by US corporate thinking and offering its employees a host of company-sponsored social and recreational activities. The relatively long lunch breaks offered to company workers, with the chance to take part in sponsored activities such as billiards, offered them the chance to spend time together from day to day.

Francesco Baldassi (Rome, 1938) framed his relationship with his wife, whom he married in 1966, in terms of passion as well as emotional and intellectual companionship:

> Gabriella was the first and only woman of my life, precisely because from the beginning she signified my interior life, my search, my evolution, my feeling, my need for affection. [...] At the beginning she was my bonfire, a pole of attraction

---

[111] A similar experience was recounted in the memoir of Ermanno Castoldi, 'Dio e il suo aiuto: riassunto di una vita minuto per minuto', ADN.

[112] Giuseppe Rigoni, *I lunghi viaggi della speranza: un autobiografia romanzata* (Brescia, 2014), p. 177. A copy is also conserved at the ADN.

[113] Rigoni, *Lunghi viaggi*, p. 191.   [114] Rigoni, *Lunghi viaggi*, p. 240.

[115] Gianfranco, MP/Adn2, ADN.   [116] MP/Adn2, ADN.

through which I directed all of my aspirations and my sentimental longings. [...]
And it wasn't her exterior or physical characteristics that set off such an effusion
of emotion and fantasy on my part, so much as some aspects of her interior being.
[...] I had someone to talk to, someone to share the pain of those days.[117]

Wading through the effusive abstractions of Francesco's declarations, we can
see that while he described her with passion—she was his 'bonfire'—theirs was
very much a union of intellect and companionship. Marrying in 1966, they
were university students together in the tumultuous days of mounting student
protest in the late 1960s. He gradually withdrew from formal education,
motivated both by the need to support his young family and his growing
disaffection with the official university system. Witnessing 1968 somewhat
from the periphery as he was by then married with children of his own, he was
nonetheless aware of the climate of activism and the feminist movement
which followed it. The couple also felt strongly enough about their future
together that they defied Gabriella's father by marrying, and set up home
together despite a lack of family support and in poor financial circumstances.
It seems fitting then that Francesco would see his own marriage in terms of
passion, love, and companionship.

Growing up in provincial Romagna in the 1960s, Massimo Bartoletti Stella
(1951, Forlì Cesena) was somewhat younger than most of the diarists and
memoirists discussed in this book. He wrote a detailed diary of his early
and mid-teenage years, giving us glimpses of how the changing culture of
the 1960s—gender roles, the influence of mass culture, and the rise of youth
culture—might impact on the sentimental life of a teenage boy. The diary is
largely a chronicle of his on/off relationship with his girlfriend and school
companion Katia. Their love grew out of companionship and friendship, as
the pair also grew up together. They mainly went to the cinema together as
they disliked dancing. Through the diary we see them trying out different
romantic postures, and Massimo worrying about how their love measured up
to his romantic ideals. Following a somewhat playful declaration of love at the
start of the relationship, the couple later on had more serious discussions
about fidelity and jealousy. At the same time their relationship was primarily a
light-hearted one of jokes and banter, and their main topics of conversation
were cinema, popular music and their parents:

I've never had a serious conversation with her, I didn't try because I know (or
thought I knew) her personality, that she liked to laugh and to make her laugh
I started the same stupid talk so that she would enjoy my company [...] It's been
almost two years since we got to know each other and we still tell each other the
same stupid things, I ask myself, can it go on like this? You ask 'what do you want

---

[117] Francesco Baldassi, 'Il ritorno'.

to discuss with her?' Answer: 'Serious things, of feelings, of many other things regarding the heart'.[118]

Massimo seemed torn between a real adolescent love based on friendship and shared interests and the expectation that romantic love should be about passionate feelings and grand, noble gestures. By the time the diary was ending in the late 1960s, his feelings about love were changing again; now he believed that marrying too young was a mistake, and he expected not to marry before he reached the age of 30. A student at *liceo artistico*, he was by this time being drawn into the youth counter-culture of the late 1960s.

For Lucio Bartolomeo (1930, Genoa) Catholic associational culture offered him the chance to get to know his future wife Carla as a friend and equal. The lay organization Catholic Action was at full strength in the 1950s, attracting roughly three million members in that decade.[119] The organization and indeed the Catholic Church more broadly played a politically and culturally conservative role in post-war Italy, fuelling Cold War politics at a local level and denigrating 'modern' values particularly when it came to the roles of women. At the same time, the Church was broadly in tune with the model of companionate marriage, seeking to understand romantic love and to frame it within a positive, spiritual light.[120] At a grassroots level, Catholicism could also have a more positive impact on young Italians, allowing them to meet and socialize in morally approved mixed gender groups.[121] After meeting her in his group of young Franciscans, Lucio took the bus with Carla every day in an effort to get to know her better:

> The tram in the morning and the bus in the evening that Carla took to return home, served as the incubators of our strong friendship first and later our love, permitting us the little intimacy that wasn't possible in the midst of our group of friends.[122]

Lucio was clear that they had come together as friends, love developing as the friendship deepened. Several pages later he mused about the nature of their love, reflecting that there had been no classic romantic moment of love at first sight, but that their feelings had developed over time. In the years of their engagement, both were involved not just in Catholic Action but in trade

---

[118] Massimo Bartoletti Stella, '1964–1968: Gli anni dell'adolescenza', DP/08, ADN.

[119] Percy Allum, 'Uniformity Undone: Aspects of Catholic Culture in Post War Italy', in Zygmunt Baranski and Robert Lumley (eds), *Culture and Conflict in Post-war Italy: Essays on Mass and Popular Culture* (London, 1990, p. 85).

[120] Alana Harris, 'Love Divine and Love Sublime: the Catholic Marriage Advisory Council, the National Marriage Guidance Movement and the State', in Alana Harris and Timothy Jones (eds), *Love and Romance in Britain, 1918–1970* (London, 2015), pp. 188–224.

[121] On Catholic culture in post-war Italy see also David Forgacs and Stephen Gundle, *Mass Culture and Italian Society from Fascism to the Cold War* (Bloomington, IN, 2007), pp. 247–59.

[122] Lucio Bartolomeo, 'Trecioli e freguggie', MP/06, ADN.

union politics and shared the same dreams and goals of bringing about a transformation in society. Theirs was a socially committed Catholicism, of the kind that could be considered part of the broader 'spirit of Vatican II'.[123]

> At the beginning of our relationship there was no 'bolt of lightning' [love at first sight] followed by overwhelming passion, but an ever-deepening affection that involved us both completely, with emotions that were new to us both, as we began our shared dreams and projects.[124]

Describing their wedding day, Lucio wrote that he regretted not being able to find the right words to tell Carla that he loved her. Overcome by the solemnity of the occasion, he awkwardly whispered to her at the altar that she 'looked like an angel'. 'I wanted to say "I love you" but I have always had trouble using that verb "to love", maybe because it seems too artificial and over used.'[125] In their case the popular vocabulary of romance seemed ill fitted to the intimacy of their companionship.

Vincenzo Rotundi (Foggia, 1927) as we saw earlier was also deeply religious; he had begun to train as a priest after spending much of his youth as a member of Catholic Action, and set aside his vocation to marry Gioy. Theirs too was a relationship that began as friendship, especially considering that Vincenzo was not openly courting when he met her. They began to spend their Sunday afternoons together and their relationship gradually deepened, becoming one of love. Reflecting in his memoir, Vincenzo addressed himself directly to his late wife, wondering: 'that day when we first met at the home of our shared friends, I was really "struck" by your presence. Even now I wonder if it wasn't the classic "bolt of lightning".'[126] Thinking back, Vincenzo tried to fit his feelings for his wife into the familiar template of the 'bolt of lightning' or 'love at first sight' even though these tropes were not an obvious fit. It is possible that the religious perspective of both Vincenzo and Lucio allowed them to create a space apart from the mainstream cultural constructions of romantic love and a masculinity strongly connected to sexual desire and dominance, similar to the way in which shared left-wing politics created a sense of companionship and equality for other couples.

Sebastiana Tarascio (Florida, Sicily, 1935) was also desperate to escape from the mainstream attitudes about love and gender that surrounded her growing up; however, her flight was not one of ideas but of geography.[127] Growing up in rural Sicily, her memoir was scathing about local courtship practices, and

---

[123] Gerd Rainer-Horn, *The Spirit of Vatican II: Western European Progressive Catholicism in the Long Sixties* (Oxford, 2015).
[124] Lucio Bartolomeo, 'Trecioli e freguggie'.
[125] Lucio Bartolomeo, 'Trecioli e freguggie'.
[126] Vincenzo Rotundi, 'Io e te insieme. Storia di una vita vissuta insieme 1957–1996', MP/99, ADN.
[127] Sebastiana Tarascio, 'Io mi racconto'.

she found the notion of 'love through glances' and the necessity of secrecy both artificial and horribly restrictive for women. As an educated woman she was able to migrate to Turin, armed with her diploma as a primary school teacher. When she finally met her husband Domenico at the age of 29 while working in provincial Piedmont, he represented for her the direct opposite of what she had rejected in Sicily. She was initially attracted to him not for his appearance but because he made her feel at ease, and she described their courtship as a gradual understanding of the other's personality. Together for three years before their marriage, theirs was a courtship with ups and downs and with arguments as well as good moments. Over time Domenico's good character gradually became more apparent to Sebastiana: 'Domenico did not reveal his character straight away. At times he was kind, open, spirited; at other times contrary, brusque, closed. But in time he showed himself to be delicate, tender, affectionate, protective.'[128] A large part of what attracted Sebastiana to Domenico was that as a man of the provincial north, he had a different character and different idea of courtship and marriage to those surrounding her growing up.

Despite Sebastiana's convictions, it was of course quite possible for a couple from a rural southern background to share a relationship of love that seemed relatively free from the traditional deeply gendered notions of courtship, sexuality, and marriage. Sometimes the principal divide regarding codes of affection and intimacy for courting couples was not regional but generational. Maria Fresu (1935/6, province of Sassari, Sardinia) described a typically southern courtship that began with glances but developed into a real love, deeply felt by both partners. Her memoir was unusual in describing such sincere and strong emotion as a woman, since the emphasis, in this tradition, was usually on the man choosing his beloved:

> Fleeting glances, smiles of complicity, were important in courtship in those days [...] We realized that we were hopelessly in love and it was lovely, I remember when I told him that yes I loved him too, he seemed crazed with joy even if we couldn't even exchange a kiss, because we were on the street and in the town it was unthinkable.[129]

The social restrictions of the time, which Sebastiana found stifling, seemed to serve only to sharpen Maria's and Antonio's feelings for each other; the glances and smiles were flirtatious while as their love developed, restraint intensified their feelings. However, her father's strictness dampened their happiness. Initially the couple hoped to keep their love secret, because once their parents knew about it, a formal engagement—with all that entailed—would have to follow. Their glances to each other in church were noted in the

---

[128] Sebastiana Tarascio, 'Io mi racconto'.
[129] Maria Fresu, 'La mia infanzia rubata', MP/Adn2, ADN.

village though, and the wedding hastened, with a date in September 1961. The disapproval of Maria's father continued. 'Nanni (her brother) accompanied me to the altar, seeing as father would not forgive me for being so much in love and my demonstrating it in all the ways possible made me seem flighty, in his view.'[130] What is curious in Maria's account is her father's opposition to the marriage simply for the depth of feeling between the couple. While the couple were openly flirtatious with each other, there was no mention of sexual transgression. Was Maria perhaps intended for another marriage arranged by her father? If so, it is curious that he protested the marriage but does not seem to have made any effort to prevent it. Maria's description of the morning after her wedding vividly demonstrates how sincere love, freely exchanged and equally felt, was perfectly possible in rural Sardinia, despite the oppressive, rigid gender norms emphasized by other sources. The fact that the couple were only able to speak freely to each other after their wedding does point to the fact that theirs was a different kind of courtship to those based on friendship and shared plans, although still one with its own distinct and real vocabulary of love. As such it seems fitting to leave the last word to her:

> The moment that I like to remember is the morning afterwards. As soon as I woke up, I realized that I was holding Antonio's hand. I stayed still listening to his breathing and looking at him in the shadow of dawn. It seemed like a beautiful dream and I cried. I cried out of a real happiness that I had never felt before. When Antonio woke up we held each other tightly and told each other all the things we hadn't been able to say before.[131]

CONCLUSION

Lieta Harrison's 1966 book *The Initiation: How Adolescent Girls Become Women* claimed to be a wide-ranging survey of Italian adolescent girls in the swinging 1960s. When interviewed about love, a number of them said that they did not believe in love at all, while others put caveats on their definition of love; it had to be 'free' or 'modern' to be desirable.[132] For these girls, marriage was also an outmoded institution: 62 per cent of those surveyed declared that they did not intend to marry. Some quotations dismissed marriage as mere 'convenience' while in the words of one 16-year-old school pupil, 'everyone marries for love, but once the marriage happens, the love is finished'.[133] Others cited the failed marriages of their parents as their reasons. These positions are an exaggerated reflection of the state of mind of the average 1960s Italian girl,

---

[130] Maria Fresu, 'La mia infanzia rubata'.   [131] Maria Fresu, 'La mia infanzia rubata'.
[132] Harrison, *L'Iniziazione*, pp. 77–87.   [133] Harrison, *L'Iniziazione*, p. 88.

but they do give us some insights into how thinking about marriage and love was rapidly changing by the 1960s.

It was not just women who might feel stifled by the traditional middle-class model of courtship shaped and regulated by family, although women's behaviour was subject to particularly close surveillance. This rigid system was being dismantled by the 1960s, with the incursion of the mass media and the social changes of the economic miracle, but it is clear that young women were still receiving contradictory and confusing messages about how they should behave. They did not need to wait any longer for a man to make the declaration of love, and might see love develop through friendship. However, sexuality was still a fraught issue for many couples; women were expected to resist sexual advances and to be passive partners, while men were expected to insist. Even in the memoirs of more liberated women, it seemed typical to minimize their own agency regarding their sexuality.

Similarly, when it came to writing about love there were strong gendered patterns. Women tended to think about romantic love in relation to dreams and fantasies for their future life, while their descriptions of actual courtship and engagement did not tend to include much detail about emotional intimacy. Considering the discord between the 'Prince Charming' of fairy-tale romance that girls absorbed in popular culture and the economics that dominated many actual courtships, women must have often been disappointed in reality. In contrast the men's memoirs were much more detailed and open in their discussions of both sexuality and romantic love and intimacy. Even in the 1960s, women's access to educational and career opportunities was not changing at the pace that it was elsewhere, and while there might have been greater equality in courtship and love, gender roles in marriage—men as breadwinners and women as housewives and mothers—remained as rigid as ever for most people.[134] We saw in Chapter 1 how, with their economic security at stake, most women could not afford to be romantic about marriage. In courtship and while engaged to marry, their outlook seems similar even if it is rarely openly expressed as such. This is not to suggest that many of the relationships discussed in the memoirs were not loving ones, but that when it came to setting down their experiences, other considerations dominated the women's accounts.

While there were strong cultural pressures on men, as on women, to conform to a certain model of masculinity, this might be tempered by politics or religion, both of which offered different models of masculinity. A strong association with Catholic culture or membership of the PCI seemed to offer men different ways of being intimate and loving, which did not emphasize sexual dominance. It is less clear that either politics or religion offered

---

[134] See Luisa Tasca, 'The "Average Housewife" in Post World War II Italy', in *The Journal of Women's History*, 16:2 (2004), pp. 92–115.

substantially different gender ideals to women. Regional differences, as well as urban, provincial, and rural settings, also need to be taken into consideration. Of course, while the gendered patterns are very clear in most accounts of courtship and engagement, there are notable exceptions, and Maria's memoir reminds us that real love and intimacy could still be experienced and communicated in a traditional rural society where courtship, love and gender roles were highly codified.

3

Where Violence and Love Meet: Honour and Italian Society

The photo story 'Love in White Overalls', which ran in *Grand Hotel* magazine over several months in 1955, seemed at first glance to be a simple story of romantic love winning out over an arranged marriage, or emotions conquering family and economic considerations (see Figure 3.1). As such it was in keeping with the magazine's mission to champion romantic love, while keeping their conservative line on sexuality. The protagonist Franca was in love with Dario, a mechanic and motorcyclist of modest means, but their happiness was thwarted in numerous and complex ways by 'bad', rich businessman De Fazio. Among other devious actions, he had convinced her mother that he was the man for her so that Franca was defying her family by choosing Dario. The love story with Dario did of course win out in the end, but on closer examination the story was not as progressive as it seemed. The love that Franca and Dario shared was a secret, forbidden love communicated through meaningful glances, as the couple rarely had the chance to speak. Both of them staked everything on their love, although they appeared to barely know each other.[1] It seemed to have little to do with the companionate marriage, and the emerging notions of a love based on friendship, equality, and shared values. At the same time, while the idea of a love based on smouldering glances and exaggerated emotions appears like simple melodrama, it was actually more realistic than it might seem.

In the southern regions of Italy, Sicily and Calabria in particular, there were specific regional traditions of love and courtship with similar elements to the story outlined above. Very often an elopement leading to marriage was the only way to turn such passion and longing into a legitimate relationship. Although these regional traditions could bleed into popular representations of romance in 1950s and 1960s Italy, they actually had much older roots. They could also have much darker connotations: in the above story the love between

---

[1] 'L'Amore in tuta bianca', *Grand Hotel*, 1955. A short story also from that year carried a similar message: Nanda Violini, 'La moglie non è un cavallo', *Grand Hotel*, 22 July 1955.

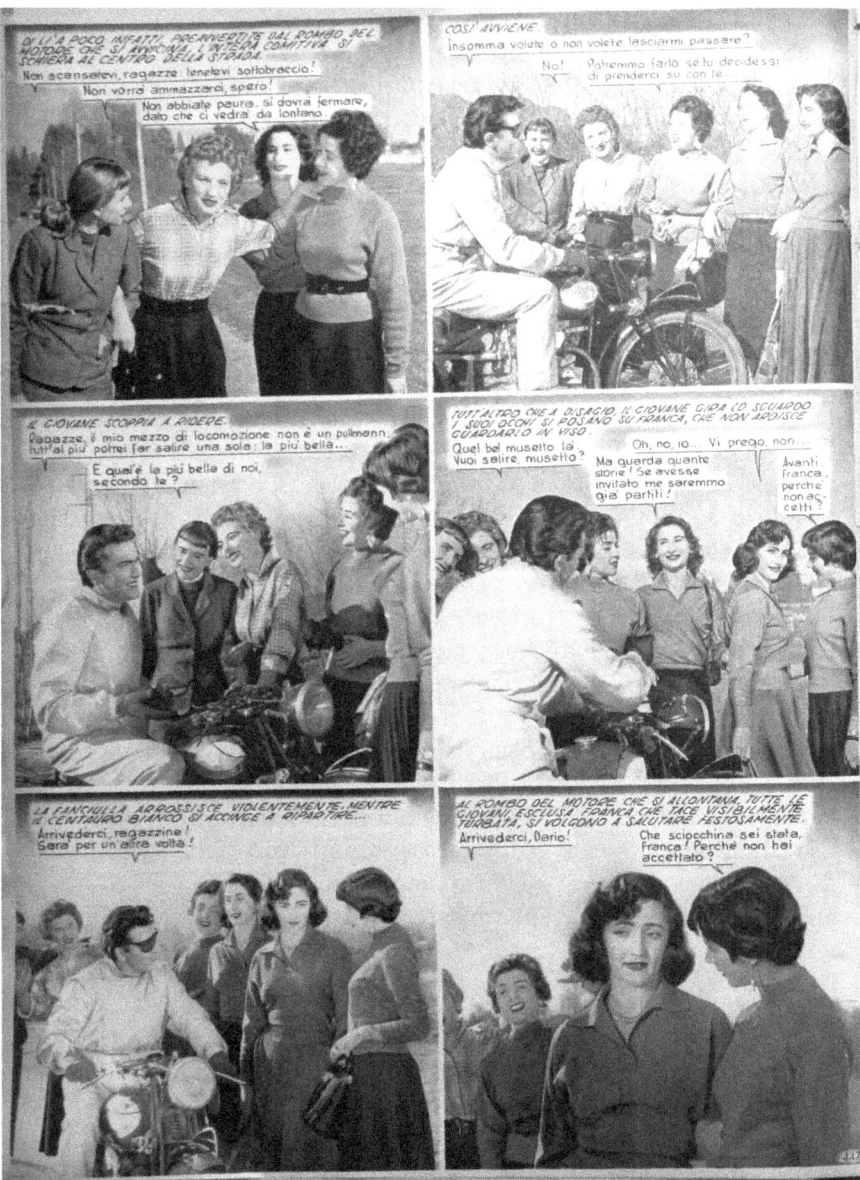

Figure 3.1. Page from an early instalment of the photo story 'Love in White Overalls'.
'Amore in tuta bianca', *Grand Hotel*, 15 January 1955. Biblioteca Braidense, Milan.

the couple seemed real enough even though it was based on very little contact or conversation. In reality, an apparent love story based solely on glances and culminating in elopement could also place a romantic veneer over violence, coercion, and control. This was particularly the case in a society where unrelated men and women were not supposed to have any meaningful contact before marriage; in these circumstances, love could be half imagined while it could also be used to excuse crimes against women. This chapter seeks to untangle the messy knot of love, longing, sexual violence, and coercion that lingered beneath the surface of some southern courtship and marriage stories. The chapter begins by exploring stories of 'love through glances' and elopement, set in the context of honour as the organizing idea for gender relations and separate spheres in southern society. It then shifts focus to examine how these attitudes and tensions came together in the story and reportage of a crime, which became emblematic of change in 1960s Italy and Sicily.

There are several reasons for using the story of a crime and a court case as the main focus of the chapter. Violence against women as we will see could often be a feature of courtship and marriage in southern society, whether kidnap, sexual violence, or the violence of forced marriage. Despite this, few men or women have spoken or written openly about how these issues affected their lives, and of those who did none were willing to be included in this book. Because local custom meant that such events were often explained away with references to love and romance, as well as honour and shame, it was no doubt difficult for women who experienced such violence to make sense of what had happened to them and to clearly articulate their own feelings. The case that forms the focal point of this chapter concerns the kidnapping of a teenage girl named Franca Viola in 1965 with the aim of forcing her into marriage. What made the case a landmark one in Italian history was not what happened to Franca Viola but the decision that she made afterwards. She refused to marry her attacker and instead brought him to trial. In doing so, she began a public discussion about honour and violence against women in Sicilian society, forcing Italian society to begin to make definite distinctions between love and passion, and coercion and violence. While it is difficult to gain a sustained insight into real experiences of these issues, an investigation of the public conversation about the case of Franca Viola and the aftermath of the trial does outline how attitudes towards crimes of honour, forced marriage, and gender violence were changing in the 1960s. As we will see, the changing understanding of love was central to the way in which crimes of honour, including forced marriage, were rejected in Italian society.

LOVE, ELOPEMENT, AND THE MALE GAZE IN SOUTHERN ITALY

The behaviour of women in rural Sicily and some southern provinces was strictly codified, with feminine virtue linked to family honour. Historians, anthropologists, and sociologists describe how in rural Sicilian and Calabrian society, women rarely left the family home except in the company of their husband, father, or brother.[2] Of course, class and circumstance would have forced some modifications to these 'rules': not all women could afford not to work and strict adherence was generally considered a mark of respectability.[3] Social spaces were, however, strictly gendered. Public spaces—the street, piazza, and bar—were for men, while the private and domestic were considered to form the feminine sphere. Even in public, women sought to lower their gaze so as to appear modest. When tradition in the south dictated that respectable women should rarely leave the house, linger in public places, or have friendships with men outside the family, one of the few ways for a couple to 'meet' was through fleeting glances exchanged on the street, until the man gathered the courage to declare his love formally to the woman's family. The growth of a 'love' through glances is a recurring theme in memoirs of men and women growing up in Sicily and Calabria as well as in magazine letters. With no other way to meet members of the opposite sex, this kind of love could be felt and experienced as real.[4]

It was also of course part of a much older European literary tradition of courtly love.[5] In the medieval tradition, a woman was idealized by a male poet and strong feelings of love sustained despite very little contact with the beloved. The love of Dante for Beatrice, immortalized in the *Vita Nova* and drawing on the earlier tradition of the Provencal poets, is the classic Italian example.[6] This kind of love was usually considered in opposition to marriage, and although sometimes adulterous, it could also be described as a pure sentiment existing above the base concerns of sexuality and procreation. In modern Italy the tradition also created a space for couples whose families were opposed to their marriages to continue in secret and defy their parents. In these traditions, the glance became strongly associated with love and longing. By implication, the glance and the gaze—both looking and being sighted— were also associated with female transgression. While Bloch traces the origins of these ideas back to the Church fathers—'since desire is engendered by, and consists in, a look, a virgin seen is no longer a virgin'—locating them also in the literature of medieval France and England, we can see the modern traces of

---

[2] Charlotte Gower Chapman, *Milocca: A Sicilian Village* (London, 1973); Linda Reeder, *Widows in White: Migration and the Transformation of Rural Italian Women, 1880-1920* (Toronto, 2003); Simonetta Piccone Stella, *Ragazze del sud: Famiglie, figlie, studentesse in una città meridionale* (Rome, 1979).

[3] Jane C. Scheider and Peter T. Schneider, *Festival of the Poor: Fertility Decline and the Ideology of Class in Sicily 1860-1980* (Tucson, AZ, 1996), p. 229–32.

[4] For a broader sample of such letters, see Gabriella Parca (ed.), *Le italiane si confessano* (Florence, 1961) pp. 119–37.

[5] See William Reddy, *The Making of Romantic Love: Longing and Sexuality in Europe, South Asia and Japan, 900-1200 CE* (Chicago, 2012) and R. Howard Bloch, *Medieval Misogyny and the Invention of Western Romantic Love* (Chicago, 1991).

[6] Dante Alighieri, *Vita Nova* (1295), trans. Andrew Frisardi (Evanston, IL, 2002).

them in the Italian honour code.[7] Under these strict social codes, it was not just how or where women appeared that was the issue; even looking was strictly circumscribed. Since women were socialized to lower their eyes in public, the gaze was socially and culturally constructed as a male gaze. For a woman to meet a man's gaze was not to be undertaken lightly, as it could be interpreted as an invitation or assent. We can see traces of these strictures in memoirs and diaries from across Italy; while visual first impressions and physical attraction are crucial to the men's narratives of falling in love, these features are much more rare in the women's writings.

The memoir of Sicilian woman Maria Lamonica (Piraino, province of Messina, 1942) is a classic illustration of how love could be cultivated through glances. Maria was forced to interrupt her education after primary school because her mother thought that it would be improper for a girl to attend secondary school in the next town. The struggle to continue her education and to gain freedom from her parents structured Maria's memoir. Confined to the family home in preparation for marriage, in keeping with middle-class Sicilian tradition, Maria was allowed to leave the house only to visit the local convent and eventually also to work part-time in a dressmaker's shop. While visiting cousins she managed to attract the attention of local man Salvatore and, although the two never spoke, he began to follow her to work. A love story thus developed through glances. 'We glanced furtively at each other from opposite sides of the pavement and then each continued on our way. Even these brief encounters made me happy. I sewed always thinking of him and as I prepared to leave I knew I would see him again and was happy.'[8] It was access to work rather than changing spaces of leisure that proved key to Maria's love story. Even these brief glances between the two were enough for people to begin gossiping about them in the town, forcing them closer together. They began to exchange love letters, and when Maria's parents came to know of their relationship, strong parental opposition further strengthened her feelings for him. However, when Salvatore travelled seventy kilometres to her aunt and uncle's home so that the couple could finally meet, Maria realized there was no real feeling between the two of them.

> He rose and began to tell me that he loved me, and all kinds of other things. But the more he spoke the more I was disappointed. I almost couldn't believe myself. I had cried and suffered so much for this boy and strangely, I didn't like him anymore. Despite everything I stayed with him. I wanted to be sure about my feelings before coming to a decision. If my parents had thought differently I could have got to know him better. I would have realized whether or not he was right for me; and he too would have realized if I was as he imagined me.[9]

---

[7] Howard Bloch, *Medieval Misogyny*, p. 100; see also pp. 100–6.
[8] Maria Lamonica, 'In un piccolo centro di provincia', MP/03, ADN.
[9] Maria Lamonica, 'In un piccolo centro di provincia'.

The idea of a love cultivated through glances was a powerful one, particularly for young men and women who had little real experience of the opposite sex. With the couple essentially isolated, town gossip and parental opposition could give extra fuel to their feelings. In Maria's memory, it was Salvatore who drove the love story forward by following her home from work and he was the one who continued to believe in it at their first and final meeting, after Maria's fantasies were quickly punctured. Her memoir was above all the story of her struggle to escape Sicily with its restrictive gender codes and courtship practices, and this rejection of Sicily clearly coloured her tone. Her account nevertheless illustrates the manner in which masculine ideas of love were linked with the male gaze and embedded in the gendered codes of Sicilian society.

Saverio, born in Calabria in the mid-1940s, also described how love could develop through glances and secret notes.[10] After spending much of his adolescence in prison, Saverio spotted Gina while on temporary release. He described how their relationship developed through glances, reminding his readers that it was not possible to simply begin a conversation with a girl on the street in 1960s Calabria.[11] Here again the love story began with the male gaze. Since dialogue was impossible, the couple began to communicate by leaving notes for each other under stones and in this way a 'miraculous' feeling developed between them.[12] This love, communicated through notes and glances, was enough to sustain Saverio when he returned to prison and indeed after his release, in a similar way to how Maria's love for Salvatore sustained her through her confined family life and her sewing work. Of course, the couple still faced the strict opposition of Gina's family to their marriage. The photo stories of *Grand Hotel* indicate that in popular culture, these very different ideas of romantic love might be blended together or co-exist with more modern notions of friendship between the sexes. The memoir sources do make it clear though that this kind of love thrived in the very specific circumstances created by the notion of family or female honour which were particularly prevalent in Sicily and Calabria.

In Sicilian and Calabrian regional folk traditions, romantic love was almost always seen in opposition to marriage, and as a disruptive force that threatened the stability and security of family interests.[13] Built into this cultural construction of love as a hidden, extreme passion, was also the promise of an extreme solution to the problem of family opposition. It was broadly accepted in Sicily and southern Italy that a couple might elope or flee together in order to force their parents to agree to a wedding. Once the couple had spent time alone together, the woman was considered to have lost her honour and

---

[10] MP/T2.   [11] MP/T2.   [12] MP/T2.
[13] Rudolph Bell, *Fate, Honour, Family and Village*, p. 91.

marriage was the only way of repairing the family honour.[14] A couple might also elope in order to save themselves the cost of a large wedding, as in their shameful state, they could not have a full celebration afterwards. It was acknowledged as an informal custom more broadly across the Mediterranean and in Turkey; Julian Pitt-Rivers notes the custom in Andalusia while a similar elopement forms the plot of the 1978 Turkish film *Girl with the Red Scarf*.[15] Among the first-person texts, there were two such accounts of elopement; one successful and one not. Saverio was one of these. After his release the couple's time together was still very restricted because of their families' disapproval, and the only solution as they saw it was to flee together. Following tradition, they were confident that if they spent several days alone together, their families would have to accept the inevitability of their marriage. Unfortunately in their case, the families asserted that Gina had not been a virgin before the elopement. Since there was no honour to repair, there was no need for the couple to marry. Even afterwards, the love cultivated through glances continued to sustain the couple, and when Gina emigrated with her family to the United States they corresponded for some time. A similar case was reported where a woman's father would not consent to her marriage even after her elopement and instead obtained a certificate stating that she was still a virgin as she had a 'particularly elastic hymen'.[16] Such anecdotal examples, even if rare, indicate that customs were never as rigid as they seemed.

Another memoirist living in working-class Brindisi, in Puglia, was more successful. Giovanni described how, frustrated with his fiancée's mother who seemed to be delaying the wedding and himself eager for sexual fulfilment, he proposed an elopement to his fiancée. She was more reluctant than he according to his account, but agreed with the plan for fear of losing him.[17] They married eight days later, the wedding taking place behind the altar 'as sinners'. Giovanni's testimony opens the question of the gender and power dynamics of elopement. Although it was generally associated with romantic love, was an elopement always a decision made freely between the couple, or might there be an element of coercion? The woman after all had much more to lose. Her reputation destroyed, she generally could not expect to find another husband should the plan fail. Elopements could easily bleed into abductions. There was also a tradition of kidnapping women to force them into marriage and it was not easy to tell the difference between an elopement

---

[14] Rudolph Bell, *Fate, Honor, Family and Village: Demographic and Cultural Change in Rural Italy since 1800* (Chicago, 1979), pp. 91–2; Charlotte Gower Chapman, *Milocca*, pp. 94–6.

[15] Julian Pitt Rivers, *People of the Sierra* (London, 1954), pp. 112–15 and *Girl with the Red Scarf* (Atif Yilmaz, 1978).

[16] Lieta Harrison, *The Wantons: A Searing Study of the Humiliation of Women in Modern Sicily* (London, 1966), pp. 58–9. Original Italian edition: Lieta Harrison, *Le svergognate* (Rome, 1963).

[17] MP/96, ADN.

and a kidnapping. In some cases a woman might wish an elopement to resemble a kidnapping in order to give the impression of virtue on her part. However, a man might also claim that a kidnapping was an elopement freely chosen by the woman, and the law was also on his side as it absolved a man of the crime of rape once he married his victim.[18] Unfortunately I found no diaries or memoirs written by women about elopement, making it very difficult to understand where, from the woman's perspective, the balance of power might lie. The answers have to be sought instead through a deeper investigation of cultural attitudes and particularly in the idea of honour.

HONOUR AND ITALIAN SOCIETY

By the 1960s, honour had long been recognized as a deeply rooted feature of Sicilian and southern society, enmeshed in the structures of both family and community. Anthropologists have continued to study it over the course of the previous century from Charlotte Gower Chapman's fieldwork in 1920s Sicily to the work of Peristiany and Pitt-Rivers on the Mediterranean region in the 1960s and 1970s, and Jane and Peter Schneider's more recent work on Sicily.[19] While family honour was based on female chastity and men's ability to protect it, it was ultimately about much more than sexual mores and was very much bound up in the wider social and economic concerns of the community. Jane Schneider posited the possible origins of the honour code in intense competition over scarce land resources in a harsh environment. In this reading, the family's ability to protect the boundaries of its land were expressed in vigilance over the sexuality of its women members.[20] Whatever the origins, honour was certainly used as economic and social leverage in Sicilian society.[21] If a woman was dishonoured, it was not only she herself who would not be able to find a husband, but her sisters too. The fortunes of the entire family were thereby affected by the loss of honour of one of its members.

Since Peristiany published his seminal essay collection on Mediterranean honour in 1966, there have been many reappraisals of the original paradigm. Many have since stressed its flexibility, emphasizing how it functioned and

---

[18] This was provided for under Article 544 of the penal code and only abrogated in 1981.

[19] Chapman, *Milocca*; J. G. Peristiany (ed.), *Honour and Shame: The Values of Mediterranean Society* (Chicago, 1966); David Gilmore (ed.), *Honour, Shame and the Unity of Mediterranean* (Washington, DC, 1987); and Jane and Peter Schneider, *Culture and Political Economy in Western Sicily* (New York, 1976).

[20] Jane Schneider, 'Of Vigilance and Virgins: Honor, Shame and Access to Resources in Mediterranean Societies', *Ethnology*, 10:1 (1971), pp. 1–24.

[21] On honour in late nineteenth- and early twentieth-century Sicilian society, see Linda Reeder, *Widows in White*, pp. 21, 47–9.

was understood at a day-to-day level, as well as how it changed over time as it came into contact with wider social and political forces.[22] Others have pointed out how honour codes were adapted to fit changing social contexts. Both Linda Reeder and Rudolph Bell have emphasized the role of migration in prompting new patterns of courtship, marriage, and gender in Sicily.[23] Linda Reeder found that widespread emigration to the US in late nineteenth- and early twentieth-century Sicily both challenged and complicated the honour code that governed rural society, since men migrated alone leaving their wives behind, their honour thus unpoliced. The 'white widows' who remained at home largely maintained their restricted lifestyles, in order to keep up appearances as respectable Sicilian women in their husbands' absence. However, migration ultimately began to loosen the rigid rules of honour, weakening the custom of killing to restore the honour of a woman and her family.[24] While codes were intended to maintain family interest, the honour code could also become surprisingly flexible when it did not serve the needs of individual families, as we saw in the cases of the thwarted elopements. Honour was therefore not an inflexible structure that stood above society or outside time; it could be reinterpreted and adapted to changing circumstances.

While honour did have a real presence in southern Italian society, it is still difficult to capture exactly what it meant to those Italians whose lives were shaped by it in the 1950s and 1960s. How did girls and young women as well as their families really perceive their supposed honour on a day-to-day basis? Both Bell and Reeder emphasized the fact that conflict brought about by threatened or lost honour, was 'colourful but rare'.[25] Gower Chapman and Reeder both stressed that women were just as invested in the honour system as men, and we know that the 'white widows' of migrant men still conformed to the honour code through their dress, movements, and behaviour while their husbands worked abroad.[26] Gower Chapman also reported that the women of Milocca felt pity for her since she, as a woman travelling alone to Sicily, had no man to protect her honour.[27] While the possibility of violence as a way of reinforcing the honour code was always present, its use was undoubtedly rare, at least while society remained relatively stable. It is suspected that honour was actually used as a cover for mafia violence in some cases.[28] However, when it

---

[22] See esp. John Davis, 'Family and State' and Maureen Giovannini, 'Female Chastity Codes', in David Gilmore (ed.), *Honour, Shame and the Unity of the Mediterranean*, pp. 22–34 and 61–74. Davis explored how honour interacted with economic and political forces, while Giovannini investigated how honour blended with gender, family, and community concerns at a day-to-day level in Sicily.

[23] Reeder, *Widows in White* and Bell, *Fate, Honor, Family and Village*, pp. 90–2.

[24] Reeder, *Widows in White*, pp. 68–73.

[25] Bell, *Fate, Honour, Family and Village*, p. 92.

[26] Reeder, *Widows in White*, pp. 55–102.   [27] Gower Chapman, *Milocca*, pp. 39–40.

[28] Jane and Peter Schneider, *Festival of the Poor*, p. 211.

came to domestic violence against women, or kidnapping leading to forced marriage, the majority of cases were probably not reported while even fewer went to trial.

The exact language Italians used to define honour in relation both to themselves and their community is difficult to pinpoint. This is to some extent due to a paucity of sources. When it comes to everyday understanding and experience of honour, sources are patchy and rare, even for the 1960s. Pitt-Rivers, analysing rural Andalusia in the 1950s, identified honour as a defining feature of that society, but he clarified that the term actually used in conversation—particularly in relation to women's honour—was 'verguenza' or shame.[29] David Gilmore, writing about Andalusia in the 1970s, reported again that the word 'honora' was rarely used in conversation as it was associated with old-fashioned, aristocratic values.[30] While 'onore' or honour was used in post-war Italy, it was most often seen in official, legal contexts; honour became defined as such when it was threatened and caused, necessitated, or explained a crime. Several films dealing with honour crime used 'onore' frequently in their dialogue; girls were dishonoured and honour had to be repaired or avenged.[31] The best known of these were Pietro Germi's Sicilian films *Divorce, Italian Style* (1961) and *Seduced and Abandoned* (1964), dealing respectively with honour crime and forced marriage. Made for national and international audiences, the screenwriters may have felt the need to name or label honour for those unfamiliar with the context. Here again we see honour defined in relation to the law, and in Germi's films to the exact legal statutes relating to honour. Letters written to advice columns in the 1950s and 1960s refer not to honour, but to shame and to honesty: a young woman might refer to her chastity by describing herself as an 'honest' or a 'serious' girl rather than an honourable one.[32] Calabrian women, speaking about growing up and preparing for marriage in the 1920s and 1930s, also spoke of shame ('vergogna').[33] Shame was also used frequently in letters to magazines, but while it had an immediate personal resonance, honour or its loss defined a woman in relation to her community.

Catholic culture was also deeply concerned with virginity in the post-war period. The canonization of Maria Goretti in 1950 was symbolic of this

---

[29] Julian Pitt-Rivers, *The People of the Sierra* (London, 1954), esp. pp. 113–15.

[30] David Gilmore, 'Honor, Honesty, Shame: Male Status in Contemporary Andalusia', in Gilmore (ed.), *Honour, Shame and the Unity of the Mediterranean*, pp. 90–103.

[31] *Divorce, Italian Style* and *Seduced and Abandoned* (Pietro Germi, 1961 and 1964); *Girl with a Gun* (Mario Monicelli, 1968).

[32] See for example Gabriella Parca (ed.), *Le italiane si confessano* (Florence, 1959). The same kind of phrasing appears in the advice columns of other magazines such as *Grand Hotel*. Whatever the veracity of the actual letters, they do provide some insight into contemporary vocabularies.

[33] Renate Siebert, *E femmina però è bella: Tre generazioni di donne al sud* (Turin, 1991), p. 211.

heightened concern for female sexual purity in a time of social and political tension.[34] Bestselling magazine *Famiglia Cristiana* referred regularly to the importance of 'pudore' or modesty for girls. While modesty referred to both dress and behaviour, it was evidently intended as a safeguard for chastity, mirroring in this way the requirements of the honour code.[35] Both Catholicism and the honour code also shared the vocabulary of shame. The shame to which many women referred in their letters to advice columns was probably at least partly a feeling prompted by religion. In their governance of young women's behaviour, Catholicism and honour were thus in an uneasy alliance. Both emphasized chastity as an unmarried woman's ultimate and only goal. However, honour was a social value while for the Church, chastity was about personal morality. The cult of Maria Goretti illustrated a further divergence. Maria's saintliness was rooted in her passive resistance, as she chose death rather than fighting her attacker, while in contrast the honour code allowed a woman to avenge her own dishonour. Interviews with ordinary Sicilians about their attitudes towards women and honour in the early 1960s also hinted at these divergences. While most declared themselves in favour of a forced marriage following rape, several also added that the couple could separate afterwards, once honour had been first restored through marriage.[36] Abortion was apparently widely accepted as a practical way of hiding the shame of pregnancy outside marriage.[37] When it came to how honour and shame were understood in post-war southern Italy, Catholicism and the honour code reinforced the values of the other in an uneasy alliance, although they diverged when it came to dealing with the consequences of sexual transgression.

Honour crimes resulting in murder were probably rare, although there were sensational occurrences in the 1960s, while domestic violence and kidnappings were underreported. How then can we account for the national concern about honour in the 1960s? Male migration to the US in the late nineteenth and early twentieth centuries had forced a measure of flexibility into the honour system, and by implication the way in which courtship and marriage were understood in rural Sicily. As a result women had also taken on more active roles in household management, engaging directly with the economy and the state.[38] There were still distinct differences between these patterns of population movement and the later upheavals of the

---

[34] See Stephen Gundle and David Forgacs, *Mass Culture and Italian Society from Fascism to the Cold War* (Bloomington, IN, 2007), pp. 255–6 and Patrick McCarthy, 'The Church in Post War Italy', in Patrick McCarthy (ed.), *Italy Since 1945* (Oxford, 2000), p. 140.

[35] Niamh Cullen, 'Morals, Modern Identities and the Catholic Woman: Fashion in *Famiglia Cristiana*, 1954–1968', in *Journal of Modern Italian Studies*, 18:1 (2013), pp. 33–52.

[36] Lieta Harrison, *The Wantons*, pp. 73–7.

[37] Jane and Peter Schneider, *Festival of the Poor: Fertility Decline and the Ideology of Class in Sicily 1860–1980* (Tucson, AZ, 1996) pp. 211–13; Harrison, *The Wantons*, pp. 123–6.

[38] Reeder, *Widows in White*, pp. 142–202.

economic miracle. Nineteenth-century male emigration was ultimately aimed at preserving the structure of families and communities in rural Sicily, and it was only from the late 1950s and 1960s, with large-scale migration of families rather than men alone to the northern industrial cities, that the social order of the rural south was really under threat. In his analysis of demographic patterns in rural Italy, Rudolph Bell found that during a time of social transition, such as in larger provincial towns in the mid-nineteenth and early twentieth century, courtship caused much greater tension and conflict between parents and children.[39] The honour system was under similar tension by the 1960s. Generational divides were heightened by the rise of mass culture and the new influences of cinema, music, and television.

The tensions between the values of the south and a changing Italy emerge vividly in many of the memoirs and diaries. The memoirs of two Sicilian women who wrote bitterly of their experiences growing up amid the restrictive gender relations and courtship customs of 1960s Sicily fit this pattern. The memoir of Maria Lamonica (born Piraino, province of Messina, 1942) was primarily an account of her struggle to receive an education, as her parents did not consider it appropriate that a girl should attend secondary school.[40] It detailed the restrictions placed on her movements and behaviour by her parents; for much of her adolescence Maria was barely able to leave the house and unable to work or study. She eventually managed to complete her education and secure a civil service position in Turin. Sebastiana Tarascio (born in Florida, province of Syracuse, 1935) wrote her memoir in 1986. We first encountered Sebastiana in Chapter 2 in Turin. She too had left Sicily to work in the northern city, because of the restrictions placed on courtship and work for Sicilian women in the 1950s: 'how stupid, sad and empty life was then for Sicilian girls', she wrote, 'only occupation: embroidery and keeping the house in order'.[41] Both of these women were unusual in that they had migrated alone for work, and only married later. In a changing society, they were able to imagine that their lives could be different and had the financial and practical means to take advantage of other opportunities. As they grew up in a society in flux and lived themselves between worlds, the conflict between family, community, and the women of their generation was probably heightened in their memoirs.[42]

We can see similar patterns in sociologies of gender in the south. In Renate Siebert's sociology of three generations of Calabrian women carried out in the

---

[39] Bell, *Fate, Honor Family, Village*, pp. 92–3.
[40] Maria Lamonica, 'In un piccolo centro di provincia'.
[41] Sebastiana Tarascio, 'Io mi racconto: bilancio di una cinquantenne', MP/87, ADN.
[42] Birgitte Solande made a similar observation in her work on Danish women's memoirs: 'Employment and Enjoyment: Female Coming-of-age Experience in Denmark, 1880s to 1930s', in Mary Jo Maynes, Birgitte Soland, and Christina Benningham (eds), *Secret Gardens, Satanic Mills: Placing Girls in European History, 1750–1950* (Bloomington, IN, 2005), pp. 254–68.

mid-1980s, the women reflected very differently on the contrast between their childhood and young adulthood in the 1930s and the changing world that they inherited in the 1960s and 1970s. As was typical at the time, one woman who had married in the 1950s had not been in the habit of leaving the house as a younger woman. She lived her life quite contentedly within the confines of the home as her mother had done. Only in later years did she begin to go out in public more often and remembered that at first she was very embarrassed to speak to men in public, blushing constantly.[43] Since society only really began to change for Calabrian women when she was a mature, married woman, there was no great tension in her adolescence between the generations, and she embraced change with trepidation rather than enthusiasm when it came. In contrast, Simonetta Piccone Stella's study of women university students in Salerno (Campania) in the early 1970s exposed sharp tensions between the women's desire to study and work and their families' strict notions about the shame of young women working and going out too much. There were class variations here too; the proletarian father was seen as a much more authoritarian figure than the middle-class one. In the words of one woman, on her experience of growing up and coming of age in the late 1960s and early 1970s, 'I was humiliated for everything: the desire to study, to have a little money, to go out, how I dressed'.[44] Tensions regarding the daughter's desire for a very different life to the one her family planned for her, in keeping with traditional southern notions of a woman's role, were in sharp evidence here. The woman in question, a sociology student, was also at this stage very active in progressive politics, creating an even sharper clash between her own lifestyle and that of her parents. The conflict seems perhaps more intense precisely because it was becoming possible for a woman to live a different sort of lifestyle by this stage.

HONOUR ON TRIAL IN 1960s SICILY

If honour was an intangible, unnamed value that nevertheless shaped the intimate and family lives of many Italians, it did occasionally spill out into the public sphere. And if it was a particularly strong part of life in Sicily and Calabria, it was not solely a feature of southern society. It was at times of political tumult or socio-economic change that honour crime came to the fore as a national issue. In 1946, barely a year after war had ended, Lydia Cirillo came to trial in Rome for the murder of her lover, the British army officer

---

[43] Renate Siebert, *E femmina però è bella*, p. 63.
[44] Simonetta Piccone Stella, *Ragazze del sud*, p. 56.

Sidney Lush.[45] On discovering that Lush was married and fearful of losing him, Cirillo shot him fatally in 1945. Although she herself first described her actions in terms of obsessive love, the case was swiftly framed by the media as one of a poor innocent Italian woman seduced by an immoral foreigner who killed in order to restore her honour. Playing along with her new role, Cirillo quickly became a sort of national heroine who by her actions had symbolically restored the honour of a nation humiliated for years by fascism, war, a brutal Nazi occupation, and the more ambiguous occupation of their Allied liberators. Released early in 1948, Cirillo went on to have a brief career in the media spotlight with interviews, photo shoots, and even cinema appearances.

It has been noted that the symbolic connection between female sexuality and national honour was heightened in times of war, when it was most visible.[46] The most notorious example of this is the public ritual shaving of women perceived to have engaged in 'horizontal collaboration'—as it was dubbed in France—with the enemy.[47] While the spectacle of shaving the heads of women 'horizontal collaborators' is associated particularly with the lengthy Nazi occupation of the central and northern regions, Porzio shows that such incidents were also numerous in central and southern Italy where they mainly targeted women who had relationships with Allied soldiers.[48] Her findings indicate that such rituals were not strictly political, but were instead an outlet for wounded masculine and national honour—in Naples the defeated military often played a leading role—bound together and intrinsically linked with the female body.[49] Cirillo's lenient sentence and brief media career were yet another reflection of what these macabre rituals indicated. In 1944 and 1945, when national honour in Italy was at its lowest point, the female body became the symbolic site through which it might be restored.

It was in the mid-1960s that honour would again come to dominate national discussions in politics and the media. While in 1946 the notion of Lydia Cirillo as avenger of Italy's lost honour met the needs of a nation humiliated by foreign occupation, by 1965 honour did not fit in any way with Italy's new identity as a prosperous industrial nation. Honour crime was now cast as brutal, antiquated, and southern, in sharp opposition to the self-consciously modern Italy of the economic miracle. This was of course despite

---

[45] See Maria Porzio, *Arrivano gli Alleati! Amori e violnze nell'Italia liberata* (Rome, 2011), pp. 3–25.

[46] Ute Frevert. *Emotions in History: Lost and Found* (Budapest, 2012), pp. 74–9.

[47] Fabrice Virgili, *Shorn Women: Gender and Punishment in Liberation France* (London, 2002).

[48] Perry Willson, *Women in Twentieth Century Italy* (London, 2010), p. 109; Porzio, *Arrivano gli Alleati!*, pp. 118–41.

[49] Porzio, *Arrivano gli Alleati!*, p. 121.

or even because of the widespread migration from the rural south to Milan and Turin, which increased the visibility of regional difference in the nation.[50] We can see these trends in Pietro Germi's two 'Sicilian' comedies of the early 1960s. While *Divorce, Italian Style* (1961) was widely interpreted as a comment on Italy's failure to legislate for divorce, its real focus was on honour crime and on the legal loopholes which made it easier for a man to murder than to divorce his wife.[51] *Seduced and Abandoned* (1964) took up a similar theme, but was widely regarded as a more serious social commentary than the earlier film. The convoluted plot line was driven by the rape of 15-year-old Agnese by her sister's fiancé. When her father discovered that she was pregnant, a solution was needed in order to restore the family honour. Her father and brother first attempted to murder Peppino before staging an abduction in order to force her into marriage without anyone losing face. Germi's primary targets were the legal codes that excused murder, abduction, and rape in the name of honour and some of his male characters were actually reluctant to take on the mantle of violent, righteous masculinity demanded by the honour code. However, the film still veered into the territory of melodrama, and was criticized at the time, despite its box office success, for being the work of a 'sudista del nord'; a northerner who sought to comment on and reform the south without really understanding it.[52]

The previous year the British Italian writer and activist Lieta Harrison had published a book on Sicily's 'dishonoured women'.[53] Although it was described as popular sociology, Harrison's research methods were unclear and the tone was sensationalist, aiming to shock with lurid detail rather than to analyse or question. Since many of her women had become murderers in order to avenge their seducers and thus restore their honour in the eyes of their communities, it appeared as if she conducted at least some of her interviews in prisons. Extracts from interviews with ordinary Sicilians followed the anecdotes, always confirming the most extreme positions. When asked for example if they would rather their daughter were an unmarried mother or a murderess, all opted for the murderess. A 'bricklayer' answered: 'A murderess, then I'd have nothing to be ashamed of.'[54] When asked if a woman should be forced to marry her rapist, all opted again for marriage, since in the words of one respondent 'you can always get over hating a man,

---

[50] Goffredo Fofi's sociology of migrant communities in Turin highlighted these tensions, discussing in particular differing attitudes to women: *L'Immigrazione meridionale a Torino* (Milan, 1974), p. 299.

[51] Mark Seymour, *Debating Divorce in Italy: Marriage and the Making of Modern Italians, 1860–1974* (London, 2006), pp. 174–7.

[52] g.f. (Guido Fink), 'Sedotta e abbandonata', in *Cinema Nuovo*, February/March 1964, pp. 127–8.

[53] Harrison, *The Wantons*.   [54] Harrison, *The Wantons*, p. 39.

but you can't get over dishonour'.[55] While attention was being drawn to the issue of honour crime, the focus was again on lurid and sensational examples.

While books and films, from Harrison's sensationalist sociology to Germi's Sicilian comedies, were beginning to draw attention to honour crime in the mid-1960s, it was a 1965 court case in Catania, Sicily which ultimately sparked a nationwide debate about the need for legal reform. When schoolteacher Gaetano Furnari murdered his daughter's lover in 1965, he was given a prison sentence of less than three years by the Catania court, sparking outrage in Sicily and across the nation about the culture of acceptance surrounding honour crime and the need to remove the provision for leniency where honour was cited as a motive.[56] Widely condemned across the nation—by Sicilian intellectual Leonardo Sciascia as by the Vatican—Justice Minister Orazio Reale immediately announced that the legal code would be reformed to remove Article 587 relating to honour. In practice this proved much more difficult to implement, as there was still considerable parliamentary opposition to the reform in the mid-1960s, with some seeing the removal of the statute as a blow to the traditional patriarchal family.[57] It was ultimately not resolved until the broader family law reform package of 1975, but the issue remained in the minds of many Italians for much of the 1960s.[58] The horror at Furnari's lenient sentence and the reported jubilation in the Catania courtroom, also ensured that what had once been seen as a national value, with potentially positive connotations in times of war and upheaval, was now cast as negative and irrevocably associated with the south.

THE KIDNAPPING OF FRANCA VIOLA

Just three days after the controversial sentencing of Furnari, and while the debate about law reform was still raging, another case relating to honour made

[55] Harrison, *The Wantons*, p. 75.

[56] The basic details of the case are summarized in Carlo Gregoretti, '587: Permesso d'uccidere', *L'Espresso*, 16 January 1966, p. 11. For more details of the case itself and of the press coverage in Sicily, see Nicola Figlioli, *Dal caso Viola al delitto d'onore: le grandi svolte degli anni '60 viste dai giornali* (Tesi di laurea: Palermo, 2004). On the sentencing, see 'Due anni e 11 mesi al maestro Furnari', *Giornale di Sicilia*, 24 December 1965, p. 1. It was also widely reported in the national media.

[57] The debates were widely reported in the newspapers in January and February 1966. See esp. 'Sotto accusa l'articolo 587: Contrastanti opinion dei palermitani', 9 January 1966, *Giornale di Sicilia*, p. 7.

[58] Leonardo Sciasca, 'Perché non possiamo dirci cristiani', *L'Ora*, 3/4 January 1966, p. 3. For the Vatican condemnation, see 'Si è legalizzato un costume primitivo', *Giornale di Sicilia*, 30 December 1965, p. 1. And on Reale's announcement, see Luan Rexha, 'Il "587"' sarà abrogato e sostituito', *Giornale di Sicilia*, 4 January 1966, pp. 1 and 12.

national headlines. On 26 December 1965, a group of young men led by 25-year-old Filippo Melodia kidnapped 17-year-old Franca Viola by breaking into her family home in Alcamo, western Sicily (see Figure 3.2). The headline in *Giornale di Sicilia*, 'They Burst in Firing Shots to Kidnap a Girl', alerted

Figure 3.2. Franca Viola, *Corriere della Sera*, 19 December 1966.
Biblioteca Nazionale Centrale di Roma.

readers to the extraordinary level of violence involved in the case.[59] This was no ordinary 'elopement' where the boundaries between love and coercion were blurred, although some elements of the familiar drama were there. Melodia and Viola had been in a romantic relationship a couple of years previously but it had ended because of her father's disapproval. Since all of the names of the kidnappers were reported in the press from the beginning they must have been known to the Viola family and made no attempt to mask their identities. They evidently never expected that the abduction would become a criminal case, but their actions that day set in train a marriage refusal which would have reverberations far beyond the private sphere, spilling out into the realms of politics, the law and public opinion.

The abduction began when two men were sent as scouts to verify that Franca Viola's father, Bernardo Viola was not at home. The eight armed men arrived soon afterwards, to abduct Franca by force. When her mother tried to resist her daughter's capture, the men fired shots in the air. Viola continued to struggle, assisted by her mother and 8-year-old brother Mariano, but to no avail. The gang dragged Franca to an Alpha Romeo Giulietta and forced her inside. Mariano would not let go of her and was taken along with her, to be released several hours later. Since her mother also clung to the outside of the car, she was dragged after the vehicle briefly and was later hospitalized for minor injuries. The kidnappers continued to fire shots as they drove, so as to intimidate their many witnesses. It was Franca's mother, Vita Ferro, who recounted the story to the police and the press, relating all of the details of her ordeal including the identities of the kidnappers. Aside from her name and age, there were few details of Franca herself in these first reports.

The case was not a unique one for Sicily in 1965. In fact, kidnappings were frequent occurrences in the local crime pages. Most girls or women were abducted in crowded, public settings, often while walking with their families, so that the crime was carried out openly with many witnesses. Despite these dramatic openings, the vast majority of kidnappings were actually solved swiftly and with minimal fuss. The day after Franca's kidnapping, a case was reported in *Giornale di Sicilia* that illustrated perfectly the ambiguity of such cases. The headline read; 'A Happy Ending to the Christmas Eve Kidnapping: Kidnapped and Kidnapper Have Sworn Their "Eternal Love"'.[60] The woman in question had been walking home when two men bundled her into a car. Her parents reported the case as a kidnapping but it seems that their primary concern was that they did not know the kidnappers' identities. If they had, they would have settled the matter themselves instead of going to the police.

[59] *Giornale di Sicilia*, 27 December 1965.
[60] 'A lieto fine il ratto della vigilia di Natale: Rapita e rapitore si sono giurati "eterno amore"', *Giornale della Sicilia*, 28 December 1965, p. 4.

The happy ending came when the couple returned to their families a few days later, declaring their love for each other. Neither family opposed the marriage and the couple swore their love in front of a magistrate to ensure that the kidnapping charges were dropped. The case thus quickly passed from 'black' to 'pink'; to use the Italian colour-coded expressions for news of crime and love.

The incident followed the classic structure of what was known as a 'fuitina' or elopement; reading these reports, it is impossible to tell now (as surely it was then) what blend of romance, coercion, or violence really lay behind each story. However, what was certain was the expectation that in all cases—with family honour at stake—the woman and her family would both accept marriage as the outcome. Such cases almost never went to court, and just as with the one cited above, they were likely smoothed over with declarations of love. It was this tension between love, coercion, and violence, and the apparent ease with which one could blend into the other in everyday Sicilian discourse, that Franca Viola's kidnappers intended to exploit and indeed used as cover in their trial.

Franca Viola's case must also be understood in the general context of violence and the state in Sicilian society. Located in the province of Trapani about twenty kilometres inland, Alcamo was at the margins of the Western Sicilian interior that was the heartland of the mafia (see Figure 3.3). With its difficult mountainous terrain, poor communications networks, and harsh climate, the interior of western Sicily had always had a fragile relationship with the institutions of the modern state. Historically land was controlled by *latifundi*, large estates owned by wealthy and often absent landowners. The weakness of state institutions in isolated rural communities reinforced socio-economic bonds grounded in family and community (and maintained through marriage alliances) with the enterprising peasant elites who would

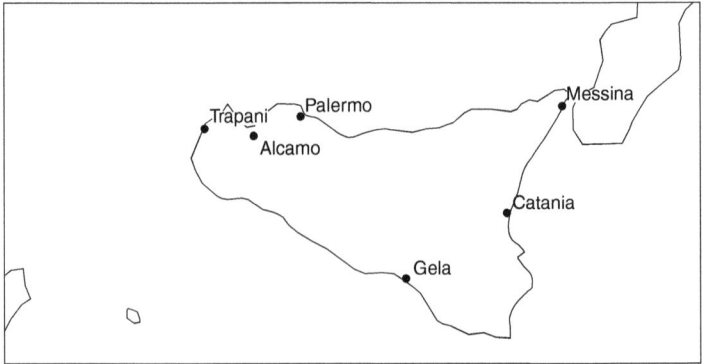

Figure 3.3. Map of Sicily.

become known as the mafia stepping into the vacuum created by absent landowners to mediate between local interests and the state.[61]

Western Sicily had been dominated by cycles of violence between bandits and mafia since the late nineteenth century, and while on the decline during fascism, the violence flared up again after the Allied invasion of Sicily in 1943.[62] The mafia had once again stepped into a power vacuum, suppressing the radical agrarian left and allying themselves with the Christian Democrats in the process. This protracted battle between radical peasants and mafia resulted in what Anton Blok described as a high tolerance for violence; those who 'had a reputation for violence and who eschewed recourse to public authorities commanded respect', and were described as 'honourable', 'respected', or 'qualified'.[63] Mafia violence and intimidation could also extend to matters of courtship.[64] While the intense violence of the late 1940s was on the decline, western Sicily in the 1960s was a society where levels of violence were high and social prestige was derived both from violence itself and from the ability to keep silent about it, solving matters 'privately' without recourse to the state. Honour had a double meaning in this society. Connected not just to women's sexual chastity and modest behaviour, it was also used to describe those *mafiosi* who could 'look after their own affairs'.[65]

Despite this high tolerance of violence, and the acceptance of kidnapping women as an apparent act of love, Franca Viola's case still breached the threshold. The level of violence used in the kidnapping, including the use of firearms and the force directed at her mother and brother, distinguished it from other cases and left little room for ambiguity about whether this was an elopement or a genuine kidnapping. The spaces in which the crime took place were also significant, since the majority of kidnappings happened on the street. In a culture where women were expected not to be seen in public in order to protect their honour, it could be argued that a woman walking in public left herself open to such dangers.[66] Franca Viola, however, was forcibly and visibly taken from her own home so that nobody could argue that she had compromised her own respectability. Although such kidnapping cases were often reported in the Sicilian newspapers, they did not generally make the national and regional newspapers in mainland Italy. Franca Viola's case did. An article in *Corriere della Sera* several days later

---

[61] On the latifundia system, see Marta Petrusewicz's study of a Calabrian latifundia: *Latifundium: Moral Economy and Material Life in a European Periphery* (Ann Arbor, 1989), pp. 92–104.

[62] John Dickie, *Cosa Nostra: A History of the Sicilian Mafia* (London, 2004), pp. 235–70.

[63] Anton Blok, *Mafia of a Sicilian Village: A Study of Violent Peasant Entrepreneurs* (Oxford, 1974), p. 211.

[64] Blok, *Mafia of a Sicilian Village*, pp. 158–60; Piero Bevilacqua, *Breve storia dell'Italia meridionale dall'ottocento a oggi* (Rome, 1993), pp. 40–4.

[65] Blok, *Mafia of a Sicilian Village*, p. 211.

[66] The film *Girl with a Gun* (Mario Monicelli, 1968) parodied this familiar notion.

underlined the serious and unprecedented nature of the crime. As in the Sicilian coverage, it focused on the criminal records of the perpetrators, on the force used in the kidnapping, and on the level of planning that went into the attack. The article concluded: 'the kidnapping should not be considered a more or less consensual elopement expected to lead to marriage. The rejected suitor planned everything down to the last details and then put his plan of criminal vendetta into action with cold determination, with the complicity of seven friends who all had prior criminal records.'[67] While Filippo Melodia would later claim the defence of the 'fuitina' or elopement for love rather than kidnapping, it was immediately evident to onlookers both in Sicily and across Italy that the Viola case had crossed a line into new territory.

Few newspapers outside Sicily carried any further news of the story that December. *Giornale di Sicilia* and *L'Ora* carried updates on 29 and 31 December. For eight days there was no trace of Franca Viola, despite a sustained police search for the kidnappers and great local interest in the case. Three of the kidnappers had been arrested at this point while the other five, including Melodia himself, were untraceable and there seemed to be few real leads until police stormed the kidnappers' hideout on 2 January. It then emerged that Melodia had been hiding with Viola near to the home of his married sister. When the police arrived, he tried to flee with her by escaping onto the roof of the house, but was quickly apprehended by police. Franca Viola was then reunited with her parents while Melodia, along with four further accomplices, was taken into custody. The full implications of all this did not become clear until a couple of days later though, when Sicilian newspaper *L'Ora* announced that 'the "marriage, Italian style" may not happen this time'.[68] Ultimately what would make this case different to the numerous other kidnappings, was that Franca Viola did not intend to accept the 'reparatory marriage' so widely expected of her in 1960s Sicily. The implication was that the kidnappers might actually be bought to trial, in the first case of its kind in Sicily.

In the days that followed, both *Giornale di Sicilia* and *L'Ora* carried further coverage of Franca Viola's historic decision. *Giornale di Sicilia* interviewed her parents and focused on their motivations for supporting their daughter when they would normally have been expected to force her into marriage.[69] Both her mother and father were praised for their moral courage in going against both deeply rooted customs and perhaps even their own community in their determination to 'break a dark tradition and prevent an unhappy marriage'.[70]

---

[67] 'Introvabile la ragazza rapita da otto giovanastri', *Corriere della Sera*, 2 January 1966, p. 10.

[68] 'Alcamo: Arrestato quattro rapitori della minorenne', *Giornale della Sicilia*, 2 January 1966, p. 1; 'Il "matromonio all'italiana" forse stavolta non ci sarà', *L'Ora*, 3/4 January 1966, p. 4.

[69] G. Impellizzeri, 'Francesca Viola non sposerà l'individuo che l'ha rapita', *Giornale della Sicilia*, 5 January 1966, p. 9.

[70] G. Impellizzeri, 'Francesca Viola non sposerà l'individuo che l'ha rapita'.

Bernardo Viola was described as both humble and moral, while Vita Ferro was determined, trusting in both God and their own work ethic that they would survive as a family should they have to leave Alcamo. Emphasizing the fact that Franca Viola had been returned to her family, rather than to freedom, the article framed the revolutionary decision as a family one rather than a courageous act of her own. *L'Ora* placed similar emphasis on the role of Viola's family in rejecting an 'uncivilized tradition'.[71] While she herself reportedly said that only marriage would save her from shame, her parents were adamant that she would not marry and had conveyed her refusal to the police, telling her not to be ashamed. 'Why then should they condemn their daughter to a life of suffering because of a belief that a girl's honour is based on her virginity?'[72] The emphasis on parental support might been an editorial decision, intended to make the refusal of a reparatory marriage more acceptable to their Sicilian readership.

However, just a few days later an interview with Franca Viola herself gave a very different narrative. In this next article it was she who was adamant in her refusal to marry, denying her parents' part in the decision, and quoted on the front page as declaring 'I will never marry him. I'm not willing to submit to violence and prejudice.'[73] Two different narratives were emerging, and their divergence would become more significant during the trial: was Franca Viola the protagonist or the pawn of her parents? Did they support her or were they preventing her from accepting a marriage that she did not oppose? The Viola family played a different role to what was expected of them in kidnapping cases. As usual though, the family dynamic was crucial, with her parents acting as mediators between their daughter and the community and society in which she lived. Franca Viola herself was more difficult to locate, even though the newspaper coverage now provided photographs, quotations, and a short interview to add to the scant details already disclosed. When the trial took place the following December, these differing narratives were exposed to national scrutiny. Emotions would also become central to interpretations of the case, as Melodia's defence contested Franca's understanding of romantic love with one which placed Melodia's actions firmly in the Sicilian love tradition.

FILIPPO MELODIA ON TRIAL: TRAPANI, DECEMBER 1966

The trial of Filippo Melodia and his accomplices began almost a year later, on 9 December 1966 in a courtroom in Trapani, a port city at the western-most

[71] 'Il "matrimonio all'italiana" forse stavolta non ci sarà', *L'Ora*, 3/4 January 1966, p. 4.
[72] 'Il "matrimonio all'italiana" forse stavolta non ci sarà'.
[73] '"Non lo sposerò mai"', *L'Ora*, 5/6 January 1966, p. 1.

tip of Sicily and Alcamo's provincial capital. It was tried in the *tribunale*, the regional court used for cases that were considered to be of too serious a nature to be entrusted to a lay jury. These usually included financial and organized crime as well as kidnapping.[74] The tribunal consisted of three judges, one of whom had the status of a judge of the court of appeal, indicating the gravity of the charges. The trial lasted for nine days, with a verdict delivered the following Saturday. The proceedings of each day were covered in detail in all the major Italian newspapers, the historic nature of the case now clearly recognized. The various lines of argument and investigation brought up in court seemed to hinge around two central questions: was Filippo Melodia motivated by love or revenge, and did the refusal to accept a reparatory marriage come from Franca Viola herself or from her father? These two apparently simple questions carried with them myriad tangled assumptions that would themselves be put on trial in the courtroom in Trapani, regarding family, men, women, honour, what it meant to be Sicilian, and even the nature of love itself.

At the outset of the trial, as in the previous January, all the newspapers seemed in agreement that the case had little to do with love (see Figure 3.4).[75] The fact that it needed to be emphasized that a violent kidnapping was not a romantic gesture, did however hint at the fine balancing line between love and violent control that always lay at the heart of the classic 'fuitina' or elopement. The coverage of crimes of honour or passion were typically laced with the vocabulary of romance and love in both Sicilian newspapers: a kidnapped woman might be referred to as a 'Juliet', the wronged mistress who resorted to murder was a 'woman in love' while the couple who wanted to prove they had taken part in an elopement rather than a kidnapping 'swore their eternal love'.[76] When it came to the reportage of Franca Viola's case it was clearly difficult to discard completely the lexicon of sentimentality and romance. Journalists found it difficult to escape it and both *Corriere della Sera* and *Il Resto del Carlino* referred to Melodia as the 'rejected lover' in their initial coverage of the trial.[77]

The southern Italian newspapers seemed to make more of an effort to consciously reject it in this instance, often using the familiar terms ironically, in order to emphasize how poorly they fitted the Viola case. Arcangelo

[74] Thomas Glyn Watkin, *The Italian Legal System* (Aldershot, 1997), p. 130.

[75] See for example 'Introvabile la ragazza rapita da otto giovanastri', *Corriere della Sera*, 2 January 1966, p. 10.

[76] See for example: 'A lieto fine il ratto della vigilia di Natale: Rapita e rapitore si sono giurati "eterno amore"', *Giornale della Sicilia*, 28 December 1965, p. 4; 'Per un amore difficile la tragedia di Malaspina: Migliorano le condizioni della giovane sposa ferita dalla 17enne inamorato del marito', *L'Ora*, 3/4 December 1966.

[77] 'Oggi a Trapani il processo per il ratto di Franca Viola', *Corriere della Sera*, 9 December 1966, p. 15; f.d., 'Ritrovata la ragazza rapita', *Il Resto del Carlino*, 4 January 1966, p. 4.

Figure 3.4. Newspaper feature about the impending trial of Filippo Melodia.
'The Girl Who Said No', *L'Ora*, 26–7 November 1966. Biblioteca Nazionale Centrale di Roma.

Palermo, writing for *Giornale di Sicilia*, referred to Viola as Melodia's 'beloved' and Melodia as Viola's 'fiancé', in inverted commas.[78] Mauro De Mauro, writing for *L'Ora* also wrote of the 'presumed (or non-existent?) love story of Filippo Melodia for Francesca Viola'.[79] Similarly, Renato Filizzola, commenting on the case in the Neapolitan newspaper *Il Mattino*, demolished the notion of any presumed link between kidnapping and romance when he expressed the hope that Melodia's sentence would discourage any more young men from choosing 'this "romantic" path, whose sentimental trappings were, to quote the penal code: persistent sexual violence, kidnap, breaking and entering into the home, physical violence'.[80] The headline to Ettore Serio's article, commenting on the closing statement of the defence on 17 December, 'The defence has only one line of argument—kidnapping for love, Sicilian style', also demonstrated impatience and a desire to distance himself from the linking of love, kidnap, and Sicily. Since Filippo Melodia's defence rested on the traditional ambiguity between elopement and rape, the language of love continued to frame the case and seep into the media coverage despite the care of southern journalists.

The defence's case rested solely on the argument that Melodia was motivated by his love for Viola and his desire to marry her, in the face of her father's cruel opposition. Viola and Melodia had been *fidanzati* for six months several years earlier but Bernardo Viola insisted that his daughter end the engagement when he found out that Melodia was a convicted thief. Afterwards Melodia emigrated to Germany for work and Viola became engaged to one Antonino Zagari in January 1965. This match, apparently arranged by her family, did not survive beyond the court case. In the meantime, Melodia had returned to Alcamo and was still obsessed with his ex-girlfriend, threatening her father and her new boyfriend while keeping her under surveillance. The defence case painted Bernardo Viola as a tyrannical father who was determined to keep the two lovers apart. In a feature published in *L'Ora* leading up to the trial, Melodia explained himself thus, his words paraphrased by the newspaper:

> In December 1964, back home from Germany, I was only able to see my ex-girlfriend when I passed by the street where she lived, without exchanging any words with her. In these recent times, since I always intended to marry the aforementioned Franca Viola in one way or another, I began again to pass by her house often. Viola did no more than look at me, but did not in fact seem offended by my manner.[81]

[78] Arcangelo Palermo, 'Franca Viola difende il "no" davanti ai giudici di Trapani', *Giornale di Sicilia*, 3 January 1966.

[79] Mauro de Mauro, 'Franca Viola: È stato così', *l'Ora*, 12/13 December 1966, p. 3.

[80] Renato Filizzola, 'La ragazza dagli occhi bassi', *Il Mattino*, 20 December 1966, p. 1.

[81] 'Lui', *L'Ora*, 26/27 November 1966, p. 2.

Here Melodia was clearly aligning himself with the Sicilian and southern tradition of a strong, secret love forged through glances. Bernardo Viola's opposition to their original engagement two years earlier added weight to this reading. Considering the cultural import of an unmarried woman not just allowing herself to be sighted but actually looking back, Melodia's assertion that Viola did not seem opposed to his silent attentions and in fact seemed to meet his gaze, was anything but casual.

Melodia's legal team attempted to paint him as the unwitting scapegoat of a courtship tradition distorted by the honour code, where parents kept their daughters locked up at home and a suitors had to kidnap his beloved with feigned violence in order to marry her or even spend any time with her.[82] In Avv. Ragusa's summing up, 'Melodia acted out of love and '"they want to jail him for 22 years for falling in love with a girl"'.[83] Commenting on the case in *Il Resto del Carlino*, Ferrante Azzali also reported scathingly on a defence that blamed Franca Viola for refusing marriage and her father for preventing the two 'doves' from 'realizing their dream of love'.[84] Ragusa in fact blamed the press for distorting a love story into one of violence. Melodia's family repeated that he had acted out of love. On hearing the verdict his father declared that 'eleven years were too many, my son loved Franca and I am sure they still love each other'.[85] Local reactions to Melodia's sentence again included some discussion about whether or not he had been motivated by love. One *Corriere della Sera* journalist found that reactions to the sentencing tended to favour Franca Viola or to be cautious in their judgement. One man he interviewed, an elderly road inspector, answered: 'I don't know the law. But I think if he loved the girl, then 11 years seems all right. If he didn't love her, then he deserved double.'[86] Even those who condemned Melodia could still conceive that he was motivated by love, and by implication that violence and love could be linked together rather than opposed to each other.

Less sympathetic interpretations of Melodia's case instead emphasized the violence of the kidnapping, casting his motives in terms of a vendetta and wounded masculinity rather than love. In fact the impression from the national coverage is that Sicilian masculinity was itself on trial. Journalists easily fitted Melodia into preconceived ideas of Sicilian men as being both

---

[82] 'La difesa ha solo un tasto: ratto d'amore alla siciliana', 17 December 1966, p. 1 and p. 20.
[83] 'Il Mafioso è Viola', *Giornale di Sicilia*, 16 December 1966, p. 16.
[84] Ferrante Azzali, 'Una sentenza riformatrice', *Il Resto del Carlino*, 18 December 1966, p. 15.
[85] '"La giustizia ha fatto il suo corso" ha detto il padre di Franca Viola', *Il Resto del Carlino*, 19 December 1966, p. 13.
[86] Silvano Villani, 'Commenti sulla sentenza per il ratto di Franca Viola', *Corriere della Sera*, 19 December 1966, p. 13.

criminally violent and controlled by their passions; ideas with a long historical tradition.[87] Another shadow that hung over the case and over the question of motive was the accusation of mafia association. Although this charge was not ultimately carried against Melodia, the suspicion lingered over the trial, while the association of violent Sicilian masculinity with the mafia seemed almost implicit in some newspapers.[88] A 1970 film based loosely on the case also depicted Melodia as a young mafia boss.[89] These depictions of deviant masculinity in the national press also sometimes tended towards racism. Melodia's actions as well as the custom he drew on were dark, barbaric, backward, African, medieval, and tribal. In their haste to display their horror that such a crime could happen in the Italy of the economic miracle, Sicily had to be cast as distant and different, in contrast to the progressive and European-minded modern nation.[90]

The defence case rested not only on Melodia's love for Viola but also on her alleged love for him. If Franca Viola had been in love with Filippo Melodia and prevented from seeing him by her father, then she could be considered an accomplice rather than a victim. Defence lawyer Ragusa asserted that Viola had loved Melodia once and had at some point changed her mind, attempting to shift the focus of the trial from Melodia's violence to the reasons for her refusal to marry. The defence team's attempts to cast the crime in terms of thwarted love rather than violence also centred on Melodia's intentions in kidnapping Franca Viola and on her rape, which took place during the kidnap. While Melodia's legal team termed the incident as a 'kidnapping with the intention of marriage', the prosecution cast Melodia's motives as purely sexual. While it was not contested that the pair had had sexual intercourse, the language used to describe and define what had happened varied widely in the courtroom and the press. The defence team argued that Viola had consented to intercourse as to the kidnapping. That it had not happened on the first day of the kidnapping was proof for them that the kidnapping had been consensual. It was also contended that at some point during the kidnapping Viola 'was convinced to submit to Filippo Melodia'. The implication here was

---

[87] See John Dickie, *Darkest Italy: The Nation and Stereotypes of the Mezzogiorno 1860–1900* (London, 1999) and Nelson Moe, *The View from Vesuvius: Italian Culture and the Southern Question* (Berkeley, CA, 2005), esp. p. 59 and p. 92.

[88] The mafia charge was repeated across the press. See for example: 'Una ragazza si rifiuta di sposare il mafioso che la rapì e la sedusse', *Il Resto del Carlino*, 9 December 1966, p. 10; 'P. M. all'attacco al processo Viola', *L'Unità*, 15 December 1966, p. 5 (Melodia was referred to as 'the young "boss"'); 'Hanno parlato dall'Ora, Corrao e Fileccia—paura dei testi mafia e il coraggio di Bernardo Viola: questi temi degli avvocati di parte civile', *Giornale di Sicilia*, 14 December 1966, pp. 1 and 16.

[89] *The Most Beautiful Wife* (Damiano Damiani, 1970).

[90] See in particular the commentary of Ferrante Azzali in *Il Resto del Carlino*. For a full discussion, see also Niamh Cullen, 'The Case of Franca Viola: Debating Gender, Nation and Modernity in 1960s Italy', *Contemporary European History*, 16:1 (2016), pp. 97–115.

that if Viola had consented even reluctantly and under persuasion, this was still proof that she was in love with Melodia and thus complicit.[91] She herself explained that she acted out of fear and the feeling that she was abandoned. While this argument was not widely accepted beyond Melodia's defence team and supporters, most newspapers still glossed over the issue of sexual violence, which was of course implicit in the kidnapping charge. While stating that Viola had not consented, the crime was still seen as one of the loss of honour, understood as virginity, rather than rape.

This was of course largely in keeping with the times, as it was only with second-wave feminism that rape would be reframed as a violent crime against the person rather than a crime against morality.[92] Most newspapers, including *L'Ora*, *Giornale della Sicilia*, and *Corriere della Sera*, used the verb 'rapire' or kidnap to name Melodia's crime. *Il Resto del Carlino* referred to Franca Viola's refusal to marry the man who 'kidnapped and seduced her', while the only newspaper to explicitly refer to rape was *La Stampa*, shifting the focus from love, elsewhere noted even in its absence, to sexual violence.[93] Framing the crime in terms of honour rather than sexual violence also allowed the defence team to minimize the crime of rape in their concluding speeches. Accepting that a guilty verdict was inevitable at that stage, Avv. Bellavista asked how long Melodia should reasonably have to serve for 'the destruction of [. . .] connective tissue'.[94] The implication was that if virginity had no social value, then there was no crime.

Franca Viola herself, aided by the many journalists covering the trial, put forward her own, competing definition of love. One of the few statements directly attributed to her was her explanation for refusing the reparatory marriage: 'I will marry the man I love'.[95] Here she aligned herself with a different definition of love, refusing the sentimental language that surrounded the kidnapping tradition and asserting her right to choose her marriage partner. It is unclear from the media coverage whether Franca was still engaged to Zagari. We know that at some point he left her, under threat from Melodia, and she married another local man, Giuseppe Ruisi, in 1968. Her parents, in their statements to the media, also aligned themselves with a

---

[91] 'Filippo Melodia condannato per il rapimento di Franca Viola', *Il Mattino*, 18 December 1966, p. 18.

[92] Willson, *Women in Twentieth Century Italy*, p. 163.

[93] 'Una ragazza si rifiutò di sposare il mafioso che la rapì e la sedusse', *Il Resto del Carlino*, 9 December 1966, p. 10; 'Respinta la richiesta di una perizia fisica sulla diciottenne che fu rapita e violentata', *La Stampa*, 13 December 1966, p. 5. *L'Unità* also referred to Melodia as 'the seducer': Giorgio Frasca Polara, 'La for a di dire no', *L'Unità*, 18 December 1966, p. 13. Some of the reportage of the trial in *Il Mattino* also emphasized sexual violence.

[94] Silvano Villani, 'La difesa chiede attenuanti per i rapitori di Franca Viola', *Corriere della Sera*, 17 December 1966.

[95] Ettore Serio, 'Gli gridai: Se mio padre non ti denuncia lo farò io', *Giornale di Sicilia*, 12 December 1966, p. 1.

different definition of love and marriage connected not to honour but to their daughter's happiness. Both of them were quoted as saying that they supported her decision not to marry Melodia as they did not want to condemn her to an unhappy marriage.[96]

The media largely supported Franca Viola and her definition of love, using the notion of love and sentiment as a symbol of modernity and freedom of choice for women, in opposition to the manner in which Melodia and his supporters made use of older Sicilian traditions of romance. In the words of Indro Montanelli, writing for *Corriere della Sera*, Franca Viola and her father, in their refusal to accept the reparatory marriage, 'have said that rape cannot be considered a surrogate for love'.[97] Montanelli reported Viola as refusing the marriage with Melodia 'because she was in love with another young man'; another probable reference to Zagari.[98] The Communist Party paper *L'Unità*, reporting on public opinion on the trial in Sicily, interviewed a number of young women who were strongly supportive of Viola's choice. In the words of one young woman in Palermo, 'seeing as she didn't love him, I really don't see what else she could have done'.[99] The narrative of Franca Viola choosing love does not exactly fit the facts: it doesn't seem as if the engagement to Zagari was a love match either, and in any case it may have already been over by the time of the trial. It was, however, a compelling narrative, and the idea of romantic love as connected to choice and freedom was a deeply resonant one for a new generation of Sicilians.

The state magistrate too spoke of a different kind of love, connected specifically to a woman's choice, in his comments on the case. He urged the judges to give Melodia and his accomplices a severe sentence, defending Viola's decision not to accept a reparatory marriage.

> 'Franca Viola chose to follow her feelings rather than the path indicated by convenience or the traditions of her town. We should all be convinced that a marriage in these circumstances is an offence to the notion of a marriage governed by feeling'.[100]

Love here again legitimized Viola's rejection of tradition: a woman could instead be guided by feeling. Such a statement is particularly resonant with the individualism of the 1960s, while it also appears to domesticate women's choices by connecting them to feeling rather than ambition or calculation. *Il Resto del Carlino*, in summing up the case after the sentencing, chose again

---

[96] G. Impellizzeri, 'Franca Viola non sposerà l'individuo che l'ha rapita', *Giornale di Sicilia*, 5 January 1966, p. 9.

[97] Indro Montanelli, 'La ragazza di Alcamo' *Corriere della Sera*, 14 December 1966, p. 1.

[98] Montanelli, 'La ragazza di Alcamo'.

[99] Giorgio Frasca Polara, 'La forza di dire no', *L'Unità*, 18 December 1966, p. 13.

[100] Quoted in f.d., 'Chiesti centoquaranta anni per i rapitori di Franca Viola', *La Nazione*, 15 December 1966, p. 7.

to focus on this line of argument. For Emilia Granzotto, writing in the article, 'The Law of the Heart', 'Franca is simply a girl who follows her feelings and detests violence'.[101] In the same paper, Ferrente Azzali commented that the sentence meant that 'Sicilian girls [...] know today that like Franca Viola, they can defend their liberty as human beings, their rights to their feelings and to the heart, and their moral dignity, rebelling against oppression and violence'.[102] Love itself was clearly on trial in the courtroom in Trapani and in the media, with Franca Viola's determination to follow her feelings and marry for love proposed in direct opposition to the cloying, sentimental language of Melodia's legal team, steeped in the southern popular romantic tradition. This battle to appropriate the vocabulary of love reflected just how much was bound up in the idea of romance and feeling; words about emotions could indicate what a woman's place was in a relationship, as well as denoting an alliance with older traditions regarding gender and marriage, or a 'new' and modern Sicily.[103]

In the face of a competing definition of love from Franca Viola herself, the fragility of the defence case became clear. While Melodia's lawyers did their best to sentimentalize her kidnap, his case was really driven by honour. It was the Sicilian honour code that Avv. Bologna argued prevented the couple seeing each other freely as they might have 'in Milan', while Melodia's crime against Viola's honour (since rape was not accepted as a crime in itself) could easily be resolved by marriage. The implication was that it was Viola's refusal and not the kidnap which put them in court. While even the defence team claimed to accept that the notion of honour was outmoded and should hold no sway over Franca Viola, Melodia's defence made no sense without it. Conversely his defence painted Melodia himself as a victim of the honour system, an interpretation which gained little traction either in court or in public opinion.

While press coverage frequently referred to Viola as dishonoured ('disonorata'), inverted commas were often used to indicate that the notion was being both ridiculed and dismissed in newspapers both in Sicily and across Italy. Interviews with young Sicilian women about the case almost always rejected this definition of honour. One young woman quoted in *Corriere della Sera* was redefining rather than rejecting the notion of honour when she said that 'if it was not she who wanted it, then there is no dishonour'.[104] *L'Unità* journalist Giorgio Frasca Polara interviewed a number of young women in Palermo who were all quoted as rejecting reparatory marriage as outdated and hypocritical, while the kidnap of a woman for marriage was condemned as treating her

[101] Emilia Granzotto, 'La "legge del cuore"', *Il Resto del Carlino*, 19 December 1966, p. 13.
[102] Ferrente Azzali, 'Una sentenza riformatrice', *Il Resto del Carlino*, 18 December 1966, p. 13.
[103] ' "Difendiamo una nuova Sicilia"', *Giornale di Sicilia*, 14 December 1966, p. 1.
[104] Silvano Villani, 'Commenti sulla sentenza per il ratto di Franca Viola', *Corriere della Sera*, 19 December 1966, p. 13.

like an object. In his summary, they said a strong '"No" to the ancient concept of honour, to violence, to reparatory marriage'.[105] While his findings on the hypocrisy of tradition and the hope that ordinary women might reject oppression were in perfect keeping with the newspaper's politics, they were still an indication of a strong rejection of the notion of female honour, at least in the public sphere.

Media commentators also put forward competing definitions of honour in order to explain the motives of the men involved in the case. While Melodia and his defence team continually attempted to frame the case in terms of love, media commentators attributed different motives to Melodia. In contrast, they cast him as the perpetrator of a mafia-style vendetta against Bernardo Viola in defence of his wounded masculine honour.[106] The defence teams attempted to paint Bernardo Viola in a similar light, accusing him of both forbidding his daughter to see Melodia and then forbidding the marriage after the kidnap, because Melodia had offended his honour. Melodia's lawyer Ragusa accused Bernardo Viola of 'paralysing Franca's passion for Filippo' by responding to Melodia's challenge to his paternal authority as a 'man of honour'.[107] As with the accusations levelled at Melodia himself, honour here carried connotations not just of a Mediterranean masculinity bound up with both sexual conquest and the sexual control of women, but of mafia connections. Honour could thus have many different meanings in the case. Defined by female sexuality, it was also bound up with a certain kind of masculinity and closely associated with criminality.[108]

In contrast, Bernardo Viola was hailed by the press both in Sicily and across Italy as the model of a more progressive, civically minded Sicilian masculinity, who stood in opposition to Sicily's 'honoured society'. On closer examination, he does not seem as progressive as the coverage suggests; whatever the truth of his role in the relationship between Franca and Melodia he did afterwards arrange another marriage for her. However, it was not his role as a father so much as a citizen that was singled out by the press, since by going to the authorities rather than settling matters himself, he was playing his part in breaking the cycles of private violence and vendetta in Sicilian society.[109]

---

[105] Giorgio Frasca Polara, 'La forza di dire no', *L'Unità*, 18 December 1966, p. 13.

[106] Guido Guidi in *La Stampa* wrote that Melodia acted not because he was in love with Viola, but because as a mafioso he could not accept that he had been rejected. Guido Guidi, 'La Parte Civile chiede una "giusta condanna" del giovane che rapì e violentò la diciottenne', *La Stampa*, 14 December 1966, p. 15. See also Silvano Villani, 'Il rapimento di Franca Viola fu una vendetta di stile mafioso', *Corriere della Sera*, 14 December 1966, p. 17 and Indro Montanelli, 'La ragazza di Alcamo', *Corriere della Sera*, 14 December 1966, p. 1.

[107] Ettore Serio, '"Il mafioso è Viola padre che non acconsente alle nozze"', *Giornale di Sicilia*, 16 December 1966, pp. 1 and 16.

[108] Blok, *Mafia of a Sicilian Village*, p. 211.

[109] 'Mia figlia Franca non sposerà mai l'uomo che l'ha rapita e disonorata', *La Stampa*, 17 December 1966, p. 9.

FAMILY AND FEMINISM: AFTERMATH OF THE TRIAL

The aftermath of the Melodia trial was quite different to that of Furnari. Melodia had been convicted and given a firm sentence. The sentences of eleven years for Melodia himself and an average of four years for his accomplices were less than what the state prosecutor had recommended but still severe enough to send a strong message about kidnap and forced marriage.[110] Satisfied that in this case the sentence was appropriate, the focus of the press coverage was on shifting attitudes within Sicily rather than on legal reform. When Franca Viola's kidnap was first reported, the debates about law reform for honour crime were in full swing. Some did link her case with honour crime, calling for a reform of the law on 'reparatory marriage' in addition to the repeal of Article 587 at the time.[111] Such voices were not numerous though, and the matter was largely left to rest after the sentencing of Melodia. Reparatory marriage was not in fact removed from the statute books until 1981.[112]

The focus of the media discussion of the trial was rather on changing attitudes within Sicily. The proof of this seemed to come just a few days after the verdict, when yet another case of kidnap was reported.[113] Mattia Clavadolo, the young woman at the centre of the case, was quoted as having said that in the same situation she would have made the same choice as Franca Viola did. When the girl was returned to her parents a few days later, she confirmed her decision not to accept a reparatory marriage and was supported by her family. While the ultimate outcome of the case is unclear, as it disappeared from the newspapers a few days later, it was reported everywhere as a sign that this 'new' Sicily was finally maturing. Indeed by 1968 the ideas of honour crime and kidnap marriage could be openly mocked in the film comedy *Girl with a Gun*—it seemed that such customs were becoming so remote from people's lives that they no longer needed to be taken seriously.[114] In reality, changes in attitude as in the law happened much more slowly.

The celebratory media clamour surrounding the verdict masked the fact that it was in reality very difficult for the Viola family to live in Trapani following the trial.[115] She was still under some pressure to marry Melodia in

---

[110] Ettore Serio, 'Melodia condannato a 11 anni', *Giornale di Sicilia*, 18 December 1966, p. 1. The state prosecutor's recommendations are outlined in: 'Un secolo e mezzo di carcere per gli imputati richiesto dal P.M.: 500 la vogliono in sposa', *L'Ora*, 14/15 December 1966, p. 4.

[111] Jemolo, 'Non è sbagliato soltanto la legge che rispetta il "delitto d'onore"'.

[112] Willson, *Women in Twentieth-Century Italy*, p. 163.

[113] A. P., 'Nessuna traccia della ragazza rapita a Salemi dall'ex-fidanzato', *Corriere della Sera*, 22 December 1966, p. 19. The case was reported widely in the regional, national and international media during that week.

[114] *Girl with a Gun* (Mario Monicelli, 1968).

[115] On the eve of the verdict, the Alcamo town council passed a motion of solidarity with Franca Viola. See: 'La cittadinanza di Alcamo solidale con Franca Viola', *L'Unità*, 16 December 1966, p. 5. A presidential honour for her father was also discussed: Ugo Ugolini, 'Alta

order to free him from prison, and threats and boycotts forced the family to move away for three years. It is also curious that while the Italian press was saturated with her name and image in December 1966, on closer glance the woman herself seems strangely absent. She never gave interviews and rarely even met the eyes of reporters in the course of the trial. She is present as slogan and symbol—as 'the girl who said no', the modest Sicilian and reluctant feminist—but her own motivations, thoughts, and attitudes are much more difficult to discern.[116] It is impossible to escape the suspicion that if Franca Viola had spoken more in public, she might have disappointed those who made her a symbol of Italian feminism from the 1970s onwards.

In 1970, Damiano Damiani released *The Most Beautiful Wife*, a film based around the story of Franca Viola, but in which the film character Francesca behaved quite differently to what we know of the historical woman. First introduced as modest, poor, and traditional, she quickly began to speak and act like a feminist of the late 1960s and early 1970s, admonishing Vito, the Melodia character, for treating her like a possession. During the rape scene, she firmly told Vito that she would rather stay a spinster than marry him. Franca Viola in contrast was reported to have accepted her marriage to Filippo Melodia as inevitable at the time when she was rescued by the police.[117] In Damiani's film, it was Francesca who remained firm in prosecuting Vito, against the wishes of her family, while the police were also reluctant to prosecute. In reality, Franca Viola's family, and especially her father, had been supportive to the extent that questions could be raised about whether the famous 'no' came from Franca herself or from her father. Neither did the extensive eight-day-long police search point towards a reluctance to prosecute, although the zeal could more likely be put down to Melodia's alleged mafia connections than a particular concern with gender violence. In its portrayal of Francesca as a modern, emancipated woman who went against her family in her quest for justice, the actual historical woman seemed to have been written out of her own story. The narrative adjustments that Damiani made in his film also hinted at changing attitudes towards the family. Showing Francesca going against her family in the film suggested that following the Italian '68, the notion of family guiding and supporting a woman in her choice no longer fitted with ideas of individual choice and romantic love. Events were soon to

onorificenza per Bernardo Viola?', *L'Ora*, 16/17 December 1966, p. 1. Franca herself refused all media attention and honour until she was awarded a presidential honour in a ceremony on International Women's Day in 2014. 'Napolitano premia donna di Alcamo che rifiutò nozze riparatrici', *La Repubblica*, 8 March 2014: Film clip available on repubblica.it.

[116] This is remarked on in Sicilian writer Beatrice Monroy's non-fiction book about the case, *Niente ci fu* (Molfetta, 2012).

[117] Franca Viola was reported to have said to the police on their capture of Filippo Melodia, 'don't shoot, he is already my husband'. Quoted in Ettore Serio, 'Il mafioso è Viola padre che non acconsente alle nozze', *Giornale di Sicilia*, 16 December 1966, p. 1.

indicate, however, that the media and popular culture narrative still had little to do with the reality of rural Sicily in 1970.

In the same year as Damiani's film was released, another abduction case made the newspapers across Italy. In November 1970, 15-year-old Carmelina Torrisi was forcibly bundled into a car and taken away by two men while out shoe shopping with her mother in the southern Sicilian town of Gela.[118] Her mother, Grazia Cassarino, was reported to have struggled against her daughter's abductors, as did Torrisi herself, but their efforts were in vain. Feeling weak after the incident, Cassarino was assisted by passers-by before making her way to the police station to report the crime. Torrisi returned home early the next morning, roughly sixteen hours after her abduction. It is unclear exactly what happened next, but some time afterwards she was rushed to hospital, after apparently swallowing the sewing needle she had been using to repair her torn skirt. Speculation naturally turned to a suicide attempt, although this was never confirmed. From her hospital bed, Torrisi narrated her story as journalists and local prosecutors pieced together the details of her case. Her abductor was one Rocco Fauciana. The son of a local shepherd, he had made a marriage proposal to her family through an intermediary which she rejected. This was possibly because of his violent past, and she was supported by her father in her decision to refuse him. The abduction was intended to force her into marriage, but following the example of Franca Viola, Carmelina Torrisi was intent on refusing a marriage based on violence and coercion.

The story became more complicated when it emerged that Torrisi's mother was complicit in the abduction, and was arrested and placed in police custody along with Fauciana himself, his sister and an accomplice who had driven the car. It was here that Torrisi's story began to diverge sharply from that of Franca Viola. While both women seemed determined to reject the reparatory marriage that was offered, Viola had the firm support of her family while Torrisi seemed to be under increasing pressure from her family to accept the marriage, particularly after her mother's arrest. Her father, Vincenzo Torrisi, was initially reported as being supportive of his daughter's decision, but journalists reported pressure from both her mother and other relatives even as Torrisi spoke from her hospital bed. Crucially, the continued detention of four people, including Torrisi's own mother, rested on her ongoing refusal to accept the marriage, a factor which must naturally have weighed heavily on her as she made her decision.

Unlike Franca Viola, who was always an elusive figure for the media, Torrisi readily gave interviews from hospital, where she remained for several weeks in an apparently uncertain although not life-threatening medical condition. The

---

[118] E. C., 'Carmela (15 anni) decisa: non sposerà il rapitore', *L'Ora*, 14 November 1970, p. 3.

longest interview was carried in *Giornale della Sicilia*, while shorter snatches of conversation with journalists were carried in other newspapers including *L'Ora* and *Corriere della Sera*. Together these interviews provide a fascinating insight into the mindset of a young woman who had undergone abduction and possibly rape. Although intent on her refusal, she was also under huge pressure from family and community to accept what was seen as the obvious and traditional solution. While Franca Viola's own words and sentiments are very difficult to discern from the numerous pages of press coverage, Torrisi's testimony in contrast was detailed and definite. Indeed her manner seemed to resemble the fictional Francesca more closely than Franca Viola herself had.

On 21 November, in the days closely following her ordeal, she seemed adamant that she would not marry.[119] When a journalist inquired if she had feelings for her abductor, she answered: 'Absolutely not. I feel nothing for him.' Asked what she would do next, she replied: 'I want to leave here, to go to Turin or Milan, somewhere else, to breathe different air, see different people and hear nothing more about any of this.'[120] Earlier, in an interview reported on 18 November, her uncle had allegedly referred to Fauciana as her husband to which she replied: 'What did you say? I have no husband.'[121] Her answers in these days were both firm and candid. In a later interview—published on 19 December, by which time her mother as well as Fauciana, his sister, and his accomplice were all in prison—her tone had shifted somewhat. Her words still clearly registered her own strong feelings, although the earlier defiance was coloured by confusion about the situation and her uncertainty about the decision she had to make. When asked if she loved Fauciana, she now answered: 'No, I feel nothing for him. But I no longer feel the hate of those initial moments.' When asked if she intended to marry him, she answered simply, 'I cannot say anything for definite, I am extremely confused.'[122] While the initial certainty that she would not marry was being worn down by circumstance and undoubtedly by pressure from relatives, her own wishes and her individual voice were still clear. In fact the interviews with Torrisi give the kind of insights that nobody involved with Franca Viola's case ever seemed to access, despite repeated attempts to interview her. That December it might indeed have seemed as if Torrisi, who readily and proudly accepted the inevitable comparisons with Viola, was the strong feminist symbol that the media had first sought in 1966.

However, after the interviews published between the 19 and 22 December, the one final mention of the Torrisi case was on 31 December when *Giornale*

[119] 'La ragazza è tornata in ospedale', *Giornale di Sicilia*, 21 November 1970, p. 10.
[120] 'La ragazza è tornata in ospedale'.
[121] Elio Cultraro, 'Gela: La 15enne respinge il rapitore che va a trovarla in ospedale', *L'Ora*, 18 November 1970, p. 5.
[122] Salvatore Parlagreco, 'Non so ancora se lo sposerò', *Giornale di Sicilia*, 19 December 1970, p. 9.

di Sicilia praised her courageous stance in their end of year news round-up.[123] No further mention of the case was ever made, as Torrisi had succumbed to strong pressure from her family and community to accept the marriage, and have the charges against her mother and the other accused dropped. Although she had spoken in clear and definite terms to the national media about her wishes and her feelings, revealing herself to be a worthy successor to Franca Viola, she lacked the one key element which was present in the Viola case: the clear and unambiguous support of her family. In 1970, four years after the conviction of Melodia, and in the absence of any meaningful law reform, a woman's wishes—or in the words of Melodia's state prosecutor, her feelings— were still not protected or respected by the law. Despite the feminist rhetoric that had surrounded the Viola case, it seemed that such noble notions as a woman's right to choose her marriage partner had little meaning if her family were not supportive. Given that Torrisi's ordeal came at the end of the year in which Damiani had elevated Franca Viola to the status of a strong-willed, outspoken feminist icon and wholly distorted the role her family had played in the case, the cruel irony of Torrisi's fate is especially noteworthy.

CONCLUSION

The trials of both Furnari and Melodia illustrated the real currency that honour still held in some sectors of Italian society. The media coverage of both trials and their aftermath revealed the struggle to define what honour could mean in the changing context of the 1960s, and how it might or might not fit with certain notions of national or regional identity. For many it seemed incompatible with the self-conscious modernity of the industrial, urbanized Italy of the 1960s, and those who acted on it represented a dangerous and violent kind of masculinity. The case of Franca Viola was, however, not just about honour. The media coverage of the Melodia trial raised questions about how Italians understood love and what lexicon they used to describe it. While regional fault lines existed when it came to love, Franca Viola's own rejection of reparatory marriage and her determination to marry for love indicated that not everyone accepted regional traditions of romance and marriage. The media coverage of the case within Sicily, in its vehement rejection of the language of love and romance, indicated a broader redefinition of marriage, gender roles and emotions in Sicilian society. Likewise, it is clear from the media coverage of honour crime, and the Viola case in particular, that honour was strongly rejected by many Sicilian journalists, activists, and intellectuals

---

[123] 'Una donna di 15 anni che fa onore alla Sicilia', *Giornale di Sicilia*, 31 December 1970, p. 5.

by the mid-1960s, while the antiquated law statutes were not regional but national in origin.[124] Important cultural shifts were certainly happening in relation to 'dishonoured women' in the mid to late 1960s. While Pietro Germi's 1964 film *Seduced and Abandoned* ended bleakly with the marriage of Agnese to her rapist and kidnapper, the more light-hearted 1968 film *Girl with a Gun* was able to give Agnese, who was also the victim of kidnap, a different and more hopeful ending. Having followed her attacker to England in order to avenge her lost honour, she was gradually able to leave behind the rigid gender codes of Sicily for the more liberated mores of England in the swinging sixties, eventually falling in love with a divorcé. The radically different endings of both films perhaps point to the opening of new imaginative spaces for southern women between 1964 and 1968, and indeed new vocabularies of romantic love. Disappointingly though, it is evident from the Torrisi case that the cultural narrative did not always reflect changed realities, and that all too often it was not sentiment or feminist sensibilities but family which still shaped the lives of many young women.

While it is evident that the notion of honour was no longer seen as acceptable by the mid-1960s, the attitudes and behaviour associated with the honour code were not necessarily discarded. It is clear from both the popular stories cited at the beginning of the chapter and the trial of Melodia, that the vocabulary of romantic love itself could point to the attitudes and behaviour associated with the honour code, as to the ideas of equality, friendship, and respect engendered in the companionate marriage. Often the messages could be confusing and contradictory; love could be passionate and liberating but still require submission and modesty from a woman. This interpretation was beginning to lose ground by the 1960s, but for some violence and love could be intimately connected rather than opposed to each other. However, the prominent role that Bernardo Viola played in his daughter Franca's famous 'no' reminds us that the kidnap marriage or elopement was at its heart a family drama. Chapter 4 will examine how outside the courtroom, the attitudes and behaviour of the honour code might, instead of diminishing, instead have been reframed in the language of the emotions. As courtship and marriage became increasingly a private matter for the couple themselves rather than their families, a woman's behaviour might be policed not by society but within the couple's own intimate sphere and bound up even further with their emotions for each other. While this chapter examined honour particularly as it related to the south of Italy, Chapter 4 will also explore the more national roots and reverberations of the attitudes and the behaviour associated with it.

---

[124] Article 587 had its origins in the 1889 Zanardelli Code of the newly unified nation. See Eva Cantarella, 'Homocides of Honour: The Development of Italian Adultery Law Over Two Millennia', in David Kertzer and Richard Saller (eds), *The Family in Italy from Antiquity to the Present* (New Haven, CT, 1991), pp. 229–44, 236–7.

4

'Love Means Jealousy': A Jealousy Epidemic in Post-war Italy?

In Pier Paolo Pasolini's documentary film *Love Meetings* (1965), the acclaimed writer and filmmaker surveyed Italians across the peninsula to capture the diverse and changing views of love and sexuality in 1960s Italy.[1] Speaking to a group of young men and women on the beach in Calabria, he asked them to describe what honour meant to them. He was met with pauses and hesitations; honour was difficult to vocalize and describe in relation to everyday life and personal feelings. However, when he asked more direct questions about sexual behaviour and regulation, jealousy was frequently mentioned in conversation. When he questioned an elderly Calabrian peasant about why it was imperative for a woman to be a virgin on her marriage while a man was expected to have a sexual past, the answer given was simple and direct: 'it's jealousy'. When Pasolini probed further, asking if things might change, the reply was negative and closed: 'always this way [...] there's no need to understand'. On the beach, he persisted with this line of questioning, inquiring as to why a woman would not be allowed to go for a coffee alone in Calabria, although such behaviour was acceptable elsewhere in Italy. A young girl of no more than ten readily answered (of Calabrian men): 'but...maybe it is because they are a little jealous'. In both of these examples, jealousy was cited as shorthand for a range of social codes and behaviours; it was named without question as their root, closing the discussion rather than opening it out further. For the Calabrian peasant, there was no need to explain further—since one either understood or not—while the notion of jealousy was clearly all too familiar even to a pre-pubescent girl. We saw in Chapter 3 how honour was difficult to vocalize, especially in the context of the changing society of the 1960s; Pasolini's interviewees suggest that at the same time it was well understood in the language of the emotions.

We do however need to be a little more careful about accepting Pasolini's conclusions—and any simple equation between honour and jealousy—at face

---

[1] *Comizi d'amore/Love Meetings* (Pier Paolo Pasolini, 1965).

value. His conversations with Calabrian people have to be understood not as direct sources, but as mediated through Pasolini's own perspective in selecting, editing, and formulating the questions. The project of charting changing attitudes towards sexuality across the peninsula was part of a broader fascination with how the economic miracle was transforming Italian society, no doubt also informed by his own sexual identity, marginalized in the conformist climate of the 1950s and 1960s.[2] Strongly immersed in the provincial northern identity of his Friulian background in his early career and then in the urban literary and intellectual worlds of Rome and the PCI, the poet and filmmaker had no specialist background nor interest in the south.[3] Neither would the musings of the elderly man or the young girl have come as any surprise to an Italian audience in the 1960s; indeed, the notion of Sicilians and southern Italians as especially jealous was a deeply rooted one. The stereotypes of southern character as emotional, passionate, and prone to violence can be dated back at least as far back as eighteenth-century travellers' accounts.[4] By the post-war period, these assumptions could frequently be found in popular culture as in the personal testimonies. Pasolini concluded *Love Meetings* with the assertion that 'there was no jealousy in the north of Italy'. Through the juxtaposition of the rural and apparently traditional south with the industrial, urban north, the documentary also suggested that, despite the assurance of the Calabrian peasant, circumstances could and should evolve over time to eliminate jealousy.

This chapter, through a survey of popular culture, newspaper reports, and first-person testimonies, will show that jealousy was not confined to the south and was in fact everywhere in post-war Italy. It will also suggest that contrary to Pasolini's implicit linking of the elimination of jealousy with industrialization, urbanization, and the north, the presence of jealousy in popular culture and the media had actually increased. There was a definite perception that it was on the rise in the 1950s and 1960s, as magazines and newspapers ran detailed enquiries on the subject of jealousy, enlisting the opinions of ordinary people, celebrities, feminists, and psychologists on the nature of this insidious emotion. The extent of the attention paid to jealousy might suggest the perception at least of an 'epidemic' of jealousy in Italy between the 1950s and the 1970s.

---

[2] See Naomi Greene, *Pier Paolo Pasolini, Cinema as Heresy* (Princeton, NJ, 1992), pp. 69–71 on *Comizi d'Amore*. The film is actually treated comparatively little in the large body of Pasolini criticism.

[3] On his intellectual and Friulian background, see Robert Gordon, *Forms of Subjectivity* (Oxford, 1996), pp. 33–40. For a broad view of Pasolini's life, see Nico Naldini, *Breve vita di Pasolini* (Parma, 2000), while Anna Tonelli's *Per indegnità morale: Il caso Pasolini nell'Italia del buon costume* (Rome, 2015) deals with the scandal of Pasolini's expulsion from the PCI for homosexual acts in 1949.

[4] See Franco Cassano, *Il pensiero meridiano* (Rome, 2007); John Dickie, *Darkest Italy: The Nation and Stereotypes of the Mezzogiorno 1860–1900* (London, 1999); and Nelson Moe, *The View from Vesuvius: Italian Culture and the Southern Question* (Berkeley, CA, 2005).

There has been evidence to suggest that the prevalence of jealousy has risen during times of rapid change and uncertainty.[5] Masha Belenky found that in nineteenth-century France, legal and cultural transformations to marriage and the family made jealousy a very public concern, continually discussed in fiction as in medical literature and marriage manuals. In both nineteenth-century France and mid-twentieth-century Italy, there was deep concern about the future of the traditional family. In France, the abolition of primogeniture in the Napoleonic Code created great anxiety about inheritance, since the law did not distinguish between the legitimate and illegitimate children of a man's legal wife.[6] Neither, throughout the nineteenth century, were single mothers allowed to pursue a legal paternity search for the child's father.[7] While the law thus policed the legitimate French family from the consequences of male infidelity, there were no such legal barriers to a wife introducing an illegitimate child to the household, which fomented anxiety about marital fidelity in French society. In Italy, the economic boom was transforming the family through migration and changing gender roles; by the 1960s changing expectations were also bringing about generational conflict between parents and children. Reforms in marriage and family law were slower in Italy, coming in the 1970s only after the major social changes. However, many matters loomed in the public mind long before that. Divorce was a matter of mainstream public discussion in the 1960s leading up to the 1970 legalization of divorce and the 1974 referendum.[8] Male anxieties were certainly whipped up in the campaign against divorce in 1974, suggesting that links between the changing legal family and anxieties about women's sexual behaviour were easily made.[9] The legal protections for so-called crimes of honour, as we saw in Chapter 3, were publicly challenged in the mid-1960s although the legal reforms did not come until 1975 and 1981. The elimination of illegitimacy as a legal category was also a provision of the 1975 family law reform act. French social reformer Pierre-Jules Hetzel argued in 1851 that jealousy was a product of gender inequality in marriage; once all legal inequality was abolished and free divorce provided, there would be no reason for jealousy.[10] This chapter will argue the opposite. It was not the legal and social imbalances between the positions of men and women in marriage that caused the national

---

[5] Masha Belenky, *The Anxiety of Dispossession: Jealousy in Nineteenth-century French Culture* (Lewisburg, 2008).

[6] Belenky, *Anxiety of Dispossession*, p. 20.

[7] Rachel Fuchs, *Contested Paternity: Constructing Families in Modern France* (Baltimore, MD, 2008), pp. 12–13.

[8] Mark Seymour, *Debating Divorce in Italy: Marriage and the Making of Modern Italians* (London, 2006), pp. 189–211.

[9] See Maureen J. Giovannini, 'Female Chastity Codes in the Circum-Mediterranean: Comparative Perspectives', in David Gilmore (ed.), *Honor and Shame and the Unity of the Mediterranean* (Washington, DC, 1987), pp. 61–74, 66–7.

[10] Belenky, *Anxiety of Dispossession*, pp. 46–8.

obsession with jealousy in post-war Italy. Rather, at its root was the anxiety and uncertainty about the ways in which traditional patterns and structures of family were being transformed. On the other hand, the close association of jealousy with love suggests that anxiety is only a part of the story. It has been noted that in late nineteenth-century England, more intimate partner violence was reported as being motivated by jealousy, as the ideal of companionate marriage became more firmly fixed in Victorian culture.[11] Indeed, in Italy too it appears that, as courtship and marriage shifted from being an arrangement between families to being one based on love and companionship, romantic love came to assume a heavier burden in relationships. The increased emphasis on love and companionship in marriage might lead to greater equality and respect in marriage, as indeed we saw in Chapter 2. It could also lead to greater possessiveness and control of women, as the anxieties about changing family structures and the strictures of the honour code became bound up in romantic love and the intimate sphere of the couple itself.

Jealousy had no single or simple meaning in post-war Italy; although the word had a certain easy familiarity for most Italians, it could signify something quite different depending on the person, time, or place. It might be an expression of love or a proud signifier of regional identity; it could equally be seen in negative terms as a passion or impulse to be controlled and repressed. Meaning and usage varied according to context while class, region, gender, and generation also impacted the ways in which it was applied and understood. While both men and women could be jealous, it was more usually understood as a masculine emotion and it was associated with quite different behaviour for men and women. Neither was it always understood strictly as an emotion. Thomas Dixon cautions against the simple conflation of terms such as passion and sentiment with the psychological category of emotion, while Giulia Sissa's history of jealousy reminds us of the range of feeling and meaning that has been contained in this one word over time.[12] In twentieth-century Italy too, *gelosia* could be used to describe both a feeling, and a range of behaviour. Monique Scheer's understanding of emotions as located in the body, and fundamentally shaped by our behaviour rather than our thoughts, is particularly useful here.[13] In legal language and crime reportage, jealousy was related to crimes of passion, and to the notion of family honour. Magazine features were more likely to discuss jealousy in the language of psychology,

---

[11] Jade Shephard, '"I Am Not Very Well I Feel Nearly Mad When I Think of You": Male Jealousy, Murder and Broadmoor in Late-Victorian Britain', *Social History of Medicine*, 30:2 (2017), pp. 277–98, 288.

[12] Thomas Dixon, *From Passions to Emotions: The Creation of a Secular Psychological Category* (Cambridge, 2003), pp. 1–25; Giulia Sissa, *Gelosia: Una passione inconfessabile* (Rome, 2015).

[13] Monique Scheer, 'Are Emotions a Kind of Practice (And is that What Makes Them Have a History)? A Bourdieuian Approach to Understanding Emotion', *History and Theory*, 51:2 (2012), pp. 193–220.

while popular film, as well as the serialized fiction of a magazine such as *Grand Hotel*, borrowed from melodrama in their exaggerated performance of jealousy as an emotion. However, the fact that there is a marked increase in the use of this word to describe varying shades of feeling and behaviour in the decades in question demands further inquiry. So-called crimes of jealousy will also be considered here; since the focus will be on reportage rather than court records, such sources straddle the boundaries between representation and experience.

Whether Italians really experienced more jealousy in these years cannot easily be measured by the historian, although this chapter will attempt as far as possible to map the public perception of a jealousy epidemic onto private experience. Since this chapter is concerned with what people themselves understood by jealousy in the post-war decades, I have included only first-person texts that explicitly name jealousy (*gelosia*) in relation to either them-selves or their partners. These texts encompass a wide range of behaviour and feeling from teenage romantic musings to intimate partner violence; at the same time accounts of domestic violence that do not mention jealousy are not included. By considering the media and popular culture sources together with the diaries and memoirs, the slippages in usage and meaning, and the extent to which language was shared and borrowed between different types of sources, becomes clearer. Indeed, we can see that popular culture provided a vocabu-lary of jealousy that could be drawn on, and perhaps even shape ordinary experience. This chapter will now turn to a closer examination of the post-war cultural preoccupation with jealousy before moving on to discuss in more detail the notion of jealousy as pathology; jealousy, crime, and control and finally the various attempts to reject and overcome this 'insidious' passion.

'LOVE MEANS JEALOUSY': JEALOUS LOVE IN POST-WAR ITALY

A hastily scribbled note in an Italian schoolgirl's diary—'love means jealousy'—in 1949 gives us some small sense of how popular culture might intersect with the personal (see Figure 4.1).[14] Born and raised in the town of Capurso, near the southern port city of Bari, Maria Maselli was 16 in 1949. Her school diary was interspersed with short phrases which sound like quotations picked up from her day-to-day life; school, friends, family, religion, and probably cinema, books, and magazines along with brief snatches of thought or observation; from football news to the local cult of the Virgin Mary. In her

---

[14] Maria Maselli, 'Diari, 1948-1957', DP/07, ADN.

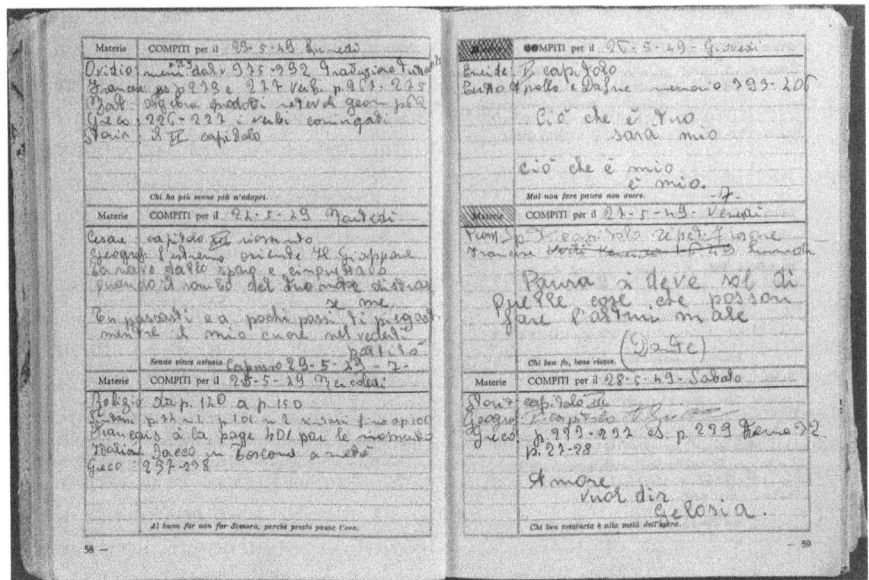

Figure 4.1. Scribbled note 'love means jealousy' in the diary of Maria Maselli, 28 May 1949.

Archivio Diaristico Nazionale.

scribbled note, Maria had most likely jotted down part of the lyrics from the popular 1947 song, *Gelosia*.[15] 'If love means jealousy', sang Nilla Pizzi, 'who will love you more than me | I tremble at the thought of a love | a love that can teach us to love like this'.[16] A rising star of Italian radio who secured her national reputation in winning the 1951 San Remo song contest, her rendition of *Gelosia* was evidently making an impression on Italian youth. The song was covered several times more, in 1969 by singer Betty Curtis, and again in the 1970s and 1980s. While the idea that love was intimately connected with jealousy was a familiar notion in 1949, *Gelosia* evidently had an enduring resonance that chimed with the ongoing public concern with jealousy in the post-war decades.[17] The notion of jealousy being intimately connected to love was a familiar trope of film and fiction, including and especially magazine fiction in these years. Whether jealous love was taken seriously, gently mocked, or more thoughtfully critiqued, it was ever-present in Italian culture.

[15] See secondhandsongs.com, entry on 'Jealousy/Jalousie/Gelosia', <https://secondhandsongs. com/performance/463879/versions> (accessed 17 June 2017). Thank you also to the editors of the journal *Snodi: Pubblici e privati nella storia contemporanea* for alerting me to this song.

[16] Song lyrics can be accessed at <http://bandaroncati.wiki.contaminati.net/index.php/Tango_ della_Gelosia>.

[17] See secondhandsongs.com, entry on 'Gelosia' (Nino Rastelli, 1947), <https://secondhandsongs. com/work/163613> (accessed 17 June 2017).

Jealousy was not of course a new discovery in post-war Italian culture. However, mentions were comparatively few in folk culture across rural Italy, despite romantic love being a common and recurring theme of folk music.[18] While romantic love had always been present largely as a disruptive force in Italian culture, it may be only as love was becoming more closely linked to marriage that jealousy, intertwined both with the exclusivity of love and the legal considerations of property and heredity bound up in marriage, really came into full force. In the cinema of the fascist era, jealousy certainly made an appearance in romantic comedies, but it was usually treated ironically or with distance, and considered an aside to the main plot.[19] In Negroni's 1931 film *Due cuori felici* (*Two Happy Hearts*), Clara invented a story about her violently jealous fiancé in order to escape from an awkward situation in a nightclub.[20] Camerini's 1937 film *Il signor Max* treated jealousy with similar levity and disdain. 'Max' was impersonating an upper-class gentleman on a luxury cruise.[21] When he had to leave in a hurry, he gave jealousy as an excuse for his abrupt exit and as a result he was teased for being 'bourgeois'; such an emotion in the 1930s seemed to have been cast aside by the wealthy and cosmopolitan. Even during fascism, when the idea of masculinity under threat was bound up in the very ideology of the regime, jealousy does not seem to have been a huge concern in popular culture.[22]

More exceptional was Poggioli's 1943 melodrama *Gelosia*. Remade in the following decade by Pietro Germi, it perhaps better fitted with the heightened sensibilities of the post-war years: from the 1950s onwards, jealousy was centre stage in Italian cinema.[23] Popular romantic comedies—from *Bread, Love and Jealousy* in 1954 (the second of Dino Comencini's romantic comedies set in rural Abruzzo) and the second film of Dino Risi's Roman trilogy, *Poor but Beautiful* (1957) to Vittorio De Sica's *Marriage, Italian Style* (1964) and Antonio Pietrangeli's *The Magnificent Cuckold* (1964)—were just some of

---

[18] See for example: Roberto Leydi, *Canti popolari italiani* (Milan, 1973); Roberto Leydi (ed.), *Le tradizioni popolari in Italia: Canti e musiche popolari* (Milan, 1990); and Brizio Montinaro (ed.), *Canti di pianto e dell'amore dell'antico Salento* (Bologna, 2000).

[19] Studies of film during the fascist era mention very little about jealousy, even in the context of gender and sexuality. See, for example, David Forgacs, 'Sex in the Cinema: Regulation and Transgression in Italian Films, 1930–1943', in Jacqueline Reich and Piero Garofalo (eds), *Re-viewing Fascism: Italian Cinema, 1922–1943* (Bloomington, IN, 2002), pp. 141–72; Peter Bondanella, *A History of Italian Cinema* (London, 2009).

[20] Marcia Landy, *Folklore of Consensus: Theatricality in the Italian Cinema, 1930–1943* (Albany, NY, 1998), p. 68.

[21] Landy, *Folklore of Consensus*, p. 91.

[22] On fascism, women, and the family, see Victoria De Grazia, *How Fascism Ruled Women: Italy, 1922–1945* (Berkeley, CA, 1992) and Paul Ginsborg, *Family Politics Domestic Life, Devastation and Survival 1900–1950* (New Haven, CT, 2014), and on the fascist cult of virility see Sandro Bellasai, 'The Masculine Mystique: Antimodernism and Virility in Fascist Italy', *Journal of Modern Italian Studies*, 10:3 (2005), pp. 314–35.

[23] On Poggioli's *Gelosia*, see Marcia Landy, *Folklore of Consensus*, pp. 229–34.

those that featured jealousy as a main mechanism for creating tension and driving the plot forward. The 'pink neorealism' of popular commercial cinema exemplified by Risi's and Comencini's work, in its depiction of the poverty and struggles faced by ordinary rural and working-class Italians albeit in a somewhat romanticized fashion, was easily able to make use of jealousy to create romantic tensions.[24] It was not only popular commercial films that took jealousy seriously in these years; Visconti's late neorealist classic *Rocco and his Brothers* (1960) also dealt with the violent consequences of extreme jealousy. The connection between romantic love and jealousy was accepted without much question in all of these films, as if the connection was a natural one which needed little examination. This was the case even when it was the excesses of jealousy which created romantic tension or dark drama and drove the plot forward. In Antonio Pietrangeli's 1964 film *The Magnificent Cuckold*, the exchanges between husband and wife reveal that a certain amount of jealousy was considered desirable in order to keep the romance in their relationship alive.[25] On discovering that her husband had been following her, Maria Grazia told him that she was impressed by the attention he paid to her. In her mind, 'when one is in love, one is always a little jealous'. The film of course would go on to reveal that striking the right balance between having just enough and not too much of the feeling, was more difficult than it seemed.

Although the couple in *The Magnificent Cuckold* were distinctly modern and metropolitan, jealousy was often associated with the south and with traditional, rural settings. While it was certainly a label imposed on the south, jealousy might also be proudly embraced by southerners themselves. Claudia Cardinale, who played Maria Grazia in *The Magnificent Cuckold*, proudly identified herself as a jealous southerner. Born in Tunisia to Sicilian emigrants, she commented in a 1959 interview for *Grand Hotel* that she would always like to know that someone was jealous of her. 'That too is a form of love, it means that somebody loves you to the point of suffering for you. In any case speaking for myself, I am like any proper southerner, extremely jealous.'[26] Such judgements of character could create, for at least some southern Italians, a positive sense of regional difference within the Italian nation, intensified perhaps by the migration waves of the economic miracle which were drawing so many Italians away from the peripheral southern regions during this period. It was in these years that southern food traditions were reinvented as national ones, while a traditional and nostalgic southern Italy was being created on screen through the popular cinema of the 1950s.[27] Just as the

[24] Millicent Marcus, *Italian Film in the Light of Neorealism* (Princeton, NJ, 1986), pp. 122–43.
[25] The final episode of the 1964 film *La mia signora* (*My Wife*), directed by Tinto Brass, Mauro Bolognini, and Luigi Comencini contained a similar message.
[26] Lino Ferrara, 'Gelosia e malinconia', *Grazia*, 10 January 1959.
[27] John Dickie, *Delizia! The Epic History of Italians and Their Food* (London, 2010); Emanuela Scarpellini, *Food and Foodways in Italy from 1861 to the Present* (London, 2016), pp. 109–40.

economic miracle was taking hold in the northern cities, cinema screens tended to portray rose-tinted images of rural Italy and the backstreets of 'traditional', working-class Naples.[28] In these films, exaggerated character traits and passions were part of the regional colour. Two of the most successful comedies of the 1960s, *Divorce, Italian Style* (1961) and *Marriage, Italian Style* (1964), set respectively in Sicily and Naples, played on the traditional stereo-types of southern men and women as jealous and possessive, passionate, and in some cases violent enough to commit murder, while unashamed of their sexual double standard.[29]

Jealousy again drove many of the plots of popular magazine *Grand Hotel*'s short stories and serialized, illustrated fiction about love, as it created a romantic tension that could be neatly resolved by the end of the story. In these stories, jealousy could lead to tragic misunderstanding or melodrama as well as to comic mishap. Reviewing the plot synopses for a sample set of issues from the first six months of 1950, 1955, and 1959, it emerges that jealousy peaked as a central storyline in 1955, with war and poverty creating much of the romantic tension in earlier years while migration, work, and changing gender roles dominated the storylines of the late 1950s. Usually, although not always, it was the man's jealousy that took centre stage, causing either a rift in the relationship or irrationally controlling behaviour on his part. His suspi-cions about his girlfriend, fiancée, or wife were also always unfounded; although the Catholic Church condemned magazines like *Grand Hotel* as immoral for their association with commercial culture and Americanization, it was in fact quite socially conservative and female infidelity was rarely an acceptable subject.[30] 'Fallen women' and single mothers could be redeemed but only in specific circumstances. In cases of male jealousy, the plot usually centred on the struggle to prove the woman's fidelity to her partner and restore his trust. In cases of female jealousy, suspicions did sometimes prove correct.

In the 1955 story 'The Thermometer of Love', the plot hinged around three sisters who were about to marry.[31] When discussing how they would keep their husband's love when married, the youngest sister Maria repeated the notion that jealousy was the real test of love. Each of the sisters then asked her fiancé what he would do if she betrayed him with another man. The older two sisters were given answers involving murder and separation. Maria instead was told by her fiancé Gianni that he trusted she would never betray him. His mild-mannered response left her unsatisfied, as she had hoped for something

---

[28] Stephen Gundle, *Bellissima: Feminine Beauty and the Idea of Italy* (London, 2007), pp. 142–69.

[29] *Divorce, Italian Style* was directed by Pietro Germi and *Marriage, Italian Style* by Vittorio de Sica. On the debates around the former film, see Seymour, *Debating Divorce*, pp. 174–7.

[30] Anna Bravo, *Il fotoromanzo*; Angelo Ventrone, 'Tra propaganda e passione: "Grand Hôtel" e l'Italia degli anni '50', *Rivista di storia contemporanea*, 17:4 (1988).

[31] Fabio Pan, 'Il termometro dell'amore', *Grand Hotel*, 26 November 1955.

closer to the jealous passion displayed by her sisters' fiancés. When they married, she was again disconcerted to find that Gianni allowed her to come and go as she pleased; she would have been happier to have him confine her to the home as a mark of his jealousy and protectiveness. Attempts to provoke Gianni's jealousy by going out and flirting with other men were again in vain. However, when Maria found a gun in the house she was finally satisfied. Refusing to believe Gianni's excuses about security on night-time walks, she was convinced that 'Gianni bought it for fear that she...finally! And that night the young wife dreamed happy dreams.'[32]

The implication was of course that Gianni was prepared to kill her if she should stray, the proof of love that Maria had been waiting for. It turned out that Gianni had no such intentions; he was in fact engaged in a plot of his own to prove to Maria how ridiculous her concerns were. At the end of the story, Maria's foolish and misguided expectations were unmasked, while Gianni also agreed to pay more attention to her. Although Maria had perhaps taken it to greater extremes, her ideas about love fitted the endlessly repeated notion that love was intimately connected with jealousy and that jealousy was proof of love.

We see it again in the 1964 film *La mia signora* (*My Wife*). Divided into five short episodes, the last one, 'The Car', involved a husband who reported his car stolen. In the end his wife testified that it was she who had taken the car to go and meet her lover. The husband immediately went to recover the car, much more concerned by its loss than by his wife's betrayal. The episode ended with his wife giving him a sharp slap; where was his jealousy and therefore his love for her? Nor was the notion confined to romantic comedy or women's magazines; the notion that jealousy was linked to love was discussed in a 1970 article in *Corriere della Sera*, after a Parisian woman was fined and given a one-month sentence for harassing her husband's work colleague out of jealousy. Although the article did ultimately argue for the need to 'civilize' this otherwise 'savage' emotion, a strong link between love and jealousy, and the fear that its absence might lead to apathy, was readily accepted.[33]

The belief that jealousy was a test of love can be seen not just in popular culture but also in the writings of ordinary Italians. The diary of Sicilian teenager Gabriella Pezzino, which she kept regularly between 1957 and 1960 from the age of 14 to 17, contained just one example of this conviction. In 1959, attempting to describe her feelings for her new boyfriend Claudio, she wrote: 'I am becoming more and more jealous [of him]'. In other passages she described feeling possessive and missing him when he was not there; her 'jealousy' can probably be seen in those terms too. For Graziella, jealousy was

[32] Fabio Pan, 'Il termometro dell'amore'.
[33] Antonio Miotto, 'Civilizziamo la gelosia', *Corriere della Sera*, 20 November 1970.

bound up with feeling, passion, and a desire for closeness. Just as Maria Maselli had accepted that 'love meant jealousy' at least enough to have copied it into her school diary, Pezzino's thinking about love was along the same lines as that of Maria Grazia in *The Magnificent Cuckold*; anyone who was really in love was at least a little jealous.

'THAT TERRIBLE THING CALLED JEALOUSY': JEALOUSY AS PATHOLOGY

Although jealousy was recognized as a normal part of romance, it was still not an emotion with which both popular culture and the media were entirely at ease. 'The Thermometer of Love' indicates how the fiction in *Grand Hotel*, along with many popular films, seemed to play into the stereotype of the jealous lover, while also undermining it.[34] The advice columns in both *Grand Hotel* and other photoromance magazines, as well as in *Grazia*, also contained repeated references to the problem of jealousy throughout the 1950s and 1960s.[35] Both men and women wrote asking for advice on how to conquer their jealousy, while women also wrote frequently seeking advice about how to handle a boyfriend's or husband's excessive jealousy. While both men and women might describe themselves as jealous—indeed many of the letters written by 'Unhappy Girlfriends' seeking advice in the anthology *Italian Women Confess*, were written by jealous women—the letters reveal that their experiences were often quite different. A young woman reader from Sardinia wrote to the photoromance magazine *Luna Park*: 'I am wealthy, beautiful, well educated, pure and honest [...] I have nothing to regret, except that I have an incurable malady: jealousy.'[36] In her case her fiancé had left her, but since they both lived in the same small town, she found it difficult to forget him and move on with her life. What she had described as jealousy seems more like distress at the ending of the relationship and perhaps an attempt to regain control over the situation and her own feelings, framed in terms of jealousy rather than pain, love, or loss. However the fact that she fitted her own experiences into the template of jealousy—imagined as an illness that affected mind and body, rather than a simple emotion—is significant, and shows the power of this word as an explanation for loss, powerlessness, or lack of control.

---

[34] The story 'Inganno per due' ('Double Deception') was about a husband who wouldn't bring his wife to Paris on a business trip, but didn't trust her to stay in Milan alone either. In the end he was punished by his wife leaving him. *Grand Hotel*, 1 October 1955.

[35] On *Grazia* see Penny Morris, 'A Window on the Private Sphere: Advice Columns, Marriage and the Evolving Family in 1950s Italy', *The Italianist*, 27:2 (2002), pp. 304–32.

[36] Gabriella Parca (ed.), *Le italiane si confessano* (Florence, 1959), pp. 215–16.

In 1959 *Grazia* ran a multi-page inquiry into what they termed 'that terrible thing': jealousy. Brunello Vandano used psychology to delve into the phenomenon of jealousy that he perceived to be plaguing the relationships of Italians. Jealousy, although clearly situated in the exclusivity of romantic love, was a pathology when experienced in excess. It was 'morbid', an 'illness', and a 'terror'. For the sufferer, the boundaries between reality and fantasy became blurred, and he or she would inevitably lose all judgement at least for one moment. Two separate examples were used to describe the experiences of men and women. A man might catch a glimpse of a woman passenger in a car and imagine that it was his girlfriend. This would then set his mind working, even if he was fairly sure it was not her; was she with friends, or a colleague? Was it an innocent encounter or not? The woman on the other hand might be jealous of her boyfriend's female friend. The differences between male and female jealousy were clear: the man's jealousy was based on the possibility of his girlfriend being out in other company, while the woman's jealousy was based on a more specific romantic rivalry. While the emotion could be experienced by both men and women, it had specific gendered paths in Vandano's view. For women it was always bound up with love, whereas for men it might also be about the desire to possess a woman independent of romantic feeling. In its most extreme form, jealousy had an intensely physical side. The experience of the man who thought he saw his beloved in a car with another man was described thus: 'now his face grows paler, his heart skips a beat and for an instant he feels an animal-like desire to bite'.[37] Eight years later, a newspaper article for *La Stampa* wrote about jealousy in a somewhat similar but even more alarmist tone. While the author admitted a category of 'normal jealousy', he was evidently convinced that it was all too easy to slip into more extreme manifestations.[38] Citing the expertise of psychoanalysis and neuroscience, he examined jealousy as 'mania', 'nervous illness', and 'pathology'.[39] The 'delirium' it produced was similar to alcoholism, morphine addiction, and dementia; although it mainly affected men, menopausal women were apparently also vulnerable.

The notion of jealousy as an intense bodily experience and even illness, while packaged here in the language of psychology, psychoanalysis, and neuroscience, had its antecedents in both popular melodrama and the more psychological cinema of directors such as Antonioni.[40] Pietro Germi's 1953 film *Jealousy* told the story of Sicilian marquis Antonio who fell in love with the peasant woman Agrippina. He felt unable to marry her because of the difference in their stations, but remained fiercely possessive of her and suffered

---

[37] Brunello Vandano, 'Le insidie dell'amore: Quella terribile cosa che si chiama gelosia', *Grazia*, 26 July 1959.

[38] 'La gelosia', *La Stampa*, 4 July 1967.   [39] 'La gelosia', *La Stampa*, 4 July 1967.

[40] See Bondanella, *A History of Italian Cinema*, cit., pp. 127–58.

from extreme jealousy. Although he arranged a marriage between Agrippina and one of his servants in order to keep her close to him, he was driven to kill this man on their wedding day by an irrational, jealous rage. The only explanation he could give for the crime was that he was driven to madness: 'I was driven crazy. Driven crazy by jealousy.' The emotion was, for him, an intense bodily experience which eventually became an illness. He fell unconscious for three days and eventually, tortured by both jealousy and guilt, lost control of both mind and body. As the film closes, we see him slumped in a chair, completely helpless and unaware of his surroundings. While the film was not a great critical success for Germi—and was indeed later dismissed by the director himself as exaggerated and excessive—the notion of jealousy as a form of illness was certainly not unique to his film.[41] A decade later, the acclaimed comedy *The Magnificent Cuckold* (Antonio Pietrangeli, 1964) portrayed it in similar terms. Although he had no grounds to do so, Andrea became suspicious that his wife Maria Grazia was having an affair, and their relationship was eventually destroyed by his intense jealousy. As Andrea's jealousy and obsession intensified, he experienced it more strongly in his body, suffering first from insomnia and then from fever (see Figure 4.2). Violent mania then progressed into a strong physical illness that rendered him bedridden. Unlike Antonio's case, Andrea's jealousy was a passing affliction which was cured; however, the course of their physical symptoms was strikingly similar.

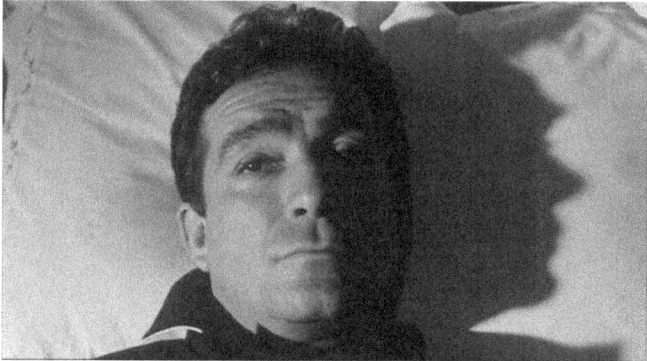

Figure 4.2. Ugo Tognazzi as Andrea, driven to insomnia by an unfounded jealousy of his wife, Maria Grazia, in *The Magnificent Cuckold.*
Antonio Pietrangeli, 1964.

[41] Carlo Carotti, *Le donne, la famiglia, il lavoro nel cinema di Pietro Germi* (Milan, 2011) pp. 79–80.

Curiously, while the idea that an excess of feeling might cause a person to fall ill is a common trope in medical literature at least up to the nineteenth century, in literature and indeed in post-war Italian film it appears unusual for men to be afflicted. In her work on jealousy in nineteenth-century France, Belenky shows how jealous women—in both the novels of Balzac and in medical treatises—experienced their jealousy as a physical malady.[42] In contrast, jealous men in literature were generally ineffectual in love, but healthy of body. Louis Bayman's work on melodrama in post-war Italian film discusses how the body becomes a canvas for the expression of emotion, with physical illness signalling emotional turmoil, suffering, and victimhood.[43] In Bayman's reading, the emotional world of melodrama signified a 'feminised emotivity' in the post-war cultural sphere, in contrast to the 'muscular masculinity' of fascism.[44] What then to make of the male characters driven to illness by their jealousy, incapacitated in mind and body? The films appear as a rather curious commentary on masculinity. Belenky found that in French society, jealousy was seen as a legitimate emotion for men—as it was connected to the legal and social status of the wife as property—but not for women.[45] The bodies of French women were thus consumed by their illicit passions, leading to illness. The meaning of jealousy was shifting over the course of the 1950s and 1960s and while many Italians saw it as intimately connected to love, we will also see later how many were beginning to reject the trope that 'love means jealousy', as well as the idea of jealousy as a masculine right. By connecting masculine behaviour with the apparently feminizing notion of a passion that debilitated body and mind, both *The Magnificent Cuckold* and *Jealousy* were exploring male anxiety about social change.

The extreme physical suffering of jealousy also contained a class commentary. Mario Camerini's 1937 film *Il signor Max* had poked fun at the 'bourgeois' jealousy of 'Max', suggesting that the wealthy cosmopolitans which whom he shared a cruise ship were beyond such base emotions as they belonged to a world where divorce and remarriage were common.[46] However, in post-war cinema the opposite could often be true. The jealous and violent lover of Pietro Germi's *Gelosia* was an aristocrat, while Pietrangeli's Andrea in *The Magnificent Cuckold* was a wealthy, urbane man who lived in a mansion with his wife and had a glamorous social life.[47] As one character remarked to Andrea's wife, Maria Grazia, 'I consider jealousy a luxury, suited to those who have both wealth and good health'. From being an emotion that was to be cast aside by those wealthy and cosmopolitan enough to do so, jealousy could be

---

[42] Belenky, *Anxiety of Dispossession*, pp. 90–1.

[43] Louis Bayman, *The Operatic and the Everyday: Post-war Italian Film Melodrama* (Edinburgh, 2014), p. 32.

[44] Bayman, *Operatic and the Everyday*, p. 34.

[45] Belenky, *Anxiety of Dispossession*, p. 47.   [46] Landy, *Folklore of Consensus*, cit., p. 91.

[47] Pietro Germi, *Jealousy* (1953); Antonio Pietrangeli, *The Magnificent Cuckold* (1964).

construed as a sort of luxury itself in 1964, the obsessive behaviour fed by idleness. Turning to fiction, we see similar themes there too. Dino Buzzati's 1963 novel 'A Love Affair' charted the obsession of a wealthy businessman with a charismatic dancer, his love and jealousy for her fed by his idleness and the empty decadence of his life.[48] Both film and fiction seemed also to be commenting on the decadence of the upper classes, whether in nineteenth-century Sicily or in the Italy of the boom.

The experience of jealousy as an illness of mind and body was not, however, merely a cinematic trope. Advice columns in popular magazines, as we saw earlier, also regularly alluded to jealousy as illness.[49] There are some personal accounts of jealousy as illness in Italian memoirs. One particularly striking example is that of historian Luisa Passerini, who has written about her experiences of love and sexuality in late 1960s Italy. Since she and her partner had strong political ideas about sexual liberation, she did not allow herself to openly feel jealousy when he experimented with other women. The feeling was instead experienced in the body, as a physical fever.[50] The second case wove jealousy into an account of mental illness, recounting the life story of 'Amatucci', a young male academic (born Rome, 1942) who met his wife in 1967 and separated in 1970.[51] Following the breakdown of his marriage, he was committed and subjected to electric shock therapy. He was convinced that his strong jealousy had destroyed both his mental health and his marriage. The memoir, written in the third person and in a somewhat opaque style, linked jealousy with psychosis and wrote of it as a kind of all-consuming force that controlled the author.[52] His wife was 'pursued by a tyrannical jealousy' and suffered the 'nightmare of a madness which was not his'. He 'suffered, in an indescribable way' and in a 'delirium' he attacked his wife, spitting in her face and hitting her.[53] While his is primarily an account of mental breakdown, it is curious just how strongly jealousy features in this drama. It is explicitly named as the cause of the author's afflictions and almost appears as a protagonist in the account, more responsible for the author's actions than was he himself.

JEALOUS MEN AND WORKING WOMEN

Jealousy might manifest itself not just on the body, whether as illness or psychosis, but if insufficiently controlled extend outwards in an episode of

---

[48] Dino Buzzati, *Un amore (A Love Affair)* (Milan, 1963).
[49] Gabriella Parca (ed.), *Le italiane si confessano* (Florence, 1959), pp. 215–16.
[50] Luisa Passerini, *Autoritratto di gruppo* (Florence, 1988), pp. 67–8.
[51] Stefano Indrio, *Amatucci* (Ragusa, 2007). A copy is also conserved at the ADN.
[52] Indrio, *Amatucci*, pp. 81–6.   [53] Indrio, *Amatucci*, p. 85.

violence. The online archive of Turin-based broadsheet *La Stampa* indicates that instances of jealousy in the daily news rose sharply in the period in question, with mentions of jealousy in the newspaper more than doubling between 1950 and 1960 in comparison to the previous decade, and remaining steady throughout the years in question.[54] These articles included reviews of plays, novels, and films as well as celebrity gossip—again supporting the idea of a national obsession with jealousy during the economic miracle years— while the bulk of them related to crime. In assessing what this means, we should first remember that the reporting of 'cronaca nera' or crime news was not officially permitted during the fascist period, while there were also restrictions on paper during and immediately after the war.[55] The increase in reporting of domestic and intimate partner violence and in crimes of passion in the 1950s could be attributed at least in part to the loosening of these restrictions.[56] There is no definite evidence to support an increase in violence related to jealousy. What the newspaper material does suggest is a heightened perception of such crimes, and an increased willingness to fit intimate partner violence into the explanatory framework of jealousy.

Jade Shepherd, in her discussion of jealousy and crime in Victorian England, noted some interesting disparities between the ways in which intimate partner violence was framed in newspapers and in court; the media tended to emphasize jealousy as a motive while it was rejected in the legal context.[57] Newspapers have their own distinct vocabularies and are in dialogue as much with popular culture as with the courtroom itself, and jealousy likely offered precisely the kind of emotional and dramatic framework that gripped readers of the crime news. These sources do however show how such crimes were understood and discussed in mid-twentieth-century Italy, demonstrating the popular resonance of the idea of violent jealousy. Turning to a detailed examination of two of these cases, we will see that although jealousy was named as a motive, the crime was not actually caused by romantic rivalry but by deeper anxieties about the changing roles of men and women.

The stabbing of Rosaria Dissipatore by her husband Giovanni La Perla in June 1959 is a particularly telling example. Both Sicilian in origin, Dissipatore had moved to Florence in search of steady employment since her husband had proved an unreliable provider. After establishing herself in Florence for some months, and finding a position in an ice-cream parlour, her husband joined

---

[54] There were 4,838 mentions between 1950 and 1950, in comparison to 1,942 mentions between 1940 and 1950. Historical archive of La Stampa, available at <http://www.lastampa.it/archivio-storico/>. Search for term 'gelosia' between 1940 and 1970.

[55] Mauro Forno, *La stampa del ventennio: Strutture e trasformazioni nello stato totalitario*, (Soveria Mannelli, 2005), pp. 125–6.

[56] On the press in the immediate aftermath of war, see Paolo Murialdi, *La Stampa italiana del dopoguerra 1943–1972* (Rome, 1973).

[57] Shepherd, 'Male Jealousy, Murder and Broadmoor in Late-Victorian Britain'.

her in the hope of persuading her to return to Sicily. When La Perla's attempts proved unsuccessful, he stabbed his wife in her sleep. Reported extensively in *La Nazione*, the crime was described as being motivated by jealousy rather than honour.[58] When La Perla was arrested and interrogated, jealousy was established as a motive. According to *La Nazione*, 'we are able to confirm not just that jealousy, in generic terms, armed the hand of the young Sicilian, but that the drama exploded precisely in relation to several facts which he learned in the last few days'.[59] Establishing the immediacy of the motive was crucial to La Perla's defence, since in order to make the case that he deserved leniency under the 'honour' clause (Article 544), he had to demonstrate that he was acting purely in the moment.[60] Curiously though, the facts that the newspaper reported were related to Dissipatore's working life, rather to any romantic rivalry. Jealousy was again used as a shorthand for the controlling behaviour associated with the honour system rooted in their native Sicilian culture, but also the tensions that migration placed on traditional gender roles. What is notable here is not just that Dissipatore had taken and kept a job against her husband's wishes, but that he was apparently unable to provide for her, whether because of the economic climate or his own ineptitude. In this case, jealousy seemed much more closely bound to male status anxiety and loss of control than to romantic love. The law would also have supported La Perla in his grievance against his wife, as until the 1975 family law reform it was the husband's sole prerogative to establish the couple's place of residence. Since La Perla was not quoted directly, it is not clear whether it was he—a working-class Sicilian migrant—or the journalist who named jealousy as the motive. In any case, the link between jealousy and violent, controlling behaviour was evidently a familiar and accepted one.

As a Sicilian, the Italian media might of course expect that La Perla would be led by his passions. It was this perceived link between volatile southern masculinity and the strains of migration that lay at the heart of Luchino Visconti's *Rocco and his Brothers* (1960) with its shocking portrayal of the rape and murder of his prostitute lover Nadia by Rocco's brother Simone. Visconti's portrayal of Simone's tragic failure to adapt to life in the modern

---

[58] In Maria Rosa Cutrufelli, Elena Doni, Paola Gaglianone et al., *Il novecento delle italiane: una storia ancora da raccontare* (Rome, 2002), p. 221, the stabbing is listed as an honour crime. However, there is no mention of honour in *La Nazione*'s coverage of either the crime itself or the trial in April 1960.

[59] 'Fu la gelosia ad armare la mano dell'uomo che accoltellò la giovane moglie', *La Nazione*, 24 June 1959.

[60] Ernesto de Cristofaro, 'Retorica forense e valori della comunità: Questioni d'onore in alcuni processi siciliani', in Francesco Migliorini e Giacomo Pace (ed.), *Gravina, Cultura e tecnica forense tra dimensione siciliana e vocazione europea* (Bologna, 2013), pp. 371–410; p. 388. See also Eva Cantarella, 'Homocides of Honour: The Development of Italian Adultery Law Over Two Milennia', in David Kertzer and Richard Saller (eds), *The Family in Italy from Antiquity to the Present* (New Haven, CT, 1991), pp. 229–44.

city played into the classic image of the southern peasant as violent and passionate; not to mention ill suited to modern life and work. However, in Anna Badino's work on the lives of migrants, we see again that the behaviour described as jealousy was clearly an attempt to maintain control over women rather than the release of strong emotion. One husband described as jealous disrupted his wife's working life through forced, repeated pregnancy. He himself was a violent alcoholic who found it difficult to hold down a job and to control the family finances.[61] The abusive behaviour continued through a series of migrations, first to Germany and then to Turin; it reads like an attempt to maintain control as migration and women's work threatened the patriarchal family structure. In a nation which was constantly on the move in the 1950s and 1960s, from rural to urban contexts as from south to north, neither were such attitudes and behaviour confined to southern men.

Around the same time that La Perla appeared in court, a remarkably similar case was heard in the Court of Assizes in Florence, which unfortunately had a more tragic ending. Bruno Agnorelli was tried for the murder of his wife Iris Gani by strangling, in September 1959. Theirs again was a typical story of the tensions of migration, changing gender roles and economic instability at the cusp of the miracle. Since their origins were not mentioned, both parties in this case were presumably Tuscan. Agnorelli had found it difficult to secure stable employment, changing jobs frequently and emigrating to France for some time to work as a hotel porter. His wife Iris Gani meanwhile had more success as a dressmaker and had managed to carve out some measure of economic independence, travelling throughout Italy for work. Gani's strangling was once again described categorically as 'a tragedy of jealousy' although the tensions between the couple, as with Dissipatore and La Perla, were connected to work and economic independence rather than romantic or sexual rivalry.[62] Agnorelli turned himself in to the police immediately after committing the crime, and readily answered police questions, 'leaving out no details but nevertheless concerned to emphasize how his hand—in committing the crime—had been guided by jealousy, by motives of honour'.[63] Honour and jealousy were firmly linked here, at least by *La Nazione*'s reporter, although the case was not explicitly linked to the south.

The memoir of Piedmontese woman Giuseppina echoes some of the tensions found in the court cases, although her story happily ended with a separation rather than a crime.[64] Both she and her husband came from humble backgrounds and seemed somewhat on the margins of provincial

---

[61] Anna Badino, *Tutte a casa? Donne tra migrazione e lavoro nella Torino degli anni Sessanta* (Turin, 2008), pp. 15–20.

[62] 'L'uomo che strangolò la moglie per gelosia comparirà in aprile davanti alla corte d'assise', *La Nazione*, 19 February 1960, p. 4.

[63] 'L'uomo che strangolò la moglie', *La Nazione*, 19 February 1960, p. 4.

[64] MP/Adn2, ADN.

northern society. She was an orphan raised in a religious institution while her husband was from a large, barely managing family. They met while he was fighting as a partisan during the war and married in 1946. The couple found it difficult to manage in the scarce economic climate of the immediate post-war years. After her husband lost his job as a cook, Giuseppina went to work and over time she would become the more reliable contributor to the family finances. By 1957 she was working in a hospital and it was she who secured her husband's new position there as a cook, encouraging him to apply despite his doubts. Very soon, however, her husband began to resent her working; his behaviour was described very precisely in the familiar vein of an obsessive jealousy. Indeed, it had traces of jealousy as malady, as psychosis. He saw 'ghosts' everywhere and exploded with anger as a colleague greeted her in the street. Working the night shift bothered him particularly and when she returned home exhausted after her shift, violent rows often awaited her. Giuseppina separated from her husband in 1966, later returning to work as a qualified nurse. Although he imagined scenes of promiscuity among those who worked the night shift, his jealousy was evidently motivated by the threat his wife posed to his status not as exclusive romantic or sexual partner but as the family breadwinner. In a rapidly changing socio-economic climate, where migration offered new opportunities as it redefined the structure and bonds of family, jealousy was the emotional and physical manifestation of male anxiety. Although in these contexts it had little to do with love, it could also map on to popular notions of romantic and companionate love as these became more closely linked to marriage in the post-war years.

'I KEPT HER CAREFULLY AS A FLOWER IN A VASE': JEALOUSY AND CONTROL

What is described as jealousy in Anna Badino's interviews with women migrants to Turin was much more than simple opposition to the women working or indeed fear of adultery. The women typically spoke of a much more generalized control over their lives. One woman was not allowed to have any friends after migrating to Turin, while a Calabrian woman who emigrated to Turin with her husband in the early 1960s was not allowed to have any contact with money at all. Not only was she prevented from working but she was not allowed to leave the house: 'I do not even know how to do the shopping because my husband was jealous'.[65] 'Jealousy' as a reason for not being allowed to do things such as going shopping, leaving the house, or

---

[65] Quoted in Anna Badino, *Tutte a casa*, p. 146.

having contact with money was named twice in the brief interview excerpt. This kind of masculine control over a woman's life, perhaps connected to the notion that such behaviour as leaving the house or handling money might be shameful, do indeed strongly echo the honour code of southern Italian society. The 'jealousy' was not prompted by anything that these women did; indeed it precluded it and prevented them from giving any cause for jealousy, understood as romantic or sexual rivalry. Restrictions on the lives of southern women migrants leaving the home were not particularly unusual—although having no contact with the family finances certainly was—and migration itself may have intensified some of these behavioural patterns.[66]

If we examine anthropological sources, interviews, and first-person testimonies relating to Calabria and Sicily, we see jealousy being used as a way of describing and justifying not just the control of wives, but also the surveillance and control exercised by parents on unmarried daughters.[67] In 1920s Milocca, in rural Sicily, when an unmarried girl became pregnant, destroying her chance at an arranged marriage with another man, her distraught mother was reported as saying: 'I kept her carefully as a flower in a vase. I never let her go out at all, I was that jealous.'[68] Sociologist Renate Siebert reported similar language being used to describe parental surveillance in fascist-era Calabria. Luisa, born in the 1930s in Calabria and interviewed by Siebert in the late 1980s also described her father as being very jealous of her, forbidding her from going out with friends and making disparaging comments about her working.[69] Twenty-first century parents do not usually describe themselves as jealous of their children in this way, but these multiple meanings and associations with love and control were evidently bound up with *gelosia* at least up to the first half of the twentieth century. In these cases the feeling mapped more closely on to the family's need to protect its own interests, by preserving the honour of unmarried daughters. As the role of family lessened in the lives of migrant couples, the pressure to maintain the gendered customs of their region fell to the couple themselves and was perhaps internalized further as romantic jealousy. The anthology *Italian Women Confess* contained a number of letters from women whose lives were restricted by their husbands' jealousy. The close relationship between masculine control, love, and jealousy is neatly expressed in one of these letters; a 24-year-old Sicilian woman married for six

---

[66] See Goffredo Fofi, *L'Immigrazione meridionale a Torino* (Milan, 1964) pp. 225–30; Linda Reeder, *Widows in White: Migration and the Transformation of Rural Italian Women, 1880–1920* (Toronto, 2003), esp. pp. 142–69.

[67] See Parca (ed.), *Le italiane si confessano*. The same kind of phrasing appears in the advice columns of *Grand Hotel* and in women interviewed for *Comizi d'amore* (Pier Paolo Pasolini, 1965).

[68] Quoted in Charlotte Gower Chapman, *Milocca: A Sicilian Village* (London, 1973), p. 95.

[69] Renate Siebert, *È femmina però è bella: Tre generazioni di donne al sud* (Turin, 1991), pp. 182–90.

years wrote the following: 'After a fairly tempestuous love, I married a man I loved, but from the first moment of life together with him he revealed himself to have a rather difficult character, forbidding me to look outside, to speak with anyone, to go outside, even with him. [. . .] I, believing it was jealousy, indulged him, thinking myself to be loved.'[70] Here we see the strong urge to accept such behaviour as a part of romantic love, followed by a gradual questioning of this logic.

Of the two memoirs that most closely describe this kind of controlling behaviour—named as jealousy—on the part of their fiancé or husband, neither was from the regions most closely associated with the honour code; one couple was Tuscan while the other was from the Friuli region in the north-east of Italy. Both women were well educated and wrote articulate and thoughtful accounts of their experiences as 'victims' of jealousy. We first met Alda Maria Dei (Florence, 1928) in Chapter 2, and her long engagement to Silvano (they met in 1947 and married in 1954) was in many ways typical of her respectable, urban artisan background.[71] However, the first year or so of their time together was also marred by Silvano's excessive jealousy of Alda. He forbade her to work outside the home, telling her instead that he preferred her to learn how to be a good housewife from their mothers. However, he really wanted her to have no reason to leave the home. Both Alda's parents and Silvano's mother Elisa were opposed to his behaviour, which he had apparently learned from his father, and with Elisa's help Alda was eventually able to regain her right to leave the home. Elisa's advice was to use subterfuge in order to gain permission for short trips to the local shops for basic goods so that he became accustomed to the idea of her leaving the house, and to gradually extend the trips and reduce the 'permission'. Elisa's plan was devised through experience, as she has spent years closed up in the house because of her husband's jealousy and was determined not to let Alda suffer the same fate. Although this plan eventually met with success, his jealousy still came out in other ways. Alda described how Silvano became jealous of other men looking at her when they were out together: 'if some boy looked at me—I was hardly Miss Italia, but not bad looking either—he would ask me if I knew him. I would tell him no, after all I knew practically nobody, but he would always make an argument of it.'[72] This behaviour made Alda fearful of receiving any male attention when in public with Silvano. Her nerves only compounded her troubles as he would then question why she blushed. This created for about a year or so, 'a life of hell' for her.[73] In her words, 'it felt like I was an object owned by somebody, an object that was precious and loved, but always an object rather than a person'. She continued that: 'I began to doubt the strength of his love for me,

[70] Parca (ed.), *Le italiane si confessano*, pp. 331–2.
[71] Alda Maria Dei, 'Graffitti', MP/03, ADN.   [72] Alda Maria Dei, 'Graffitti'.
[73] Alda Maria Dei, 'Graffitti'.

absolutely refusing to accept the axiom love = jealousy.'[74] Alda, describing her experiences in the late 1940s and early 1950s, was quite familiar with the popular notion of jealous love, although she chose to reject it completely. It clearly did not fit with her own ideas of love, nor those of her family. Alda's solution was to flee to Rome for a few days in order to test Silvano's love for her. In the end her adventure only lasted an afternoon and she didn't leave Florence, but she considered Silvano's distress a measure of her success, as he had proved that he 'loved her and did not just consider her a piece of property'.[75] Alda's memoir does not contain much further mention of Silvano's jealousy in the more lengthy and detailed account of their happy, loving marriage, although one wonders whether the problem could have been solved so neatly.

A Friulian woman writing under the pseudonym of Aerre, born in 1942 and coming of age in the early 1960s in the provincial north of Italy, described a similar experience of jealousy with her first boyfriend Angelo, whom she left after two years at the age of 18.[76] Several years older than she, Angelo was an orphan who worked as a pizza chef and initially she fought to have her family accept him. However, despite his charms, problems began to surface in their relationship. In her words, 'the problem with our "affectionate friendship" was his jealousy, which oppressed me, which made me feel like I was no longer free'.[77] She was only allowed to leave the house with Angelo or a family member, and the only place they went together was to the cinema. She was forbidden from talking to her friends and felt that she had 'become his property'.[78] While Alda firmly rejected jealousy as being in any way positive or loving, Aerre's memoir shows how it might be possible to accept such behaviour and to rationalize it as a part of romantic love. She wrote about how she initially rebelled against these strictures, then accepted them in order to be with Angelo. 'I lived blessed and happy talking of marriage but one morning...I woke up and thought about my life: I was little more than seventeen and I was thinking of marriage (?): if he was jealous now, what would it be like afterwards?'[79]

It was at this point after two years together, that she decided to leave Angelo. The language of mania and madness seeps into her words: she wondered if she was crazy to have considered such a claustrophobic life, or whether he was 'mad' to have demanded it of her. Aerre writes that she had no regrets, immediately going out dancing with friends and talking about regaining her freedom. Angelo reacted by threatening suicide in an 'insane gesture'; dressed in black, he was planning to visit his parents' tomb and to end his life there.[80] Horrified by this 'melodramatic side of his character', Aerre's resolve

---

[74] Alda Maria Dei, 'Graffitti'.   [75] Alda Maria Dei, 'Graffitti'.
[76] Aerre, 'Esisto anch'io', MP05, ADN.   [77] Aerre, 'Esisto anch'io'.
[78] Aerre, 'Esisto anch'io'.   [79] Aerre, 'Esisto anch'io'.   [80] Aerre, 'Esisto anch'io'.

to end the relationship was strengthened by his reaction.[81] Angelo's actions show that he certainly was taken in by the notion that love, passion, jealousy, and madness were all closely associated. Indeed Aerre's account, with its repeated references to madness and to melodrama, seems to echo the popular discourse about jealousy in these years; her memoir raises the question of whether such public discussions and representations reflected or actually shaped real experiences.

Both Alda and Aerre firmly rejected what they described as jealousy in their relationships, even though each of them also accepted it for some time. However, while Aerre's account emphasized freedom and found that the experience of jealousy destroyed any feelings she had for her fiancé, Alda Maria on the other hand found that Silvano's jealousy made her doubt his love for her. While Aerre wanted freedom, Alda Maria wanted reassurance that what Silvano felt for her was really love. While both of these women considered themselves in a position—through family support, upbringing, education, or personality—to reject jealousy, others were not so fortunate. Lavinia, born near Rome in the early 1930s, described her sadness and desperation on marrying her jealous fiancé in 1957, after four stormy years together.[82] Following their marriage, his jealousy resulted in violent reactions when she wore make up or pretty dresses. Her memoir wrote of continual displays of jealousy and psychological battles, and like Alda she experienced all of this behaviour as the desire for possession rather than an expression of love. After over a decade together, she finally decided to separate.

Although all rejected the idea of jealousy as a positive quality, or one with any connection with love, they still accepted jealousy as the appropriate label for their partners' behaviour. We can see from the attitudes and behaviour described, which ranged from preventing the woman from working or leaving the home to controlling her appearance, that the jealousy had little to do with specific romantic (or sexual) threats or rivalries; if anything the men seemed to be jealous of the women's attempts to realize their roles as active citizens, in the world of leisure and work, in a society where gender roles were in flux. While women themselves might have accepted the connection between jealousy and love in the abstract—as in the teenage diaries of Maria Maselli and Graziella Pezzino—the reality of life with a jealous partner seemed to have little connection to romance.

So far all of the accounts of jealous male partners have described the relationship from the woman's point of view. The memoir of Francesco describes remarkably similar behaviour, but from a male point of view, giving us an intriguing insight into the inner workings of jealousy. Francesco grew up in a town near Naples and earned his university degree before his marriage in 1968.

---

[81] Aerre, 'Esisto anch'io'.   [82] MP/10, ADN.

The personal narrative constructed in his memoir was one in which jealousy was very much intertwined with love, playing a defining role in his courtship with his future wife. He first laid eyes on her when he was 18 and she several years younger, and their furtive, meaningful glances developed into love. His feelings for her were described in strong, emotive language: she was the love of his life and he thought of nobody but her.[83] The connection between love and jealousy was a natural, implicit one for him; of course he had such feelings. The intensity of his jealous love also tested the boundaries of sanity, at least in his telling; jealousy and love drove him crazy. Their relationship was tempestuous, mostly as a result of his strong jealousy for her, which she found oppressive. They also kept their love secret for several years and this made it more difficult for him to trust her since she was able to socialize more freely than she would have done as Francesco's official fiancée.[84] All of this caused Francesco great pain and at one point he suspected her of infidelity. When he confronted her, she was full of remorse. Implicit for both partners was the notion that even if the woman was not intending to commit infidelity, it was up to her not to attract suspicion with her behaviour. The burden of proof rested on her to show her fidelity through her dress and manner rather than on the man to prove her adultery.

The lovers' exchange, even if half imagined and only half remembered, reflected the broader pattern of how jealousy was thought about for men and women. Letters to agony aunts asking for advice about jealousy were frequent; while men sometimes wrote, the letters more frequently came from women with jealous partners. Any reader who wrote asking for advice in this situation was generally advised not to tolerate it and preferably to end the relationship before the couple married. For example 'Rosabianca', writing to *Grand Hotel* from Turin in 1955, was told that it was not normal for her boyfriend to prevent her from going out and seeing friends because of his jealousy.[85] She was advised to speak to her parents and reconsider whether she wanted to marry him. However, the reply to her letter contained an important caveat; her boyfriend had no reason to be so jealous of her, especially considering that she was such a well-behaved, 'serious' girl. Jealousy in a man was definitely something to be avoided and controlled, although equally a woman should not give a man cause for jealousy.

OVERCOMING JEALOUSY: CLASS, GENDER, GENERATION, AND 'MODERNITY'

While the pressure for women to accept male jealousy as part of a loving relationship was strong, it is also clear that such behaviour—and the idea that

[83] MP/06, ADN.   [84] MP/06, ADN.
[85] Letter from 'Rosabianca', *Grand Hotel*, 15 January 1955.

it had anything to do with love—could be decisively rejected both by women themselves as by agony aunts and writers of popular fiction. While the onus was often on women to decide whether to endure or to reject the 'oppression' of their partners' jealousy, the project of overcoming jealousy might also begin with the jealous self. In 1950, a man writing under the pseudonym 'Excelsior Roma' sought advice on how to conquer the strong jealousy he felt for his girlfriend.[86] Although he was not given much useful advice on how to go about it, he was told in no uncertain terms that it was something he must do. Although 'Excelsior Roma' gave the impression of a strong compulsion over which he had little control—reflecting the familiar representations of jealousy as madness and malady—he also had an awareness that his jealousy was something which he *should* control and indeed sought help in doing so. In the same years as jealousy was apparently on the rise in Italy, there was a renewed need to combat and control it. This section will examine the different campaigns to overcome jealousy, and consider the apparent contradiction that jealousy was often unacceptable although ubiquitous in late twentieth-century Italy.

Although apparently unfashionable, at least in public, in the 1930s, we have seen how jealousy was firmly back in focus by the 1950s. Following the socio-economic transformations brought about by the boom, the need to bring about a legal redefinition of the family in line with new social realities was a major theme of public debate in the 1960s. An important aspect was the eventual abolition of the crime of adultery, which had penalized women much more heavily than men.[87] Ruled to be unconstitutional in 1968, it was several more years before Law 559—which provided for a prison sentence of up to a year for the adulterous wife—was finally repealed, after extensive parliamentary debate.[88] Female adultery was meanwhile becoming a more accepted topic in popular culture and the media; while it was unthinkable in *Grand Hotel*'s fiction in the 1950s, women's magazine *Arianna* carried an extensive insert on the topic in 1972.[89] While they were careful to stress that they did not condone adultery, the feature explored the many and complex reasons a married woman—and older women in particular—might have an affair, acknowledging her need for sexual fulfilment. Meanwhile film and fiction—from Buzzati's *A Love Affair* to *La Dolce Vita*—were exploring and

---

[86] Letter from 'Excelsior Roma', *Grand Hotel*, 30 December 1950.

[87] Female adultery was criminalized while male adultery was only a criminal act if the affair was carried out in the family home, see Perry Willson, *Women in Twentieth Century Italy* (London, 2010), p. 124. The parliamentary debates are available online in the library of the *Camera dei Deputati*. See for example discussions of 8 July 1971, 13 October 1971, 11 November 1971, and 1 December 1971.

[88] Unione Donne in Italia, Archivio Centrale. Tema: Divorzio famiglia: busta 6, fascicolo 87, 'Dichiarazione sulle sentenze della corte costituzionale in maniera di adulterio'.

[89] L'Adulterio. Insert in *Arianna*, 184: April 1972, pp. 97–110. Unione Donne In Italia, Archivio Centrale, busta 9, fascicolo 129.

highlighting the new possibilities for casual amorous encounters in an Italy that was increasingly prosperous and freer in its mores. The debates about divorce from the mid-1960s to the 1974 referendum also carried the familiar refrain that divorce would lead to a rise in female adultery, rendering Italian men 'cuckolds'. Expressed by some of the interviewees in Pasolini's *Love Meetings*, these fears were exploited—albeit not always successfully—by Christian Democrat politicians in their campaign against the referendum.[90] The early 1970s also saw continued debate in parliament and in the media on a whole series of long-awaited family law reforms which would establish the equality of both marriage partners and the abolition of the husband as legal 'head of household'.[91] After years of debate and over a decade of campaigning by feminist organization Unione Donne Italiane (UDI), these reforms were finally codified in the 1975 rewriting of the civil code. Most remaining inequalities between marriage partners—such as a wife needing her husband's permission to apply for a passport—were abolished at this point.[92] Changing attitudes towards adultery in particular can be connected to how jealousy was represented in society and popular culture; on the one hand jealousy was considered increasingly less acceptable in a society where women were being regarded as equal marriage partners. On the other, it could also represent a reaction against these new ideas and attitudes, and indeed a way of expressing such concerns in an oblique, indirect fashion that in its connection to romantic love might not immediately seem reactionary.

We have already seen how there were no clear-cut boundaries as to who might experience jealousy in terms of class or geography; while often associated with the rural south, it might also be considered a sign of urbane frivolity and idleness. We can, however, see some clear connections to generational identity. *Tempo* magazine's 1959 interview with a group of Milanese teenagers saw almost of them reject jealousy as retrograde, old-fashioned behaviour that had no place in their lives.[93] In the interviewer's words, 'the first reaction to this word was a row of smiles of superiority'.[94] While the journalist questioned whether these teenagers could be in love if they were not jealous, his interviewees considered that relationships should be based on equality and camaraderie, rejecting older gender codes and ideas of gender relations. There was a sense in the article that jealousy was lessening in Italian society. One young

---

[90] *Love Meetings* (Pier Paolo Pasolini, 1964); Maureen Giovannini describes how the notion of the 'cuckold', considered to be particularly important to Sicilian society, was exploited in the Christian Democrat campaign, although as far as she could see unsuccessfully due to the politicians' outsider status. Maureen J. Giovannini, 'Female Chastity Codes in the circum-Mediterranean: Comparative Perspectives', in Gilmore (ed.), *Honor and Shame*, pp. 66–7.

[91] See press clippings, Unione Donne in Italia, Archivio Centrale. Tema: Divorzio Famiglia.

[92] Willson, *Women in Twentieth Century Italy*, p. 159.

[93] 'I giovani e l'amore' (discussion with psychologist Dino Origlia), *Tempo*, 23 June 1959.

[94] 'I giovani e l'amore', *Tempo*, 23 June 1959.

woman answered that she thought that people expressed jealousy less often because it was no longer 'in style' rather than because they didn't feel it. It would have been impossible for a man to express jealousy in her circle, because he would be dismissed as 'a bore, an anti-social, an individualist, a fanatic', and thus presumably unsuitable as a boyfriend or husband.[95] It was because of the strength of the association between love and jealousy in popular culture and in the media that these young Italians felt they had to reject the notion with such vehemence.

Luisa Puliti's memoir of her open marriage in the 1950s and 1960s suggests that, despite the PCI's conservative family policies, progressive politics might also provide a path to overcoming jealousy in the self. Both communist activists in Rome, Luisa and her husband Paolo were open with each other about their affairs, and according to her own account Luisa genuinely did not feel jealous of Paolo's lovers.[96] The counter-culture of 1968 saw a much more extreme 'revolt against feelings', with many activists completely rejecting the idea of romantic love.[97] Jealousy was not mentioned in interview excerpts with activists, although the efforts they made in rejecting any hint of love as possession, swapping sexual partners with studied casualness, suggest that it certainly lurked in the background. While we have seen how popular culture could certainly reinforce individual feeling, we also saw a conscious move to reject the familiar trope of jealous love by those interviewed in *Tempo*, at the cusp of the 1960s. The '68 generation of activists took this much further, their extreme efforts to overcome any feelings in relation to sex indicating that they revolted not just against political, social, and educational structures but also, and perhaps most fundamentally, that theirs was a revolution of feelings.[98]

In the long run, it seems that little ultimately changed. In 1974, the same year as the divorce referendum, women's magazine *Annabella* ran a feature on jealousy which assumed that the emotion was somewhat out of step with contemporary Italy, but potent all the same (see Figure 4.3).[99] *Annabella* reported a recent survey which seemed to confirm that 'jealousy is an unfashionable sentiment', since all those surveyed under the age of 25 declared themselves not to be jealous and found the emotion 'ridiculous'. However, it was despite and perhaps because of the myriad ways in which codes of gender and sexuality were changing in Italian society that jealousy was such a powerful force in Italian relationships and was even, according to *Annabella*,

[95] 'I giovani e l'amore', *Tempo*, 23 June 1959.
[96] Luisa Puliti, *È nato un bambino di sesso femminile* (Viterbo, 1994), p. 61.
[97] Rebecca Clifford, 'Emotions and Gender in Oral History: Narrating Italy's 1968', *Modern Italy*, 17:2 (2012), pp. 209–21, 218.
[98] See Rebecca Clifford, Robert Gildea, and Anette Warring, 'Gender and Sexuality', in Robert Gildea, James Mark, and Anette Warring (eds), *Europe's 1968: Voices of Revolt* (Oxford, 2013), pp. 239–57.
[99] Emilio de'Rossignoli, 'La gelosia', *Annabella*, January 1974, pp. 10–17.

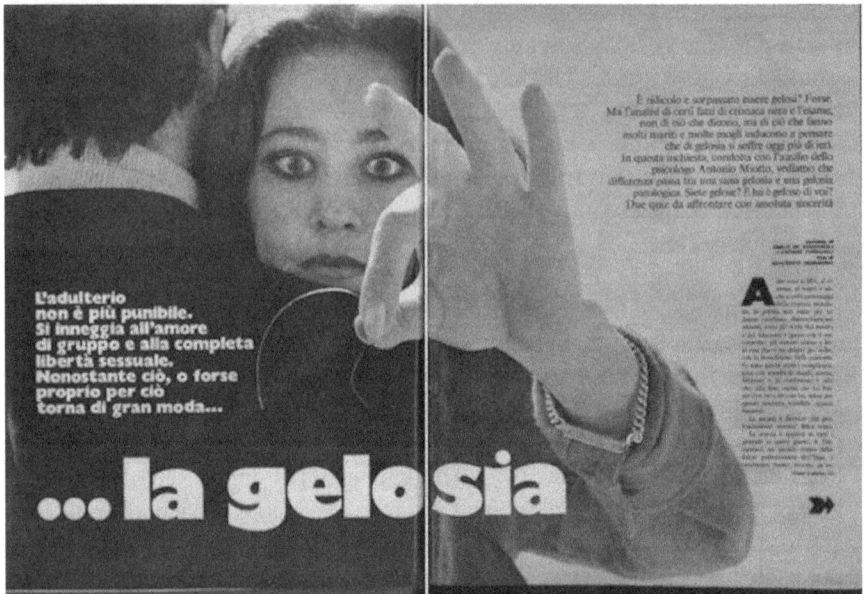

Figure 4.3. 'Jealousy', *Annabella* magazine, January 1974.
Biblioteca Nazionale Centrale di Roma.

on the rise again in the 1970s. Langhamer notes a similar phenomenon in 1960s Britain: more permissive attitudes towards sexuality resulted in a rise in infidelity. However, at the same time young Britons in 1969 put a greater emphasis on infidelity and jealousy as causes of marital failure than the previous generation.[100] Jealousy played a curious role in the emotional lives of 1960s youth; loudly rejected for its association with misogyny and the control of women, it could also be a way of naming responses to anxiety about changing codes of gender and sexuality, while benefitting from the increased emphasis on honesty and exclusivity in love.

By the late 1960s and early 1970s, jealousy was also becoming something of a feminist issue. The feminist magazine *Effe*, set up in 1973 and edited by Gabriella Parca, made these points much more explicit when it published an in-depth feature on jealousy in March 1974.[101] It collected five different women's testimonies on their experiences of jealousy in intimate relationships. Experiences ranged from the Sicilian woman whose father had spent many years in jail for murdering a man who had simply gazed at his wife, to the apparently more modern couple who had decided to have an open marriage.

---

[100] Langhamer, *The English in Love*, p. 199.
[101] Willson, *Women in Twentieth Century Italy*, p. 153; Lara Foletti (ed.), 'La gelosia. Sostantivo plurale maschile', *Effe*, March 1974, pp. 28–31.

However, when the wife began to have an affair, her husband found himself unable to control his violent jealousy. The editorial conclusion was that jealousy was bound up with misogyny since it was really always about possession. 'And since jealousy is born from possessiveness or the desire for possession, and thus from the fear of being deprived of an object, how could women be jealous? Jealousy is a masculine problem, not one that regards us.'[102] Jealousy was experienced differently by men and women; however, both the testimonies collected in the article itself as well as throughout this chapter indicate that jealousy was certainly experienced by both sexes. The jealousy described by the women in the *Effe* feature as in the advice columns was usually related to their lack of power in relation to their partner; jealousy was the only way for them to express the autonomy they sought in the relationship. These gendered patterns indicate yet again how the emotional language of jealousy could sometimes be the only socially acceptable way for men and women to assert their power or express their lack of control in a relationship. In its assertion that women could not be jealous, *Effe* was clearly arguing against its own evidence; more properly the journalist was asserting that any real feminist should not be jealous since she should not feel bound by the inherent misogyny of romantic love. In considering jealousy as both an emotion and a tool of misogyny, and in doing so failing to tease out the contradictions, the *Effe* feature also alerts us to just how slippery jealousy was for late twentieth-century Italians. Despite the best efforts of 1960s youth, political activists, revolutionaries, and feminists, was jealousy simply ungovernable?

CONCLUSION

It should by now be evident that Pasolini's assertion that there was no jealousy in the north of Italy contained little truth. Although there was a clear link between jealousy and the honour code, this chapter has shown that its roots were much broader than this. The survey of jealousy in post-war film and magazines—whether fiction, documentary, or magazine inquiry—indicates at least the perceived prevalence of the behaviour associated with jealousy in post-war Italy. It could clearly have multiple and shifting meanings, whether regional, generational, or gendered; it might be proudly claimed as a sign of love or an indication of southern heritage, or dismissed as a tool of misogyny. It was difficult to pin down and replete with contradictions. While it can be mapped on to a particular style of masculine behaviour associated with

---

[102] Lara Foletti (ed.), 'La Gelosia: Sostantivo plurale maschile', *Effe*, p. 31.

honour and control, it was—despite *Effe*'s assertions—not an emotion to which women were entirely immune. It was scorned by the young Milanese interviewed by *Tempo* magazine in 1959, and yet paradoxically on the rise according to *Annabella* magazine in 1974. Often associated with the south, jealousy could also be used as a way of ridiculing the wealthy and urbane bourgeoisie of the economic miracle, as in *The Magnificent Cuckold*, where the emotion was associated not with ignorance or 'backwardness' but with idleness. The notion of jealousy as a pathology also offers intriguing insights into the ways in which Italian society and culture were absorbing and responding to the enormous social and cultural changes brought by the post-war boom.

The memoirs and diaries give us some evidence of how jealousy was experienced in ordinary lives and by both men and women. Although women might associate jealousy with love in the abstract, the overwhelming experience of jealousy for women was control which sometimes escalated into physical and psychological abuse. The language in the first-person sources also mirrored the cultural representations of jealousy as illness and madness, posing some intriguing questions about how popular culture might offer a framework and a language for articulating emotions and behaviour. Crime reportage again fitted violence against women into the familiar vocabulary of crimes of love and passion, even when we can see that what was at stake was often women's work and a much longer-term need to control, rather than a spontaneous eruption of violent passion. Just as with the cases of kidnap marriage discussed in Chapter 3, a certain understanding of romance saw jealousy as an extreme manifestation of love rather than its opposite. Considering just how closely jealousy was intertwined with love in the popular imagination—from crime news to magazine love stories—it is perhaps no surprise that the project of overcoming jealousy in the self was such a difficult one.

Jealousy was evidently connected to much deeper anxieties about how family structure and gender roles were changing between the 1950s and the 1970s. The fears expressed around the 1974 referendum that divorce would render Italian men 'cuckolds' is a clear indication of how anxieties about social change were expressed in terms of a threat to masculinity and sexual power.[103] While such concerns may have bubbled under the surface as the economic miracle began to transform society in the 1950s, these debates and associated fears were articulated more publicly in the 1960s, as traditional gender codes and family structures were being rapidly dismantled in the eyes of both society and the law. Both attitudes towards and legal definitions of adultery, honour, family, marriage, and divorce were all changing in these years. The prevalence of the allegory of jealousy as illness points to the difficulty

---

[103] Giovannini, *Female Chastity Codes.*

of expressing such unease in an Italy which was self-consciously positioning itself as 'modern' and 'European' and by implication distancing itself from the behaviour associated both with the south and with the past. It was perhaps precisely this desire to distance Italy from what were seen as southern emotional styles, while failing to deal with the contradictions and tensions within Italian masculinity itself regarding the changing family and new gender roles, that resulted in the curious and contradictory jealousy epidemic of the post-war period.

5

'The Marriage Outlaws': Experiences of Marriage Breakdown Before Divorce

In 1954, one of the biggest scandals relating to post-war morality emerged from the nascent world of sporting celebrity. Fausto Coppi, champion cyclist and five times winner of the Giro d'Italia, was arrested for adultery with his secretary Giulia Occhini-Locatelli. His fall from grace was captured and dissected very publicly in a society which was only beginning to embrace celebrity and the mass media.[1] Although on the statute books as a crime, it was unusual for adultery charges to be brought in the 1950s. In this case, it was the very public nature of the affair which had prompted Occhini-Locatelli's husband to prosecute. In the conservative, Catholic climate of the provincial north, the couple had openly lived together and even shared a hotel room on occasion. At the time of the trial, Occhini was also pregnant with their child. Since adultery was not in itself a crime for men, Coppi was charged with 'conduct contrary to family order', while full adultery charges were pressed on his pregnant lover. Occhini was also demonized by the press, while Coppi was portrayed as a family man who had been led astray. The fallen national hero, the scandal nevertheless took its toll on him and he appeared cowed and shamed in court, his voice 'low, a little hoarse, contrite'.[2] He was cross-examined about why he left his wife, whether he would return to her, and why he had made such a public show of posting his wedding ring back to her. For Coppi, the crime was not the adultery, so much as his determination to break up his family in order to form a new one. His justification was that he had 'an obligation of loyalty towards Occhini', pregnant and repudiated by her husband.[3] Framing his decision in the language of duty rather than love, he

---

[1] John Foot, *Pedalare, Pedalare: A History of Italian Cycling* (London, 2012), pp. 97–124. On the post-war media, see Stephen Gundle and David Forgacs, *Mass Culture and Italian Society from Fascism to the Cold War* (Bloomington, IN, 2007), pp. 95–123.

[2] Mario Cervi, 'Fausto Coppi spiega in tribuna perche si allontanò dalla sua famiglia', *Corriere della Sera*, 13 March 1955.

[3] Quoted in Mario Cervi, 'Fausto Coppi spiega in tribuna perche si allontanò dalla sua famiglia'.

sought even in the midst of his public humiliation to dress his circumstances with what respectability he could.

Both Coppi and Occhini were given short prison sentences but each also suffered more severe consequences. Occhini was prevented from seeing her daughter from her first marriage again while Coppi's career was dealt a heavy blow by the scandal and he died in 1960. The story reveals much about Italian attitudes towards marriage, family, adultery, and separation in the 1950s. While adultery was unforgivable for a woman, Coppi only suffered such public consequences for leaving his wife and entering into a new union with Occhini. What is perhaps most curious though is how Coppi explained his actions, invoking duty rather than love to justify what must in fact have been a passionate love affair. He had married in 1945, at a time when marriage was associated more with family and shared household than with romantic love. This is not say that that love was not part of marriage or that people did not marry for love, but that it was understood differently in a world where marriage was supposed to be for life. The rigidly conservative Catholic climate of the early 1950s was soon to give way to the prosperity and rapid social change of the boom, creating a new world where Coppi's solemn ideas about duty would give way to new ones about emotion, choice, and freedom. For those marrying in the mid-1950s, from the cusp of the economic miracle onwards, new ideas about love would ultimately shape not just how relationships began but how and in what circumstances a marriage might end. Coppi and Locatelli had the misfortune to conduct their affair in a society where social attitudes seemed static, although they were on the brink of change.

MARRIAGE, SEPARATION, AND DIVORCE IN POST-WAR ITALY

Italian culture in the mid to late twentieth century placed an enormous importance on the institution of marriage, both as the bedrock of family life and social stability, and as the ultimate prize sought in romantic stories. We have seen how the pressure on women to achieve fulfilment through wedded bliss was especially intense, with such messages transmitted by family, popular culture, and the Catholic religion. It was only gradually from the mid-1960s that other messages began to filter into the mainstream. Of course, no amount of pressure on Italians to marry was able to guarantee the happy ending promised by the stories of *Grand Hotel*, and although those whose marriages did not last were at the margins of official culture, they were numerous. Although divorce was not made legal until 1970, and later confirmed by the 1974 referendum, an awareness of the scale and consequences of marriage breakdown was growing in the preceding decades. The possibility of a divorce law had been debated in Italy since the nineteenth century although set aside during the fascist period, and it was first raised again by Socialist Deputy Luigi Sansone in 1954, the same year of the Coppi–Occhini arrest for adultery.[4] At that point Sansone estimated that about four million Italians were 'marriage outlaws', unable to make their new relationships and families official under the law even though their marriages were effectively over.[5] When Radical deputy Loris Fortuna presented a second divorce bill to parliament in 1965, he estimated the 'outlaws' at five million, amounting to 10 per cent of the population.[6]

It is not surprising therefore that experiences of separation, cohabitation, and divorce feature in the first-person texts of our diarists and memoirs. Out of those surveyed in this book, a total of twenty-six wrote about the experience of divorce or separation, while a further two experienced cohabitation with a married man. This chapter will examine their experiences in light of the growing public conversation about marriage breakdown and the divorce campaigns of the 1950s and 1960s. It will not attempt a detailed history of the political and legislative path to legal divorce; that story has already been told by historians.[7] Rather, it will attempt, through an examination of these intimate histories of separation, divorce, and cohabitation, to examine how attitudes towards marriage were being reshaped in the post-war decades. The 1970 divorce law evidently had a real impact on those lives affected by marriage breakdown. However, the campaigns for divorce also shaped how all Italian couples thought about their relationships, shaping notions about authenticity and durability in love relationships and in marriage. The divorce campaigns themselves, ongoing for over two decades before the 1974 referendum, reflected the social moments from which they emerged. In 1954 Luigi Sansone's 'little divorce' campaign aimed to offer salvation only to those in the most extreme and desperate circumstances.[8] The reasons he suggested included one spouse serving a long prison sentence or being committed to an asylum, abandonment through emigration, or following attempted spousal murder. The emphasis was on freeing people from the legal chains of marriages which existed only on paper.

The idea of divorce by mutual consent could not yet be raised in public and was indeed uncommon anywhere in the post-war West, before the divorce law

---

[4] For a long-range history of the Italian road to divorce, see Mark Seymour, *Debating Divorce in Italy: Marriage and the Making of Modern Italians, 1860–1974* (London, 2006).

[5] Seymour, *Debating Divorce*, p. 168.

[6] Fiamma Lussana, *L'Italia del divorzio: La battaglia fra stato, Chiesa e gente comune, 1946–1974* (Rome, 2014), p. 83.

[7] Seymour, *Debating Divorce*; Fiamma Lussana, *l'Italia del divorzio*; Domenico Letizia, *Storia della Lega Italiana per il Divorzio* (Rome, 2014).

[8] Seymour, *Debating Divorce*, pp. 168–73.

reforms of the late 1960s.[9] By the time Loris Fortuna's bill was presented to parliament in late 1965, attitudes were beginning to shift and this new bill permitted divorce after a period of separation of at least five years. Fortuna's public campaign was launched in the radical magazine *ABC*, and prompted an avalanche of letters to the editor.[10] As an 'office worker' from Florence wrote, 'It is love which justifies marriage. Marriage is merely a public agreement for the protection of children, the other duties can only be valid if there is feeling.'[11] This was increasingly the way in which ordinary Italians were beginning to approach marriage in the 1960s. The linking of love and marriage, so persistently made in the 1950s by popular culture, paradoxically created the strongest argument for divorce.[12] Some of the loudest voices against the notion of marriage for life came from the 1960s youth generation, as shown by the scandalous 1966 article of the Milanese girls' secondary school Liceo Parini in *Zanzara* magazine.[13] Lieta Harrison's survey of 1960s Italian girls also revealed cynical positions about marriage, which was usually dismissed either as the 'tomb of love' or as an arrangement based on economic interest, rather than a love match.[14] Many had looked at their parents' marriages and found them lacking. It has been well documented too how the 1968 generation developed different ideas about love, monogamy, and durability.[15]

Although this chapter will include some brief marriages formed in the late 1960s, when attitudes about gender, emotion, and marriage were in turmoil, the generation who met and married during the years of the economic miracle are firmly at its core. Although the 1960s generation readily accepted the changing nature of commitment, the seeds of these ideas were sown in the experiences of those who met and married in the previous decade. More than ever this generation was sold the dream of a marriage based on romance and love through magazines, romantic fiction, and films, even though they might have married under different circumstances themselves. For those who did

---

[9] On British divorce law reform, see Claire Langhamer, 'Adultery in Post-war England', *History Workshop Journal*, 62:1 (2006), pp. 86–115, esp. pp. 93–7.

[10] Seymour, *Debating Divorce*, pp. 189–92; Fiamma Lussana, *L'Italia del divorzio*, pp. 79–80 and 169–216.

[11] Quoted in Fiamma Lussana, *L'Italia del divorzio*, p. 186.

[12] Claire Langhamer also observed a strong connection between the rise of romantic love and increased divorce rates in late 1960s and 1970s England. Claire Langhamer, *The English in Love: The Intimate Story of an Emotional Revolution* (Oxford, 2013). Anthony Giddens also made a similar argument about 'confluent love' in late twentieth-century Western society, in *The Transformation of Intimacy: Sexuality, Love and Eroticism in Modern Societies* (Cambridge, 1993), pp. 62–4.

[13] Fiamma Lussana, *L'Italia del divorzio*, pp. 86–9; Anna Tonelli, *Comizi d'Amore: Politica e sentimenti dal '68 ai Papa boys* (Rome, 2007), pp. 26–30.

[14] Lieta Harrison, *L'Iniziazione: Come le adolescenti diventano donne* (Milan, 1966), pp. 81–8.

[15] On romance and 1968, see Rebecca Clifford et al., 'Gender and Sexuality', in Robert Gildea (ed.), *Europe's 1968: Voices of Revolt* (Oxford, 2013), pp. 239–57.

marry for love, the companionate marriage by its nature could never measure up to the reality of the lives of men and women in the 1950s and 1960s. Based on equality and companionship, it was ill suited to a world where spheres of work and leisure were separated for men and women and becoming increasingly so with the move away from the shared economy of the rural household and towards that of the industrial wage earner and the housewife.

This disjuncture between ideal and reality was particularly acute for the women of the rising middle classes who in many cases would be the first women in their families not to work. They were also among those most likely to have embraced the notion of the companionate marriage. The dominant media perception in the run-up to the 1974 referendum was that women would vote against divorce, and indeed such gendered assumptions were exploited by the anti-divorce campaign with their assertions that the new law would lead to women being used and discarded 'like a plaything'.[16] An examination of personal stories of marriage breakdown reveal that in contrast to the popular, although misguided narrative, it was overwhelmingly women who took the initiative in separation or divorce proceedings.[17] Given the nature of our sources, it can also be said that women were perhaps more likely to write about such experiences and to structure their life stories around them. Those few men who did write in detail about separation or divorce described strong feelings of loss and failure. The women in contrast tended to see the separation as a kind of liberation, albeit an ambiguous one.

Most of the marriages we will examine did not actually end until several decades after divorce came in; some in the 1970s, many more in the 1980s, and one as late as 1991.[18] Even as the public pressure for a divorce law was growing, it was still very difficult to be a single mother in the 1960s and even the 1970s. The recognition of being unhappy in marriage, and making the decision to leave, were clearly quite separate things. Indeed despite the strength of the majority voting in favour of divorce in 1974, the law by no means opened the floodgates as was widely feared, and divorce rates in Italy have always remained comparatively low.[19] In addition, many described only legal separation and not actual divorce even after the law was passed. Legal

---

[16] Quoted in Fiamma Lussana, *L'Italia del divorzio*, p. 128. On women and the divorce referendum see also Maud Bracke, *Women and the Reinvention of the Political: Feminism in Italy, 1968–1983* (London, 2014), pp. 70–1.

[17] Of the twenty-six texts, nineteen were written by women. Of these, in thirteen cases the woman instigated proceedings herself, while in one case the decision was mutual. In the other women's memoirs it was not mentioned who ended the marriage. In four of the seven men's texts, they wrote that it was their wife's idea to end the marriage. Only one man wrote of leaving his wife, while in the other cases the circumstances were unknown.

[18] Two also fall slightly outside our date range—one born in 1924 and two in 1927, marrying in the mid 1940s—but their experiences are valuable enough to be considered here.

[19] Seymour, *Debating Divorce*, p. 213.

divorce in Italy was a difficult and lengthy process, with separation as the necessary first step. This chapter will explore how and why some people— usually women—did decide to leave their marriages in a society which was so hostile towards people who did not fit the traditional family model. The experience of work was often central for these women, as it gave them both economic independence and an identity. For several women, the turning point was feminism. In almost all of the memoirs, there was some description of how the marriage did or did not measure up to the ideal of a love marriage. This accounting with romance indicated a new reflexiveness about what made a good relationship and indeed an openness to the idea that one could or should seek satisfaction and happiness in marriage. This chapter therefore offers an alternative history of the Italian road to divorce. Rather than being centred around the political and media campaigns for divorce, it examines how intimate thoughts and feelings about marriage were changing from the 1950s to the 1970s, both informed by and informing the public conversation about divorce, but also by changing ideas about love itself, suggested by the mass culture of the economic miracle. In order to illuminate the social world of Coppi, Occhini, and others of their generation, caught between the war and the great transformation of the economic miracle, we will begin with an examination of legal separation in the immediate post-war decade.

BEFORE THE MIRACLE: LEGAL SEPARATION 1947–55

Although divorce was not legal until 1970, Italians had always been able to avail of legal separation. This process provided for the division of assets, spousal maintenance, and the custody and care of children, although it did not of course allow remarriage. Growing numbers of Italians were going to the courts in post-war Italy in order to formalize the end of their marriage. Over 5,000 separations were granted in 1951, more than four times the number granted ten years previously, although still of course only a fraction of the estimated number of marriage breakdowns.[20] Patterns varied widely by region, with couples in the urban north historically being much more likely to resolve their marital situation in court than those in the south, both rural and urban, and in the strongly Catholic Veneto region.[21] This section will examine a small sample of separation cases brought to court in Turin between 1947 and 1955 in order to examine how and why marriages ended, before the social and

---

[20] Fiamma Lussana, *L'Italia del divorzio*, p. 41.
[21] Seymour goes into detail only about separation in the nineteenth century in *Debating Divorce*, pp. 62–75.

economic transformation of the economic miracle.[22] With between 1,100 and 1,200 cases presented annually in these years, Turin's family courts were among the busiest in Italy. This was not surprising given its status as a large and growing industrial city with a large working-class population, which had also suffered heavily from war damage and trauma. A close look at twenty cases brought to court in each of the years 1947, 1950, 1953, and 1955 reveals that women were more likely to instigate legal proceedings to end a marriage, and increasingly so coming into the mid-1950s.[23] Cases were divided into judicial separations and separations by mutual consent. Since the law favoured men in terms of custody, property, and maintenance, women generally had to demonstrate cause and go to court in order to gain favourable terms and be awarded maintenance. Although we know less about separations 'by mutual consent', since they did not go to court, it can be assumed that most were not decided in the woman's favour. This is not to say that women did not instigate them, and a woman might renounce the right to maintenance in order to escape a bad situation. The general pattern in post-war Turin is that the judicial separations were mostly requested by women, with the number of judicial as opposed to mutual separations climbing over the period in question.[24] This suggests that while women always dominated in taking such cases to court, the number of women who were prepared to fight their cases rather than simply accepting the terms offered grew between the late 1940s and early 1950s. This is not especially surprising; even going back to the mid-nineteenth century, it was predominantly women who requested judicial separations.[25] The pattern also holds further into the twentieth century, as shown in a study of separation cases in late 1960s and early 1970s Naples, while the margin narrowed somewhat towards the end of the twentieth century.[26]

The judicial separation files generally give a reasonable amount of detail, and sometimes a lot, on the cases. Of course, these documents are very different from the memoirs, since they are legal testaments designed to

[22] Verbali di separazioni coniugali, Tribunale civile e penale di Torino: Mazzi 103–192, Archivio di Stato di Torino. Turin was chosen for two reasons. The first is that it was actually possible to view the records of these cases. Because of strict interpretations of Italian privacy law, I was not granted permission to view these records for most other cities and regions. Held at municipal level, the completeness of the record holding also varies very widely. In addition, Turin makes a good case study because of its relatively high rates of personal separation cases, set against national numbers.

[23] Sample set of twenty cases dated August/September for 1947, 1950, 1953, and 1955. Month chosen at random but kept consistent across the years so as to eliminate any possible seasonal variation.

[24] In 1947 seven women and four men brought cases of judicial separation while there were nine cases of 'mutual separation'. In 1955, thirteen cases of judicial separation were brought by women and three by men, while four were mutual or consensual.

[25] On the nineteenth-century figures, see Seymour, *Debating Divorce*, p. 67.

[26] Luca Salmieri, 'Genere e conflitto: Separazioni giudiziali a Napoli', *Polis*, 16:1 (2002), pp. 5–34, p. 14.

make a case to a judge. The cases are presented in the officious and verbose style of the solicitor, and their clients' voices are rarely heard directly. In order to make the strongest cases possible and to meet the legal criteria for a separation, the clients and their spouses had to be carefully presented so as to gain maximum sympathy from the judge.[27] Certain criteria for 'good' and 'bad' husbands and wives had to be met in each case.

The reasons most commonly cited by women in judicial separations were domestic violence and failure to provide for the family, or often a blend of both, while abandonment was also a frequent 'cause' for women. The greatest cause for men was adultery, and increasingly over time, the wife's 'character'. The impact of war is clear in the 1947 cases; many deal with issues of separation, adultery, and abandonment due to the social upheaval of the military conflict. From the 1950s onwards, the most common reason cited by women was domestic violence, followed by the failure to provide for the family. Often both were cited together, suggesting that domestic violence itself was not considered cause enough. Many of the testaments in the case files stressed that the woman had been beaten for no reason, or for minor reasons in order to pre-empt the suggestion that she had somehow deserved it. As the social disorder of the immediate post-war years dissipated, abandonment moved into third place. In late 1960s Naples, 'failure to provide' did not appear as a cause and the most commonly cited reason was abandonment—probably a reflection of the new-found affluence of the boom years.[28] Evidently the hundreds of women in post-war Turin who cited failure to provide as a cause for separation were acting from a position of real economic necessity which continued at least into the mid-1950s.

It is also worth considering the gendered and class dynamics of marriage in post-war Turin, as these offer further insight into the reasons a legal separation might be sought, when it offered no possibility of remarriage. In late 1960s Naples, the typical couple requesting a separation were the 'manual worker-housewife pair'.[29] Although there were fewer housewives in the pre-economic boom Turin files, the class profile is similar. While there were the odd middle-class or professional couples who requested a separation—always consensual rather than judicial so that intimate details were not revealed in public—the couples were overwhelmingly working class. The typical man was a manual or industrial worker, while the woman was usually a dressmaker or industrial worker herself. It is clear that men had much greater autonomy within marriage than did their wives. The cases frequently cited adultery,

---

[27] Rachel Fuchs has a particularly interesting discussion about how to read legal documents as sources for social and family history in her book *Contested Paternity: Constructing Families in Modern France* (Baltimore, MD, 2008), pp. 5–8.

[28] Salmieri, 'Separazioni giudiziali a Napoli', p. 12.

[29] Salmieri, 'Separazioni giudiziali a Napoli', p. 15.

frequent absences from the family home, gambling, and socializing away from the home, but these were usually secondary causes rather than the central ones. It was clear that such behaviour alone did not make a man a 'bad husband' in legal or perhaps even social terms. The frequent cases of abandonment also point to the relative freedom that working-class men had to simply walk away from their families and start again, particularly during and immediately after the war. Even in cases where maintenance payments were ordered by the court, it was doubtless still very difficult to enforce them and in some cases even to trace the disappeared spouse. While social circumstances granted men great freedom within marriage, women could often only resort to legal means to assert their autonomy or indeed to make financial provision for their families, through court-ordered maintenance payments. Given the difficulties involved, it is unlikely that these women would have pursued a legal separation if not from a place of real necessity.

Cases were also notably built on the conviction that husbands and wives were not fulfilling their proper roles in marriage, meaning at the most basic level that men provided for their families and women remained faithful. Of course, this is at least partly due to the official nature of the sources and the strict legal criteria for separations. What we see in these sources are examples of people fitting their own marriages into official templates, although they do give us a sense of how people understood their own experiences against these official narratives. Paul Betts, in his study of divorce cases in the German Democratic Republic (GDR), noted how in the 1950s couples generally cited the failure of husbands and wives to play their traditional roles as breadwinner and housewife, while by the 1960s the language had altered to include judgements of sexual satisfaction and love, or their lack.[30] Although it is not possible to trace the Turin separations after 1955, in Italy too, understandings of marriage shifted in the late 1950s and 1960s from complementary gender roles in the traditional household to include notions of love, satisfaction, intimacy, and companionship.[31] We will now turn to the memoirs in order to examine how these new ideas impacted on marriage and marriage breakdown.

MEMOIRS OF MARRIAGE BREAKDOWN: FORCED AND ARRANGED MARRIAGES

It was unusual for forced or arranged marriages to end in separation or divorce. This probably should not surprise us, because the social and familial

---

[30] Paul Betts, *Within Walls: Private Life in the German Democratic Republic* (Oxford, 2010), pp. 88–109.

[31] Files for personal separations are not available to view in the Turin Archivio di Stato after 1955.

worlds of these couples did not conceive that marriages could end, except through death. Such marriages were mainly held together by obligation to family and tradition rather than romantic love. Only three women memoirists were in this situation, and two were among the eldest. We will examine these somewhat exceptional women first before turning to how matters changed over time. Although these women had typical marriages in some ways, their backgrounds were also somewhat unusual, likely making them more predisposed to seek an escape route. We have seen how arranged marriages were common everywhere in rural Italy certainly up to the 1960s, although arrangements could be more rigid in Sicily and southern Italy. Forced marriage was also more common there, and although diminishing, still present up to the late 1960s and 1970s. Indeed, the only two Sicilian women who feature in the list of twenty-six separated memoirists were in arranged marriages.

Carlina Lorenzini's (1924, Argentina) experience shows how forced marriage based on sexual violence did not just happen in Sicily.[32] Her childhood was spent in Argentina, and following the family's return to Italy she enrolled as a student at the University of Pisa where she met her future husband—a man of Polish origin whose family had suffered under fascism. Their relationship began as a modern courtship based on love and companionship. In Carlina's words: 'I was in love with him, I appreciated many aspects of his thinking [. . .] but there were also shadowy zones which I did not understand, prejudices which did not fit with my own ideas and which pushed us to frequent arguments.'[33] A courtship between two university students who were unafraid to argue about their ideas nevertheless fits well with later patterns of courtships based on friendship. Carlina graduated and began to work as a teacher; however, her plans for the future were changed quite suddenly when her *fidanzato* raped her in her home while her parents were out, making her pregnant and forcing the couple to marry, in accordance with the norms of middle-class society in the 1950s. Writing about the incident in her memoir more than five decades later in 2005/6, she described her feelings thus:

> When he left me I felt nausea, the need to vomit, desperation: today you could say that I was raped, against my will; I don't know what my thoughts were then [. . .] I just know that I didn't want to, in that moment I hated him and . . . the following month I realized the consequences. Love, disappointment, desperation, immense sadness for my parents who were quite stricken and who didn't deserve this betrayal [. . .] We married on 20 January 1951.[34]

Years later Carlina's husband told her that he had acted under suspicion that she was not a virgin because 'that's what you did then'. The marriage was not a happy one; they went to live with his parents and there were tensions between

---

[32] Carlina Lorenzini, 'Il ritorno', MP/07, ADN.   [33] Carlina Lorenzini, 'Il ritorno'.
[34] Carlina Lorenzini, 'Il ritorno'.

the generations. Moreover, her husband proved himself lazy and did not continue his studies so that Carlina supported the couple by working as a teacher for some time. He also had a tendency to beat her. The details of the divorce are not included in the memoir. All that is known is that the divorce happened many years later after the couple had raised their children together. Carlina's sad experience blends elements of the old and new, the progressive and the retrograde. As a female university graduate in the late 1940s, she was unusual. For some time she was also the breadwinner, supporting the couple while her husband studied and found work. However, their outwardly progressive relationship was in reality anything but, and the basic principles of the 'kidnap marriage' and the equation of honour with virginity were clearly not confined to the southern rural peasantry. Such incidences may have been much more common in all circles but very rarely discussed. Carlina herself acknowledged that in 1950 she lacked the language by which to properly understand or describe what had happened to her. A clear understanding and categorization of such a violent act as rape would only come later, with the campaigns of second-wave feminism.

The second-eldest woman of the twenty-six, and one of the few Sicilian women, also married in quite unusual circumstances. Giuseppina Caravello (1927, province of Ragusa, Sicily) fell in love as a teenager with an unsuitable man whom she was not allowed to marry.[35] She then decided to become a nun but left the convent in 1960, returning to her family. As an older woman in her late thirties there was now real pressure on her to marry, and in 1968 she accepted an arranged marriage with a distant cousin. The marriage turned out to be abusive. He was also epileptic, and kept his condition from her until after the marriage. She described her difficulty in living with him, managing his illness and his moods and the tensions of sharing a home with her in-laws. She left him after ten years of marriage, feeling free to do so only after her mother's death. She had also been working as a teacher since 1973 and the confidence, independence, and economic security she gained from work were key to the decision to leave her husband and live alone. The confidence and the economic autonomy gained through working, as a bridge to gaining the courage to leaving an unhappy marriage, was key to many of the separation stories recounted in the women's memoirs.

Unlike Carlina Lorenzini, Giuseppina did recount in some detail how she slowly made the resolution to leave her husband and put the separation into place. She wrote of how she informed her husband of the decision to leave, and of his utter indifference. On her instigation they then both went to a solicitor to ask for a consensual separation, and a few days later she hired a van to remove all of her belongings to her new home. Hers was very much

---

[35] Giuseppina Caravello, 'Storia di una vita tutta sbagliata', MP/02, ADN.

the story of a decisive move for independence, with her job giving her both the confidence and the economic means to leave her marriage and live independently. In these respects, her story has very much in common with the memoirs to be discussed below. As a Sicilian woman who escaped an arranged marriage, her story was also an extremely unusual one. It likely had to do with the age at which she married and perhaps even her experience as a nun, during which time she worked in orphanages around Sicily. In these years, the convent offered one of the only acceptable ways for a woman to be single, and to work, in her society. The memoirs of these two women offer insights into the mindsets of women who both endured forced, arranged, and abusive marriages, and ultimately left them, documents that are unfortunately all too rare.

The experience of Lauretta Cavinato (1938, San Giorgio delle Pertiche, province of Padua) was recounted in Chapter 1.[36] Married in 1960, hers might not have looked like an arranged marriage from the outside, and was more typical of post-war arranged marriages in incorporating some elements of modern courtship. She did not dislike the man she married, but felt quite strongly that he did not measure up to her own expectations of romantic love. Her experience shows how familial strategy was in conflict with personal ideas about romantic love in the society of the boom. Although not given voice at the time, this discordance coloured the marriage. The circumstances leading to her decision to separate are in some aspects typical of other women who left their marriages in the 1960s and 1970s. Hers was not an abusive marriage and the tensions and challenges of the early years were common to many young couples beginning their lives together in the early years of the boom.

Lauretta's husband worked at FIAT in Turin and initially the couple lived there with his family. She was careful to describe that her husband was 'happy, able and affectionate' and she accepted her new role as wife, 'tranquil' if not content. Tensions arose between the older and younger couples with regard to finances. In order to gain some economic independence, Lauretta found a job in dressmaking, but when her father-in-law insisted that he should manage her salary too the couples argued and the generations parted ways. Lauretta described her happiness when she and her husband finally had a home of their own. Although they had very little starting out, she used her own savings to buy two steaks to make a celebration dinner with tomatoes, fried potatoes, and some good wine. Lauretta too took a job at FIAT and the couple lived well. Both in well-paid, secure jobs in 1960s Turin, they decided to have their first child after almost four years of marriage. Lauretta described her initial happiness at becoming a mother, and in the early years of her daughter's life she was content to stay at home with her.

---

[36] Lauretta Cavinato, 'Cocco e il fratello', MP/02, ADN.

Tensions began to arise in the couple's sexual life as Lauretta's appetite for sex diminished after her daughter's birth and she felt pressured into it by her husband. She felt strongly that 'you should have sex for pleasure and not out of duty'.[37] She also increasingly wanted something more in her life. Satisfied that her family was complete with the arrival of her second child, her thoughts increasingly turned to work and a longed for independence. She took professional training courses, went back to school to complete middle school, and took various different jobs. Her husband unfortunately did not understand her motivation to work, and there was increasing tension in the household. 'It was not so much the money that I missed because I did know how to live with very little, but rather the desire to have what my heart missed.'[38] Marital tensions over a wife who worked or wanted to work came up very rarely in the testimonies for the Turin separation cases, but were increasingly to become a theme of women's memoirs about marriage breakdown in the following decades. While the working-class women of late 1940s and early 1950s Turin most likely worked out of necessity, Lauretta's generation was the first to experience the affluence of the boom. In these years, the housewife became the ultimate symbol of the modern affluent family, signifying a husband who could afford to keep his family on his salary alone.[39] It is likely that Lauretta's husband was baffled by her desire to work when family finances were comfortable, but for Lauretta working was about much more than money.

Although she continually tried to convince her husband that her job would not change anything for the family, it certainly signified independence in her memoir. Her ability to manage both family and work gave her the confidence and the assurance that she could manage alone. 'It was in this way that I began to think about preparing myself for independence, in any case I kept the house going myself, and it was I who took care of the children in everything, with just a little money it could be managed.'[40] While tensions increased at home over several years and Lauretta considered different routes to her coveted independence, it was her decision to open a bakery which brought matters to their conclusion. Her husband, wary of the financial risk of the venture, requested a division of assets. She responded angrily and decisively: 'you can't accept that I am doing something for myself? Then each of us can take our own path, the house was there (above the bakery) and so it was.' In the end the couple made an informal agreement that Lauretta would stay in the family home as that was where their children preferred to live, with her husband taking lodgings opposite them. Some time later he decided to move, taking half of the furniture with him, and it was then that Lauretta contacted a solicitor to make the

---

[37] Lauretta Cavinato, 'Cocco e il fratello'.   [38] Lauretta Cavinato, 'Cocco e il fratello'.
[39] See Luisa Tasca, 'The "Average Housewife" in Post World War II Italy', *The Journal of Women's History*, 16:2 (2004), pp. 92–115.
[40] Lauretta Cavinato, 'Cocco e il fratello'.

separation official. Although Lauretta gave no precise dates in her memoir for these events, it is clear from the ages of her children that the legal separation happened in the late 1970s or early 1980s. Although divorce would have been legal at this point, Lauretta also speaks only of separation. Neither did she remarry; although she had had several companions, she was still single when she wrote her memoir in 2001.

'WE SPOKE, WITHOUT EVER UNDERSTANDING EACH OTHER': ROMANCE, MALAISE, WORK, AND THE 1960s WOMAN

The separation story of Giuseppina Caravello was unusual for a woman of her time and place, while that of Lauretta Cavinato had a lot in common with the experiences of other separated women, with one key difference. The vast majority of marriages which broke down were described not as arranged marriages but as love matches. Compared to those women quoted in previous chapters, many of the memoirists who separated were particularly definite and vocal about the love they felt on meeting and marrying their spouses. Women, often reticent in speaking about love in courtship, tended to emphasize it in stories leading to separation. Maria Vanzi (Empoli, Tuscany, 1931) married in 1952 and requested a legal separation in 1972. On meeting her husband she described experiencing the 'flash of lightning' that in Italian signifies love at first sight.[41] Vincenza Parrella (Acerenza, province of Potenza, 1938), attempting to explain how she entered an abusive marriage at 19, wrote: 'I fell in love with him, madly and irrationally, in a way that's only possible at that age.'[42] The memory of happy times was of course heightened by the quotidian and often difficult and sad reality that followed, but the emphasis placed on love and romance was also firmly of its historical moment.

It was in the 1950s and 1960s that the idea of marriage for love became something that people believed they all could and should expect in their lives. Reinforced both by popular culture and the increased informality of relations between the sexes, it was also incorporated into Catholic teaching about marriage.[43] Claire Langhamer has shown how, in England, the increased emphasis on love as a foundation for marriage contributed to the sharply rising divorce rates after the 1969 divorce law reform.[44] The growing conviction that if men and women should marry for love, they also had the right not

---

[41] Maria Vanzi, 'La mia vita. Flash di ricordi', MP/Adn2, ADN.
[42] Vincenza Parrella, 'I miei figli…percorsi di memoria', MP/97, ADN.
[43] See Angela Sorgato, *Tu, io e il nostro amore* (Milan, 1971) and others.
[44] Langhamer, *The English in Love*, pp. 175–206.

to remain trapped in a marriage without love, was the key argument expressed in the ordinary testimonies collected in the official legal report and reflected in the Church of England report.[45] This led to the inclusion of the principle of 'irretrievable breakdown' in 1969, so that a divorce could be granted without demonstrating cause. Public and political opinion in Italy evolved at a similar pace; and while earlier divorce bills required cause, the 1970 law recognized this principle by allowing divorce after five years of separation. Marriages that were made in the late 1950s and early 1960s were often the first ones to be predicated on such fragile grounds as feelings rather than social, economic, and familial concerns, and the memoirs give us an intimate picture of how these legal and political redefinitions of marriage both reflected and shaped social realities.

While some of the marriages described in the memoirs were abusive, it was much more common for women to describe a creeping awareness of dissatisfaction or malaise in their lives at the starting point of their decision to separate. In her study of urban middle-class wives during the economic miracle, Enrica Asquer attempted to trace the roots of the dissatisfaction felt by so many. In assessing the differences between expectations and the reality of married life, she found that for many women it was not domestic life itself, but rather how the couple spent their leisure time, that was key.[46] Women envisaged spending time together as a married couple, but the reality was that men still tended to socialize together and engage in active citizenship while women remained grounded in home and family. The vision of quality leisure time spent together as a married couple speaks again to the notion of companionate marriage in the context of the growing emphasis on individual satisfaction and increased leisure time in the affluent society of the 1960s. As we have begun to see, the reality was that work was key in giving women a sense of collective identity and active participation in society. Without it, they might not have strong social and support networks of their own. It is isolation that emerged as the overarching theme in the following testimonies, and the need to bridge this isolation was crucial to imagining an escape route.

The short written statement of Milena reads more like an oral testament than a written memoir.[47] There is no precise dating in the text, but we know that her experiences take place within the economic miracle years. Her mother was a rice worker in rural Lombardy—one of the few groups of female rural labourers who were famously politically organized—and the testament is bookmarked at one end by the political struggles of the rice workers that she

---

[45] Langhamer, *The English in Love*, p. 191.

[46] Enrica Asquer, *Storia intima dei ceti medi: una capital e una periferia nell'Italia del miracolo economico* (Rome, 2011), pp. 129–31.

[47] MP/T2, ADN.

grew up with, and at the other end by her discovery of feminism in 1970s Rome.[48] Enrica Asquer's work probed the dissatisfaction of middle-class women with their confinement to the domestic sphere, but is clear from Milena's text that this sense of dissatisfaction or malaise crossed class boundaries. Although her education likely did not extend beyond elementary school, her background left her predisposed to left-wing politics and women's activism. Her marriage began as a great love, prompting her to leave her family and move to Rome; all was described as a privilege and an adventure: she wrote of feeling like a princess in a fairy tale. Like some of the Milanese women Asquer interviewed, Milena initially deemed it a great privilege to be the first woman in her family not to work during her marriage, in contrast to her mother who had not even been able to take any maternity leave.[49] However, this impression did not last long. The couple had two children, but over time Milena found it challenging to be confined to the domestic sphere. It was when she began to vocalize these feelings to her husband and was confronted with his lack of understanding that the marriage began to fail.

Milena was clear that what lay at the heart of the marriage breakdown was a failure of communication between the spouses, her husband's inability to take seriously her interior crisis. Milena became pregnant again, and her husband's happiness at the prospect of a third child was met with her desperation. With three children, Milena was certain that the marriage was over. For the daughter of rural landless labourers, who had grown up in the post-war deprivation that preceded the economic boom, the security of being provided for and the apparent luxury of not having to work must have been difficult to renounce, however dissatisfying the reality of being a housewife turned out to be. Her husband was also praised for being a good father and worker. By traditional standards, he was the perfect husband, and Milena would under no circumstances have qualified for divorce under the very limited criteria suggested by Sansone's 'little divorce' bill in 1956. Her memoir is a clear testament to the increased weight given to romantic love from the 1960s onwards. While some of the language used suggests the influence of popular culture with its strong emphasis on the idea of romance—love, fairy tale, princess—her ideal was also that of the companionate marriage, with mutual respect and communication at its core. Her greatest complaint about her husband was his inability to listen.

Elisabetta Battistini (Rome, 1941), whom we first encountered in Chapter 2, also described how her personal dissatisfaction and her husband's lack of understanding prompted her decision to separate.[50] Her marriage in 1966

---

[48] On the oral political culture of the rice workers, see Diana Garvin, 'Singing Truth to Power: Melodic Resistance and Bodily Revolt in Italy's Rice Fields', *Annali d'Italianistica*, 34 (2016), pp. 373–400.

[49] Enrica Asquer, *Storia intima dei ceti medi*, pp. 132–3.

[50] Elisabetta Battistini, 'Del divorzio ovvero massacre di un'identità', MP/96, ADN.

came after several years of living the relatively liberated lifestyle of a single woman working as a secretary in 1960s Rome. At the age of 25, and after a year and a half together, she married a Sardinian architect in an extravagant and fashionable Roman wedding. The couple returned to Sardinia straight after their marriage. Elisabetta thought the move would only be temporary when in fact it lasted seven years. She was also convinced that leaving her life for her husband and future family was the right thing to do for love.

> I left my job in order to get married, I was convinced that if I wanted to start a family I would have to dedicate myself totally to it and I decided also, as a supreme act of love, that I would leave my city, my family, my friends, everything, to follow my husband.
> This was my first mistake.[51]

Just as in Milena's testimony, the strength of the initial love was in sharp contrast to what came afterwards. Each of the women was careful to emphasize the strong feelings that motivated their decision to marry and move with their husbands, and in both memoirs marriage was presented a positive and definite choice. While Milena, the daughter of rural labourers, also found economic security in marriage, Elisabetta may also have been searching for the strong and stable family life she did not herself have as a child.

The roots of Elisabetta's dissatisfaction in marriage lay in the decision to relocate to Sassari, in Sardinia, leaving behind friends and family in Rome. While the economic miracle was in full swing in 1960s Rome, its effects only penetrated Italy's outer margins more slowly. Attitudes to women, particularly in relation to work and family, were quite different there and it would certainly have been out of the question for a middle-class, married woman to work.[52] Elisabetta described the stark contrast between the rhythm of working life in Rome and her new domestic life in Sassari. Although only three months passed before her first pregnancy brought her joy again, her memoir gives the impression of an endless stretching of time:

> My life had changed from one that was extremely dynamic, full of appointments and organized around work, to a completely different one, in another city, among people who were completely different, above all in their mentality. I adapted to the new rhythm, everything happened more slowly, I took care of the house with the help of a servant in the morning, I learned how to cook, I kept everything tidy. [...] I was in another dimension, half drowsy; from the bedroom window to the bathroom one facing the internal courtyard I could hear the wind whistling strongly and it was an anguished sound that I had never heard before and that filled me with sadness in the long winter afternoons.[53]

---

[51] Elisabetta Battistini, 'Del divorzio ovvero massacre di un'identità'.
[52] Asquer, *Storia intima dei ceti medi*, pp. 135–40.
[53] Elisabetta Battistini, 'Del divorzio ovvero massacre di un'identità'.

Asquer also remarks on the peculiar form of 'domestic time' in her oral testimonies, blurred and formless in contrast to the regular linear clock time of the world of work.[54] It is through the distortions of time that we get a real sense of Elisabetta's unease in her new life, her drowsiness and her sense of being in another world conveying an acute sense of being utterly disconnected.

Elisabetta had suffered mental illness in her adolescence and soon after her wedding made her second suicide attempt. Central to her motivation was her feeling of having made a mistake and of being trapped. However, she was still careful to emphasize her love for her husband then and afterwards. Her dissatisfaction was clearly rooted in the boredom and isolation of her domestic life. She said that afterwards, 'I tried to forget my sadness, I wanted to work, just taking care of the house seemed reductive, it bored me'.[55] She read a lot and took to flower arranging, until pregnancy and the impending birth of their child began to occupy her. Elisabetta had two children and dedicated herself completely to them. In her memoir she admitted to no feelings of regret or dissatisfaction in motherhood, determined to give her children the normal childhood that she herself had never had, since she did not know her father. It was as they grew older that she began to feel again a strong desire to become more involved in the life of the city. Opportunities were limited in Sassari and the couple eventually returned to Rome on Elisabetta's instigation, where she began to work again as a primary school teacher.

Elisabetta's gradual but growing sense of dissatisfaction and her conviction that despite marrying for love the couple were not in fact compatible, led her to request a separation in 1982 after sixteen years of marriage, followed five years later by a divorce. She described her annoyance at having to do the bulk of the childcare and her husband's disgruntlement at having to return to Rome, but found it difficult to pin down both the exact moment when her dissatisfaction began and its precise causes. Again she emphasized how she had married for love, but things had not turned out how she had planned. 'I had married him for love because he was kind to me and I felt happy with him. It wasn't like this. I wasn't happy with him and maybe he was not happy with me. In a word we were incompatible.'[56] Their relationship followed the classic trajectory of the marriage that crumbled, built solely on the fragile foundations of romantic love, or what Anthony Giddens termed 'contingent love'.[57] More than that though, Elisabetta's memoir shows how the ideal of a marriage based on companionship and equality could never be fully realized in a society which relegated men and women to separate spheres, public and domestic, after marriage.

---

[54] Asquer, *Storia intima dei ceti medi*, pp. 142–5.
[55] Elisabetta Battistini, 'Del divorzio ovvero massacre di un'identità'.
[56] Elisabetta Battistini, 'Del divorzio ovvero massacre di un'identità', p. 40.
[57] Anthony Giddens, *The Transformation of Intimacy*, pp. 62–4.

Giovanna Bartolozzi (Florence, 1936) married in 1959.[58] She met her husband Franco when she joined the local 'communist circle', going mountaineering with a group of young people who were as interested in exploring the countryside as they were in left-wing politics. Theirs began very much as a friendship and the relationship that resulted was rooted in companionship and shared interests. They also had open discussions and made informed decisions together about sexuality and birth control. The companionate marriage which they entered into was one very much grounded in the associational culture and grassroots left-wing politics that pervaded much of the urban and provincial centre-north in the 1950s.[59] She described how their marriage was beset with economic tensions. They started their family at the height of the economic boom and felt under pressure to overextend themselves financially in order to have the coveted consumer items of the period: washing machine, car, television. However, Giovanna identified her husband's lack of understanding when she had an abortion in the mid-1960s as the root of their marriage breakdown.

At this stage the couple already had two children and felt that their family was complete; the condom they used had broken. The decision was made to have an illegal abortion, performed by an 'unscrupulous obstetrician' in the family home.[60] Franco had taken their two children out and Giovanna was left alone for quite a few hours after the obstetrician had left; weak, bleeding, and traumatized by the experience. He did not understand Giovanna's upset when he returned home later than planned, and as far as she was concerned his lack of understanding of what she had gone through with the abortion was the beginning of the end of their relationship. She found it difficult to connect with him sexually afterwards, commenting bitterly afterwards on how she saw not 'love' but 'egoism' and absorption in his own sexual pleasure in their intimate life from then on. Giovanna went on to have further health problems which affected their sexual life, while Franco began an affair. His infidelity signalled the eventual end of their marriage. In their case the decision to end the marriage was mutual. There were several periods of separation, and it seems the couple already lived apart by the time Giovanna began the proceedings for a divorce in 1980.

Dissatisfaction with domestic life, lack of understanding, sexual discord, unplanned pregnancy: the marital problems the women have described so far were not especially unusual ones. What did set them apart was their decision to end the marriage. Despite the ongoing public debate about divorce in the late 1960s, it is clear from the low numbers availing of the 1970 law that the

---

[58] Giovanna Bartolozzi, 'Ricordi indelibili', MP/04, ADN.
[59] On left-wing associational culture in the 1950s, see Forgacs and Gundle, *Mass Culture and Italian Society* pp. 259–68.
[60] Giovanna Bartolozzi, 'Ricordi indelibili', MP/04, ADN.

decision to end a marriage was still not one that was easy, common, or readily accepted in many sectors of society.[61] The women who wrote memoirs about these experiences also saw divorce or separation as one of the defining events of their lives, and felt it necessary to write about it and submit their text to the National Diary Archive, thus sharing their stories with a wider audience. What was it that motivated them to take the drastic, difficult, and pioneering step of ending an unhappy marriage? Although Italian women typically did not re-enter the workforce when their children were older, the majority of these women memoirists did so. Work was indeed key in most of these memoirs, and besides the obvious economic benefit, having a job gave the women a sense of identity, confidence, and crucially in many cases, a support network.[62]

The opposition of a husband to his wife's desire to work played some role in many of the memoirs about separation, suggesting that such attitudes were common across Italy from the late 1940s through at least to the late 1960s. These examples of course add to the evidence collected in Chapter 4 when tensions about women working were expressed in the language of jealousy. Such tensions crossed class and regional boundaries, while the economic miracle brought its own tensions. The fact that the housewife was one of the key status symbols of the boom years could create social pressure for the husband to act as sole provider for the family, even when household finances did not really allow it. This created tensions in some households. In Genoa, Giorgio told his wife to give up her job upon their marriage in the mid-1950s, saying that it was now his role to support her, although the couple had barely enough money to set up home together. While they had an apartment, they did not have enough money to furnish it and basic necessities such as gas and electricity were a strain, both financially and ultimately on their relationship.[63] Work could thus play an important part in marriage breakdown, whether it was that tensions over work or finance created marital conflict or that work provided women with the financial, social, and psychological means to prepare for life outside marriage.

THE IMPACT OF FEMINISM: ACTIVISM AND AWARENESS

Some of the women who worked not only gained self-assurance but also encountered new ideas which helped them to make sense of their experience

---

[61] Seymour, *Debating Divorce*, pp. 213–14.
[62] A further example is Maria Vanzi (married 1952 and requested a separation in 1972), whose work was key to giving her the confidence to end the marriage.
[63] MP/93, ADN.

and ultimately to make the decision to leave their husbands. Vincenza Parrella (Acerenza, province of Potenza, 1938) met her husband in Bari at the age of 19 and married a year later in 1958, moving to Rome shortly afterwards. What began as a relationship of love quickly turned into an abusive marriage. Her husband Tonino used rape, forced pregnancy, and economic neglect as the tools of his oppression. As a poorly educated woman from a southern family background living an isolated life in Rome, Vincenza possessed neither the means nor the confidence to leave him. The couple had two children together, and despite Tonino's opposition to her working Vincenza was obliged to seek employment in order to support the family. While she worked in various part-time positions when her children were younger, accepting informal childcare from her mother and sister, she took a full-time, stable factory position in 1973, and was proud that through her work they were able to afford their first family holiday in 1975.

When she entered the factory, Vincenza quickly became politicized, joining the trade union Confederazione Generale Italiana del Lavoro, the PCI and, the left-wing feminist women's organization, UDI. Trade unionism was indeed a typical bridge towards feminism in the 1970s.[64] She also made many friends and even went back to evening school to complete middle school. Although she remained married at this stage, she was gaining the tools through her socialization in the factory and her gradual integration into the world of feminist politics to eventually leave Tonino. Feminism in the early 1970s was a strong and growing movement in Italy; the UDI had its roots in the post-war politics of the Left and was still closely linked to trade union politics.[65] Indeed, trade unionism formed a typical bridge towards feminism in the 1970s.[66] She eventually began proceedings for a legal separation in 1995 after discovering that Tonino had sexually abused their daughter. It is clear from her memoir that her involvement in trade union politics and militant feminism was key to being able to make this step. She owed the fact that she managed to survive the emotional pain of her daughter's abuse and her marriage breakdown to the support of friends, but also 'to trade union politics and activism, which in the factory absorbed me with all the problems that continually needed to be tackled, and thus prevented me from thinking. To the women of the feminist movement who hugged me tightly when they saw me, full of solidarity, comprehension, affection.'[67] Vincenza went on to play an active role in feminist campaigns against sexual abuse in the family. Feminism

---

[64] Bracke, *Women and the Reinvention of the Political*, pp. 72–3.

[65] On the history of UDI see Molly Tambor, *The Lost Wave: Women and Democracy in Postwar Italy* (Oxford, 2014), pp. 22–46 and Aida Ribero, *Una questione di libertà: Il feminismo degli anni settanta* (Turin, 1999), pp. 51–64.

[66] Bracke, *Women and the Reinvention of the Political*, pp. 72–3.

[67] Vincenza Parrella, 'I miei figli...percorsi di memoria', MP/97, ADN.

provided her with strong support networks and gave political meaning to her own sad experience.

While Vincenza discovered feminism through trade union politics, and indeed there was a strong history of such links since the late 1940s, by the 1970s feminism was also taking much broader roots in Italian society. One of the distinguishing features of Italian second-wave feminism was the extent of the grassroots activity it inspired, with many thousands of women becoming involved in collectives across the country, where they experimented in new ways of living as well as contributing to activism in women's health, sexuality, politics, and work.[68] In many cities a Women's Bookshop provided a place to congregate, read about new ideas, and hear talks on feminist topics. In this way even women who were not typical activists might be drawn into the peripheries of the movement.[69]

Milena, who felt suffocated by her responsibilities as a wife and mother, found her life utterly transformed by her discovery of grassroots feminism in Rome.[70] Milena's increasing dissatisfaction with her life coincided with the growth of feminist collectives in 1970s Rome, providing spaces for like-minded women to gather in solidarity and activism.[71] While women of all backgrounds were involved, including some married women, Milena was unusual as one of the few members of such groups to have children.[72] Given the Italian feminist emphasis on sexual difference and separate female spaces it is perhaps not surprising that her involvement led her to question her marriage. She likely took part in consciousness raising, a practice in which women shared stories of their intimate lives and questioned the patriarchal structures of marriage and motherhood.[73] She described her radicalization in some detail. Although aware of being strongly judged for her feminism which others also linked to her marriage breakdown, she described above all the transformative effect that feminism had on her life. She emphasized the exhilaration she felt in the weekly meetings with like-minded women who were examining their relationships with their husbands and children, and their lives more generally. The moral and psychological support she received from her feminist friends was clearly key to feeling able to leave the marriage.[74]

---

[68] Bracke, *Women and the Reinvention of the Political*, p. 1.

[69] On the development of Italian feminism, see Aida Ribeiro, *Una questione di libertà*. On one middle-class Sardinian women who was drawn into the margins of the feminist movement, see Enrica Asquer, *Storia intima dei ceti medi*, p. 230.

[70] MP/T2, ADN.

[71] On one of the most significant Roman feminist collectives, see Mariapia Pizzolante, 'Il Pompeo Magno da "piccolo gruppo" a "collettivo"', *Snodi: Pubblici e privati nella storia contemporanea*, 5 (2010), pp. 99–108.

[72] Bracke, *Women and the Reinvention of the Political*, pp. 92–3.

[73] Bracke, *Women and the Reinvention of the Political*, p. 94.   [74] MP/T2, ADN.

The lack of proper punctuation and syntax made Milena's writing dense and a little difficult to understand but her style reflected an education that was likely very basic, as a working-class rural girl growing up before the boom. It also conveyed the force of her feeling when she reflected on the feminist collective and the important role it played in her life. We do not know how Milena came to be involved in the feminist collective, although her experience is evidence of the group's success in publicizing the concerns of feminists and reaching out to a wider female public.[75] Although Milena may not have appeared to be the typical 1970s militant feminist, lacking any background in activism or left-wing politics, her mother's experiences of collective action and female solidarity as a rice worker in post-war Lombardy clearly made her receptive to radical politics. The theme of solidarity and support between women was also a common thread running through her narrative. It is clear that she saw her involvement in the movement and her subsequent choices as taking her very much outside the boundaries of respectability, and her decision to leave her husband was made more difficult by the fact that she was also separated from her children for some time afterwards. Although Milena's experiences are not typical, her memoir does demonstrate the power of the feminist movement in making sense of the experiences of ordinary women and in empowering them to make life-changing decisions.

In the case of Giovanna Bartolozzi (Florence, 1936), feminism seems primarily to have helped her make sense of her life after the breakdown of her marriage.[76] Her background perhaps made her more receptive to feminist ideas. Both she and her husband had been involved in the PCI since their youth and Giovanna had continued at least intermittently to be involved in politics. Over the years that her marriage was breaking down, she made continual notes about her state of mind, a practice which has echoes of the 1970s feminist emphasis on self-knowledge or in its Italian version, *autocoscienza*.[77] It seems likely, due to her political awareness and her later involvement with feminism, that Giovanna would at least have been aware of the practice. Her involvement in a feminist collective was also a definite support as she made the decision to ask for a divorce in 1980. Her discussions at the collective helped her to make sense of her marriage breakdown: 'It was obvious that much of the blame was my own, attending the feminist collective helped me to see all the mistakes I had made, the fear of being alone, fear of not managing.'[78] While the first two women involved with feminism found that it helped them to gain the confidence to leave their marriage and live

[75] On the Pompeo Magno collective's publicity initiatives, see Mariapia Pizzolante, 'Il Pompeo Magno', pp. 104–7.

[76] Giovanna Bartolozzi, 'Ricordi indelibili', MP/04, ADN.

[77] See Aida Ribeiro, *Una Questione di libertà*, pp. 155–80 and Bracke, *Women and the Reinvention of the Political*, pp. 65–6.

[78] Giovanna Bartolozzi, 'Ricordi indelibili', MP/04, ADN.

independently, the benefit for Giovanna was mostly psychological, giving her the self-awareness she felt that she lacked. In all cases it is clear that the feminist movement of the 1970s, both in terms of the sense of solidarity and belonging that membership of a collective brought, and in the new ideas to which women were exposed, had a very real impact on the lives of these women, whose backgrounds varied from southern working-class woman to bourgeois Tuscan socialist.

NEW VISIONS OF LOVE AND FAMILY: POLITICS, GENERATION, AND MARRIAGE BREAKDOWN

All of the women who chose to leave a marriage in the 1960s and early 1970s, whatever their reasons, described how difficult it was. Although their actions were bold and decisive, they were aware that the society they lived in would not be tolerant or forgiving of their actions. Lavinia had wanted a separation in 1960, three years after her marriage, but was persuaded by her uncle not to leave her husband. He told her that it would be very difficult for her as a separated woman and that even if she lived as a saint, she would be judged.[79] She eventually obtained a legal separation some years later in the 1970s. For many of these women, there was not one single decision, but many moments which led to the final one. Many more women, like Lavinia, may have wanted to leave, or tried to leave, but were not able to go through with it. The experiences of the women who did separate or divorce are not especially reflective of mainstream Italian society, which did not tolerate marriage breakdown easily, despite the divorce campaigns of the 1960s. Milena was convinced that, in the 1970s, she was one of the first women in Italy to ask for a separation, so alien was the notion to her neighbourhood in Rome. Giovanna Bartolozzi's feminism seemed to evolve from her earlier political activism, but even she found the decision to separate an extremely long and difficult process.

Some did, however, live outside the bourgeois norms of 1950s Italy, and were already, in this age of social conservatism, conformism, and strong religious values, beginning to imagine new ways of living and loving, as couples and as families. We saw in Chapter 2 how Italian communism was wary of progressive sexual politics, and particularly so when it came to divorce. Although Italian communists had a strong involvement in the divorce campaigns of the 1960s, the party remained cautiously uncommitted on the issue in the 1950s. In the deeply conservative climate of the early Cold War,

---

[79] MP/10, ADN.

party leader Palmiro Togliatti was reluctant to challenge the traditional Catholic family, despite having a personal stake in the matter. Since 1946, Togliatti had been having an affair with much younger party activist, Nilde Iotti, eventually leaving his wife Rita Montagnara for her and obtaining a legal separation in 1951.[80] The party went to great lengths to keep all details of Togliatti's private life out of the press, for fear that a scandal would damage them, while the affair was of course an open secret within party circles.[81] Guido Morselli caustically commented in his novel *The Communist* on this climate of hypocrisy and 'double standards' in the post-war party.[82]

Luisa Puliti's memoir shows how, despite the social conservatism of official Italian communism, politics could sometimes encourage alternative attitudes towards commitment.[83] We saw in Chapter 2 how Luisa got married in 1952 to a communist activist who brought her into the party. After the wedding, they moved to Rome where they both worked for the party. After several years and one abortion later, Luisa gave birth to their son, Guido. Their lives continued to be focused on the party rather than on creating a traditional family life, and neighbours noted their eccentricity. Certainly by the 1960s they also had an open marriage. At one point, Luisa left Paolo to live with an older man, while their son Guido remained with Paolo. Luisa candidly wrote that she felt no guilt about leaving them both. When the relationship ended after three years, it seems that she did return to the marital home. One of the episodes detailed in her memoir is her arrest at a protest march against the Vietnam War, marking President Johnson's visit to Rome in December 1967. Her husband and son were there to greet her proudly when she was released from her short prison stay. Some years later, when Guido was in his late teens, Luisa and Guido both left Paolo, going to live alone together. Paolo cohabited with a companion, Elena, and a legal separation followed. The relationship always remained amicable, and Paolo was apparently still prepared to return to Luisa if Elena had left him.

Their marriage, unusual even in progressive political circles for the 1950s, set a model for the culture of 'free love' that emerged everywhere in Western Europe in the late 1960s. It also contains echoes of early twentieth-century left-wing experimentation with free love which communists appeared to have buried or forgotten after 1945.[84] The post-war revolutionary tended to remained hostile to any attempts to rethink monogamy and the family,

---

[80] Anna Tonelli, *Gli irregolari: Amori comunisti al tempo della guerra fredda* (Rome, 2014), pp. 71–85.

[81] Tonelli, *Gli irregolari*, pp. 80–1.

[82] See Maria Casalini, *Famiglie comuniste: Ideologie e vita quotidiana nell'Italia degli anni cinquanta* (Bologna, 2010), pp. 140–2.

[83] Luisa Puliti, *È nato un bambino di sesso femminile* (Rome, 1999). A version of the manuscript is also held at the ADN: MP/91.

[84] Ginsborg, *Family Politics*, pp. 23–6 and 49–51.

dismissing sexual experimentation as bourgeois decadence.[85] The broader culture of student politics and protest culture did certainly leave its mark on the relationships and marriages of the younger generations though, and particularly those engaged in student politics and protest culture around the Italian '68.[86] We see some hints of their impact on ordinary marriages, particularly in relation to fidelity and commitment, in a couple of the memoirs. The two shortest marriages were described in the memoirs of two men; Stefano Indrio (Rome, 1942) and Riccardo Varanini (Portoferralo, province of Livorno, 1945).[87] Both completed university degrees in the late 1960s and met the women who would become their wives in this milieu. Stefano, who was a university lecturer in Rome, married in a civil ceremony in 1967 and by 1970 had requested a legal separation. This act only formalized what had happened, as his wife had already left him by this point. It seems that a combination of infertility and Stefano's deteriorating mental health—as explored in Chapter 4—caused the marriage breakdown. Nevertheless, it seems likely that the changed cultural climate of the late 1960s, particularly for university educated Italians, contributed to Stefano's wife feeling able to leave the marriage after a relatively short time together.

Riccardo Varanini's experience yields a little more insight into the world of student activism in late 1960s Italy, and its possible impact on gender relations and expectations in marriage. A law student in the late 1960s, Riccardo was a registered member of the PCI and very much involved in the world of student activism. He describes himself as having much less experience of women and sexuality than of politics, which absorbed most of his time. In one anecdote, he asked a girl to go away with him to Marxist summer camp rather than to the beach and she refused. He experienced 1968 thus: ''68 arrived and it was a great liberation—sexual too—for everyone but for me it was nothing of the sort, rather I had a great sense of inadequacy combined with a strong desire to study and keep up with my exams and a great sadness as a result'.[88] Despite not developing any deep or lasting relationships during his years of study and activism, he described the great sense of camaraderie and collective purpose that he gained—a sense of being part of an important and exciting moment.

[85] Eros Francescangeli, 'The Bride in Red: Morality and Private Relationships in the Italian Revolutionary Left—the Case of the Maoist Group Servire Il Popolo', *European Review of History: Revue européenne d'histoire*, 22:1 (2015), pp. 101–19.

[86] On student culture and 1968 in Italy, see Robert Lumley, *States of Emergency: Cultures of Revolt in Italy from 1968 to 1978* (London, 1990). On the sexual and gender politics of the Italian '68, see also Rebecca Clifford, 'Emotions and Gender in Oral History: Narrating Italy's 1968', *Modern Italy*, 17:2 (2012), pp. 209–21. On sexuality and 1968 more broadly, see Rebecca Clifford et al., 'Gender and Sexuality', in Robert Gildea et al. (eds), *Europe's 1968: Voices of Revolt* (Oxford, 2013), pp. 239–57.

[87] Stefano Indrio, 'Amatucci' (Ragusa, 2007); Riccardo Varanini, 'La mia vita è qualcos'altro', MP/11, ADN. A copy of Stefano Indrio's text is also held at the ADN.

[88] Riccardo Varanini, 'La mia vita è qualcos'altro'.

He met his wife Rita several years later in 1970, but recognized her then as 'one of the girls who had made an impression on me' in the days of student activism, and they were able to share their memories of those times.[89] It seems likely that Rita was somewhat involved in or at least aware of the nascent Italian feminist movement. She was in any case much less enamoured of the traditional model of marriage and family for which Riccardo longed. He keenly felt 'the need to create his own family structure, to finally have a real relationship, and the desire to marry and have children became the central, irrefutable aims of my life'.[90] He saw Rita as the way of realizing these ambitions of family. She, however, was more reluctant to become involved with him and much less inclined towards marriage; she was completing her thesis while battling ill health and was wary about committing her time to a relationship. Neither did she want to waste time with someone as sexually inexperienced as he. When she became pregnant before their marriage, Rita had an abortion despite Riccardo's opposition. Eventually Rita became less opposed to the idea of marriage; 'marriage was knocking at the door, Rita was convinced that I wasn't such a bad idea'.[91] The wedding took place in February 1972. The couple had a son in 1973, who in Riccardo's account was desired more by him than by Rita. While 'the marriage distracted us both, it did not stop Rita's evolution, positive regarding work, less positive regarding men'.[92] She became a journalist and her career continued to develop. Riccardo found out later than she was also having affairs. Her decision to end the marriage in 1977 came as a huge shock to Riccardo even though other friends had already seen the signs.

> The result was that I was brutally knocked over by the news in June, which came together with the request to start thinking about finding somewhere else to live. [. . .] In any case the shock was violent and unexpected, her announcement was as brutal as it was final: she couldn't keep living like this, she had a great desire to live, more, live with her new love, I was destroyed.[93]

The emphasis of much recent historiography of the sexual politics of 1968 has been—and correctly so—on the misogyny that often underlay new codes of sexual liberty, with women often put under pressure to conform while traditional gender roles and hierarchies were often reproduced within activist groups and circles.[94] However, we can see here and in the memoirs of the older women discussed earlier, how new ideas coalescing around the emergence of Italian feminism from the long '68 offered women new models of

[89] Riccardo Varanini, 'La mia vita è qualcos'altro'.
[90] Riccardo Varanini, 'La mia vita è qualcos'altro'.
[91] Riccardo Varanini, 'La mia vita è qualcos'altro'.
[92] Riccardo Varanini, 'La mia vita è qualcos'altro'.
[93] Riccardo Varanini, 'La mia vita è qualcos'altro'.
[94] Clifford, 'Emotions and Gender in Oral History', pp. 209–21. Gildea et al., *Europe's 1968*.

work, marriage, family, and love. While those whose lives were shaped by these ideas were still in the minority, these examples demonstrate the power of new ideas and models of femininity to reshape gender relations, family, and marriage in the late 1960s and particularly in the 1970s. The memoirs of the women we have examined so far always tend to style separation as an act of liberation however difficult or complicated. Riccardo's memoir shows the emotional impact from the male point of view. According to his account, the separation was an experience simply of loss and sadness.

'WITHOUT ONCE THINKING THAT I WAS AN ADULTERER': ADULTERY, MARRIAGE, AND COHABITATION

The memoirs of Luisa Puliti and Riccardo Varanini raise questions not just about sexual politics and commitment, but also about fidelity and infidelity. Did an affair have to signal the end of a marriage, or might it be ignored or forgiven? Did commitment mean staying together in the marital home, or did it also necessarily incorporate sexual fidelity? These were potent questions for Italians in the mid to late twentieth century, as the answers were becoming increasingly less obvious. In the case of Luisa Puliti, sexual fidelity was evidently not a requirement of marriage as both she and her husband continued to have affairs for many years before their legal separation. In the case of Rita, Riccardo Varanini's wife, she too had affairs and left her husband to be with her new love after a few short years of marriage. Did love and fidelity have different meanings for the 1968 generation? Did a greater emphasis on sincerity and, in Claire Langhamer's words, 'authenticity' mean that for those marrying in the 1960s, it was no longer tolerable to be married to one person while in love with somebody else?[95] While the experience of neither couple is typical of Italian society in the 1950s, 1960s, or 1970s, the differences between their experiences do perhaps hint at some broader shifts in how marriage, emotion, and commitment were understood from the 1950s to the 1970s.

We saw in Chapter 4 how the spectre of adultery loomed large in the popular jealous mind during the post-war period. It was certainly perceived to be threatening the institution of marriage in some vague sort of way. Adultery cropped up regularly in the memoirs of marriage breakdown (and indeed in those of couples who stayed together), but it was rarely the primary

---

[95] Claire Langhamer, 'Love, Selfhood and Authenticity in Post-war Britain', *Cultural and Social History*, 9:12 (2012), pp. 277–97.

reason that a marriage ended. The women who separated or divorced certainly mentioned their husband's almost inevitable affairs, but they were only one of many factors and hardly ever the decider. This was also the case for women filing for separation in Turin, while adultery was the most common reason cited by men in cases against their wives. In the late 1940s and early 1950s many of the cases filed by husbands betrayed the anxiety, disorder, and desperation caused by the wartime separation of husbands and wives, with anxieties centred on the wartime conduct, real or imagined, of their wives.[96] In other cases separation tended to follow very soon after the marriage, as soon as the adultery became known.[97]

All of this is of course entirely in line with Italy's strong double standard with regard to male and female sexuality, and these attitudes were regularly reinforced in the advice columns of popular magazines. Women who even contemplated betraying their husbands were dealt with extremely severely, while tolerance and resignation were advised to the wives of unfaithful men. An 'unhappy wife' who wrote to *Grand Hotel* in 1950 for advice about her affair was strongly reprimanded and instructed to think of both her children and her poor lover, who should be freed to find a wife of his own.[98] Later that year another reader was told that her husband strayed not through his own fault but that of the immoral girls who preyed on him. All she could do was to put the affair behind her and make the best of things.[99] Although the occasional challenging voice penetrated the magazines, the advice remained firm over the decade.[100] This double standard was equally reflected in *Grazia*, with its more middle-class, urban readership.[101] An unmarried woman who wrote into the magazine about having a lover was treated with horror. Meanwhile the amorous adventures of another reader's husband were lightly dismissed; his adventures were not 'corna' (slang for infidelity) but 'cornetti' (smaller and less serious).[102] Letters from unfaithful women were few though, and while adultery was endemic among men this was still largely accepted as a part of marriage, rather than a threat to it. It seems likely that the 'tide of adultery'

---

[96] See, for example, cases 910 and 911, 1947. Verbali di separazioni coniugali, Tribunale civile e penale di Torino: Mazzi 103–192, Archivio di Stato di Torino.

[97] For example case 825, 1950. The couple married in June 1949. He quickly discovered her infidelity and immediately filed for separation.

[98] On the readership of *Grand Hotel*, see Anna Bravo, *Il fotoromanzo* (Bologna, 2003), p. 81.

[99] Letter from 'Senza speranza 13', *Grand Hotel*, 2 December 1950.

[100] See for example the letter titled 'Chi ha ragione', *Grand Hotel*, 14 February 1955. This reader asked why infidelity was judged differently for men and women, asserting that according modern values both genders should be treated equally.

[101] On the tone and readership of *Grazia*, see Penny Morris, 'A Window on the Private Sphere: Advice Columns, Marriage, and the Evolving Family in 1950s Italy', in *The Italianist*, 27 (2007), pp. 304–32.

[102] 'Coda di cavallo studentessa di filosofia', 20 March 1955; 'Con la dolcezza', 15 July 1955; 'Corna e cornetti', 4 January 1959.

that the Archbishop of Canterbury identified in 1950s England did not threaten Italian marriages in quite the same way, and that the jealousy in Chapter 4 was reflective of deeper and more abstract anxieties rather than anything more concrete.[103]

While male adultery might be tolerated as long as a husband always returned to his wife, did he also have the power to break up a family unit and create another? The answer, in the 1950s, was negative. We saw in the case of Fausto Coppi how he traversed the moral boundaries of his world not through adultery itself but through his intention to leave his wife and begin a new family. While the separation cases demonstrate that men did abandon their families and start new ones, and had indeed done so throughout history, such acts were firmly outside the bounds of respectable, and certainly middle-class, behaviour. New ways of thinking about marriage, grounded in individualism and emotion rather than family, gradually began over time to offer new ways of thinking about second unions. If marriage, moving into the 1960s, was linked to love, it could only last if it was sustained by love. It might begin to follow then that new unions, also built on love, could be formed.

Sophia Loren's long trial by the Italian media, beginning in 1957 and lasting until the mid-1960s, gave some indications about how the conversation about marriage and divorce might begin to change. In October of that year, Loren married her producer Carlo Ponti in Mexico. Already married, Ponti's foreign divorce was not recognized in Italy and the marriage was therefore invalid. Outrage mounted in the press as a private citizen denounced the couple for bigamy and they risked facing trial in Italy should they return. However, although the reaction was similar to that which had faced Coppi and Occhini several years earlier, the language that framed the case was already beginning to change. The diva's mother was reported in one interview as saying 'what else could they do?' as if, rather than being restrained by obligation and respectability, they were driven helplessly by their feelings.[104] The couple had a long road to public acceptance in Italy. Tried for bigamy in absentia in 1960, they annulled their marriage in 1962 and finally remarried in 1965 after Ponti obtained a divorce in France. As the years went on though, Loren was increasingly able to frame her own story not in terms of shame, but of love. She made the couple's love for each other the cornerstone of the respectability and approval she sought for her marriage. Her language was defiant and she did not only challenge the moral codes of the 1950s but help to reshape them in the changing society of the boom. In a 1959 issue of *Grand Hotel* which carried an interview with Loren, the magazine also carried a photo story connecting divorce with romantic love.[105] One character begged

---

[103] Quoted in Langhamer, *The English in Love*, p. 194.
[104] 'Le difficili nozzi di Sophia Loren', *Epoca*, 6 October 1957, pp. 36–40, 40.
[105] 'Ponti-Loren sotto accusa', *Grand Hotel*, 17 January 1959.

her lover to divorce his wife in order to satisfy their love: 'divorce your wife. We'll marry. Only then can we be happy.'[106] This was an unusual step for a magazine which normally towed the Vatican line on morality. With the rise of the companionate marriage, and the increasing emphasis on personal autonomy, love, and fulfilment, the idea that romantic love did not just end single life by way of marriage, but might also propel individuals towards new relationships, was beginning to take hold.

Most Italians could not afford a foreign divorce like Loren and Ponti. Before 1970, the only option facing most couples was that of cohabitation. Common law marriage had been practised long before the twentieth century, and was tolerated particularly well in some regions, such as Emilia-Romagna, where anticlericalism was common among the peasantry and working classes. However, it was still very much beyond the bounds of both respectability and middle-class morality in the 1950s and 1960s. Anna was born in the early 1930s and grew up in Rome.[107] She had an unconventional childhood with a largely absent father and lived quite a liberated life in her early twenties, working and renting an apartment with female friends. However, when, at 25, she met a married man who was separated from his wife, her family was bitterly opposed at first to the new relationship. Defiantly, the couple decided to cohabit after some years together, and in Anna's memoir her choice felt justified by their happiness together.

Livia Colasanti's (Rome, 1937) memoir describes in even greater detail the efforts a co-habiting couple might have to go to in order to give their union the respectability that it lacked in the eyes of society.[108] Livia began work at the age of 15, taking a secretarial training course in the evenings. Her politics were left-wing and she even took part in a trip to Czechoslovakia in the early 1960s organized by a left-wing company 'for propaganda purposes'.[109] In 1957 she met her partner Dario. He was separated and had a child from his marriage. Livia went to live with him in 1964, when she was pregnant with their child, although their relationship ended little more than a year later. Her father had died several years previously and she mused that she would not have had the courage to cohabit had he still been alive. Although Livia's mother and sisters knew the truth, a sham wedding was organized in order to maintain face with the extended family on her father's side. The story was invented that the couple had married just outside Rome in a private ceremony, and a small reception for relatives was organized afterwards in a café on the Tiber. 'Just like in a real wedding, Dario and I even went to Florence on a fake honeymoon afterwards'.[110] In Livia's case, she made it clear that both her immediate family

---

[106] 'Labbre sconosciute', *Grand Hotel*, 17 January 1959.   [107] MP/07.
[108] Livia Colasanti, 'Il sapore della cioccolata', MP/10, ADN.
[109] Livia Colasanti, 'Il sapore della cioccolata'.
[110] Livia Colasanti, 'Il sapore della cioccolata'.

and neighbours knew the reality of her situation; the show was for certain members of the extended family. Moving into the 1960s and 1970s, the tolerance for such second unions did increase gradually. Giuseppina Caravello, who left her husband in 1978 after ten years of marriage, cohabited for four years afterwards with another man. Even living in Sicily in the late 1970s and early 1980s she was able to say that, 'for four years I lived with that man, without thinking about anything, without once thinking that I was an adulterer'.[111] Doubtless the campaign for divorce which culminated in the 1974 referendum contributed to the changing attitudes towards separation and cohabitation.

CONCLUSION

In 1974 over nineteen million Italians and almost 60 per cent of the electorate voted to retain the 1970 Fortuna–Baslini law which provided legal, no-fault divorce.[112] Often cited as a victory of secular Italy over the Catholic Church, or as the event by which Italy proved its 'modernity', it was also the outward signal of a quieter and more gradual revolution in the history of feelings and intimate life.[113] Following the passing of the 1970 law, life did not change overnight for very many Italians. While there were the typical stories of couples finally able to marry after decades of waiting for a divorce, the numbers using the law were not great by European standards. For many of the men and women we have discussed, the decision to separate was a slow-burning one. Since a no-fault divorce could only take place after a separation of five years, it was still by no means a fast or simple solution, and indeed many of the memoirists spoke only of separation, not divorce. What the referendum result did signal was that over the course of the previous two decades, attitudes towards not just divorce, but marriage itself, had changed irrevocably. The significance of the law was not just in the lives it impacted directly, but in the way in which it reshaped how many millions more approached both their own marriages and the notion of marriage itself.

We have already seen how the vocabulary surrounding marriage in the media was shifting quite rapidly from the duty and obligation that characterized Fausto Coppi's attitude both to his wife and his mistress, to Sophia Loren's defiant proclamations of the power of love. By the mid-1960s, modern consumerist society was providing yet another lens through which to view and measure marriage: that of satisfaction, happiness, and pleasure. In 1966

---

[111] Giuseppina Caravello, 'Storia di una vita tutta sbagliata'.
[112] Seymour, *Debating Divorce*, p. 221.
[113] Lussana, *L'Italia del divorzio* and Seymour, *Debating Divorce*.

readers of *Annabella* magazine were asked whether happiness in marriage was important to them, a question which would have been unthinkable a decade earlier.[114] A majority—and slightly more women than men—answered in the affirmative, valuing personal happiness over the more abstract good of marriage. Actress Anna Maria Guarnieri echoed the sentiments of many *Annabella* readers when she said 'marriage must be pleasurable, otherwise it is better to continue working and living alone'.[115] Such attitudes only had meaning once marriage was beginning to be a choice rather than a necessity for women. The idea that marriage should be freely entered into, and if necessary exited, was a strong part of the commentary around the Fortuna bill in 1966, although it had been unthinkable a decade earlier. Several of the letters to *ABC* magazine, where Loris Fortuna first launched his proposal, stated that the writer would not marry until the law was changed to permit divorce. The idea of marrying for romantic love, pushed so strongly in the 1950s when Italians (and especially women) had little choice about whether to marry or not, paradoxically made the strongest argument against lifelong marriage.

We have also seen that contrary to the Catholic and Christian Democrat perception of divorce as a tool to be callously used by men against women, it was overwhelmingly women who made the decision to leave their marriages. Men seldom seemed to take the initiative in ending a marriage and often wrote of much stronger negative emotions when their marriages broke up. Women tended to write of separation in more ambivalent terms, and made the decision to end a marriage for many different reasons. In the separation files, we saw how many women went to court out of necessity, in order to be able to provide for their families or prevent an abusive spouse from living in the family home. When it came to the memoirs, the majority wrote not of violence and abuse but of love gone sour. The fact that romantic love featured so strongly in their accounts of courtship and early marriage suggests that the companionate marriage was difficult to realize in a society where men and women were far from equal. None of this is to suggest that separation was an easy path for women to take, and well into the 1970s theirs would have been difficult and marginal experiences. It seems that for the few, exceptional women who wrote of marriage breakdown and separation in the 1960s, 1970s, and even into the 1980s, romantic love led them into marriage, while it was the politics of feminism as well as the more concrete experience of work that provided them with a path out again.

---

[114] Lietta Tuornabuoni, 'Lei e lui oggi in Italia', *Annabella*, 20 January 1966, pp. 23–9.
[115] 'Lei e lui oggi in Italia', p. 27.

Conclusion: Individuals, Families, and Nation

> At the age of 58, I decided to write my diary [*sic*] even though all these years have passed and also so that my memory did not deceive me and so it is that since the past has not been quite so sparkling for me, I wanted to relive the days of my youth. [...] we lived in Castiglione Alto where all the families were like ours that is large and poor, because in those times we were all the same.[1]

This is how Laura Massini began her handwritten memoir in 1988, after almost sixty years of living in the small Tuscan seaside village of Castiglione della Pescaia. Laura's rural girlhood was characterized by hardship, work, and cramped living conditions but also by fashion, dancing, swimming, and sewing bikinis. As we saw in previous chapters, her youth came to an end with her marriage in 1950, hastened by pressure from her parents who struggled to provide for their large family, and by Laura's own fear of remaining a spinster at 20. Material circumstances did not improve immediately following the wedding as Laura's husband, a wounded war veteran, struggled to find work and the couple could not afford their own home for some time. Laura was obliged to work as a farm hand throughout her pregnancy and early mother-hood in order to support the family, until her husband found work in Genoa as a seasonal migrant.

By the early 1960s, Laura's village was itself beginning to be transformed by the economic miracle into a bustling seaside resort and local work finally became available. In 1965 the couple began to manage a bar, opening their own restaurant in 1968. The couple were able to move into a modern apartment with their daughter and to acquire those coveted objects of the boom: a car and a television. These later years of Laura's memoir, narrated at a breathless pace, are an almost continual description of work, and indeed Laura was writing at a time when she was supposed to be resting, due to exhaustion and ill health. Although she and her husband did benefit materially from the

---

[1] Laura Massini, 'Domani è un altro giorno', MP/91, ADN.

economic miracle, her relentless pace of work was geared towards helping her daughter to achieve a better life than she herself had had. There was not much time in her life to reflect on love or happiness in her marriage, and the ambivalence she felt towards her marriage was only teased out through some linguistic detective work. Neither did Laura ever leave her village for Italy's cities, making her less likely to encounter new ideas or have the collective experience of work that some women had in later life, although the economic boom did come to her through tourism.

With such a strong focus on work, for survival and later material improvement, there was perhaps no real space in her life for dissatisfaction to develop either. In this sense Laura's experience was in stark contrast to the memoirs of the women who married during the late 1950s and 1960s for love and companionship, only to be plunged into a domestic isolation which they were schooled to view as a privilege. We have seen in the memoirs that the women who married in the 1960s were much more likely to write about dissatisfaction or lack of love in their courtship and marriage, while the women who married in the 1950s tended to mention love as a seamless, barely examined component of their stories. This was despite the fact that those marrying in the 1960s were more likely to have had some discretion in choosing their partner, in contrast to those who married in the previous decade, often under pressure from family either to marry quickly or to marry the right suitor. Of course, even those women who chose their marriages did not always marry for love. Several of the women who married in the 1960s were quite candid in their admission that they had married to escape parental influence and establish an independent life rather than for love. Others felt pressured into continuing with courtships that their hearts were never, or were no longer fully, in. In retrospect some might also have been able to detect in their memoirs what their younger selves did not realize was missing in the relationship. Arranged marriages did still happen in the 1960s, although we have seen how the boundaries between arranged marriages and love matches were not always clearly defined.

As time went on, there was certainly much greater reflection about love in the women's accounts, and when held up against personal experiences and feelings, romantic ideals almost always fell short. Although not always reflected in their life choices, ideas about love and romance are nonetheless present in the personal writings of these women. In some cases these disappointed expectations might become the germ of a later decision to end the marriage. The diaries and memoirs are in this way a window onto a quiet, gradual transformation of feelings, attitudes, and expectations. This transformation began in the raised expectations of life and love that were brought by the economic miracle, and by focusing on intimate life this study has pushed us to redraw the parameters of societal change: the seeds of the divorce referendum were sown long before the 1970s.

These subtle changes in attitudes and feelings from the 1950s to the 1970s were less easy to detect in the memoirs and diaries of Italian men, who as we saw were much more likely to be open and candid about feelings of love, attraction, and passion than were the women. This was doubtless due to the distinct manner in which men and women each came to marriage, with men generally experienced and worldly, while women tended to be younger and often still lived at home. It is also important to remember that in a society where marriage and motherhood was the only path open to most women, economic security had to be considered in addition to or ahead of love. In addition, these gendered differences spoke to the greater freedoms that men had within marriage. We saw how men were much less likely to ask for a separation or divorce than women, and conversely more likely to write about loss and pain in relation to marriage breakdown if their partner did leave them. Their lives were evidently not defined by marriage in the same way as was a woman's, but it was clear from the men's memoirs and diaries that men did very often make a huge emotional investment in their marriage. It may also be that since marriage was not so closely linked to practical and financial matters for men as for women, men were more able to dwell on the emotional side of courtship and marriage. Although their movements and life choices were not as restricted as those of women, men were still under considerable pressure to conform to certain standards of masculinity, and this could be seen most clearly in men's discussions of sexuality in courtship. The tropes of masculinity so artfully ridiculed by Marcello Mastrioanni in the 1960 film, *Bell'Antonio* still very much informed 1950s and 1960s courtship. Just as women were pressured to resist pre-marital intimacy, men were expected to demand it.[2] These attitudes and sometimes quasi-formulaic exchanges can be seen in the advice columns as in memoirs and diaries of courtship. The examination of jealousy also revealed just how much ideas of manliness and romance were bound up with masculine control and possessiveness. Of course not all men conformed to this model of aggressive virility, and the two dominant sub-cultures of the post-war years, Catholicism and Communism, offered men in particular a sort of emotional refuge from dominant ideas of manliness.[3] Religious men wrote of pride in remaining virgins until marriage, and deepening spiritual love which first replaced and later enhanced their sexual relationships, while communist men were more likely to write about equal partnership and mutual agreement in relation to sexual and other matters.

While ideas about love, gender, and marriage were absorbed from politics and religion as from films, magazines, and television, the dominant influence

---

[2] Mauro Bolognini, *Bell'Antonio* (1960).
[3] This concept is succinctly outlined by William Reddy in his roundtable interview with Jan Plamper: 'The History of Emotions: An Interview with William Reddy, Barbara Rosenwein, and Peter Stearns', *History and Theory*, 49:2 (2010), pp. 237–65, 244–6.

in most of the memoirs and diaries was always that of family. Even those who acted in opposition to family—whether marrying young to defy parental ambitions for them or eloping because of parental disapproval—still had their experiences defined in some respect by family. Those men and women who struggled with obstacles to love, whether illness or class difference, found that objections came from the family of their intended, and as we saw, were usually respected. What was changing was how people defined themselves in relation to their families over the course of the economic miracle period. We can see this particularly in relation to women, whose lives tended to be much more closely intertwined with family until their marriage than were the lives of men. Some of the women marrying in the late 1940s and 1950s, like Laura Massini, found it difficult to articulate both their own feelings and a sense of agency separate from their parents' wishes, even writing decades after the events. A decade later we saw how Lauretta Cavinato, pressured into an arranged marriage by her family, was very definite in her own mind about not wanting the marriage, even though she did not actively resist the path chosen by her parents.

The transformations wrought by the economic miracle did not simply result in Italian society becoming more individualized and families diminishing in importance. Any observer of twenty-first-century Italy would know this simple binary could not be true for the 1960s. Parents themselves strategized to enable their children to move away from the land and enjoy a more modern, affluent lifestyle than they themselves had. We can see this in Lauretta's experience of arranged marriage in 1960: her suitor was chosen precisely because he had a good job in Turin's FIAT factory and therefore offered her a chance to escape her rural Venetian background.[4] Neither did her marriage look like an arranged marriage from the outside. Lauretta had a three-year long-distance engagement during which she exchanged regular letters with her fiancé, like so many other girls whose intended had migrated to the city. To the casual observer of the time, hers may well have appeared like a more modern courtship than it was. Rather than individuals always striking out on their own to reap the benefits of the miracle, families could work together to ensure what parents saw as the best outcome for their children. Indeed, we can see the beginnings of what Ginsborg identifies as the 'long, thin' family of late twentieth- and twenty-first-century Italy—characterized by closeness and cooperation between the generations and fewer children—beginning to take shape in these years.[5] It was still usual in many regions, particularly the traditional sharecropping regions of northern and central Italy, for the different generations to live together after marriage, and this did not necessarily

---

[4] Lauretta Cavinato, 'Cocco e il fratello', MP/02, ADN.

[5] Paul Ginsborg, *Italy and its Discontents: Family, Civil Society, State 1980–2001* (London, 2001), p. 74.

change with migration. Lauretta and her husband lived with his parents in Turin for a time, while other urban families wrote of adapting homes or making living arrangements on the basis of sharing with parents or in-laws. In Laura Massini's memoir we can see how her continual work ethic was motivated by the drive to give her daughter, the only child she mentions, a better life than she herself had, and the latter years of her life were spent caring for her only grandchild. Although the relationship of men and women to their families did shift and adapt over time, with individual feelings and actions assuming greater importance, it remained difficult to escape the pervasive nature of the Italian family.

Indeed, we saw how the greatest symbol of the power of feelings in 1960s Italy—Franca Viola's famous 'no' in 1965—was in reality due largely to the role played by her family. Without the support of her father Franca Viola would very likely not have been able to remain firm in her refusal, and we saw how her decision to 'follow her feelings' was partly articulated through her father. The sad case of Carmelina Torrisi, who some years later was pressured by members of her family into accepting a marriage with her attacker, points to the centrality of family even after the historic example set by Franca Viola. Without the support of her parents, Carmelina Torrisi's feelings were worth very little to the media or to the state. We can also see once again how Sicilian families were not the simple bulwarks of tradition that might have been assumed. It could be said that in 1965 and 1966 it was the Viola family rather than Franca as such who advanced the cause for the transformation of feeling in modern Sicilian society. Families could adapt, support, and even encourage new customs, and mores but decisions were still made with the family interest firmly in mind.

At the same time, the Franca Viola case forced the messy issues of gender relations and masculinity, love, and domestic violence out of the intimate world of families, homes, and couples and into the public realms of the courtroom, the media, politics, and the law. By the mid-1960s, the economic miracle had transformed Italy from a poor, rural country recovering from its fascist past into an urban, industrial nation. The international branding of Italian food, film, and fashion, combined with the economic strength of the boom, gave Italy the self-confidence to project itself on the international stage as a modern, European nation. The confrontation with the realities of forced marriage and sexual violence in Sicily brought Italians face to face with the remote, southernmost tip of their territory. A region historically cast as dark, impenetrable, and backward, Sicily seemed to many Italians of the 1960s almost African in contrast to the European gaze of the modern nation.[6]

---

[6] John Dickie, *Darkest Italy: The Nation and Stereotypes of the Mezzogiorno 1860–1900* (London, 1999); Nelson Moe, *The View from Vesuvius: Italian Culture and the Southern Question* (Berkeley, CA, 2005).

For the Italian press, Filippo Melodia became the embodiment of this dark and violent southern masculinity, itself an idea with a long history both in Italian culture and in the travellers' accounts of Northern Europeans. The language used to describe the case spoke of darkness and distance: both the crime and the culture surrounding it were quasi-African, medieval, and backward. In an Italy which saw itself as modern, progressive, and European this was not casual language. Neither were its implications entirely abstract. It was the language of a nation which struggled to understand the southern migrants who now populated its northern cities and fuelled the economy of the boom.[7] By distancing Melodia's crime from 1960s Italy in both time and space, the press was excluding certain groups from the shared imaginary space of the national community.[8] We can see from the case of Franca Viola just how much the boundaries of what was acceptable in the modern nation were policed in the language of the emotions. In this way it is clear how ideas about national character might be bound up with feelings and how closely national communities might overlap with emotional communities.

In our exploration of jealousy, we saw how the feelings and behaviour that informed Filippo Melodia's behaviour towards Franca Viola were by no means confined to Sicily or southern Italy. They were in fact closely entangled with what was understood as jealousy in post-war Italy. Encompassing love and control, passion and possession, *gelosia* seemed to combine much of the behaviour associated with the idea of family honour on the one hand, and with both new and old ideas of romantic love on the other. Post-war Italy had a curious and contradictory relationship with jealousy. Proclaimed in popular culture as the affirmation of true love and a driver of passion, it also made people uncomfortable in certain times and places. Some maintained that a certain amount of jealousy was necessary and good, but care was needed so that healthy, measured jealousy did not turn into excessive jealousy, manifesting itself as illness and madness. Other groups, particularly young Italians, feminists, and 1968 radicals, sought to distance themselves from jealousy altogether because it did not fit with their ideas about modern love, sexuality, and gender relations. A slippery foe, jealousy was not so easy to eradicate. Despite the efforts of the 1968 generation to separate sex from feelings and love from possession, *Annabella* magazine observed that jealousy was on the rise in 1974 while popular films of the 1970s half-seriously rehashed the old tropes.[9] Clearly the feelings, attitudes, and behaviour that allowed honour crime and forced marriages to happen in modern Italy were not confined to

---

[7] Goffredo Fofi, *L'Immigrazione meridionale a Torino* (Milan, 1964).

[8] Benedict Anderson, *Imagined Communities: Reflections on the Origins and Spread of Nationalism* (London, 1983).

[9] Ettore Scola, *Dramma della gelosia: Tutti i particolari in cronaca/Jealousy, Italian Style*, 1970; Mauro Severino, *Amore vuol dire gelosia*, 1974.

the southern margins of the nation but persisted both in people's minds and in national culture. The year 1981 finally saw the legal abandonment of the idea of honour, and the outlawing of the so-called reparatory marriage. The lingering presence of jealousy in late twentieth-century Italian culture reminds us that feelings are rather more difficult to govern than legal codes and customs might allow. An examination of how Italians wrote and spoke about love, honour, and jealousy from the late 1940s to the 1970s is also a salient reminder of just how closely interlinked the sphere of intimate life was with the public sphere of law, media, politics, and the nation.

What this book has done is to place the personal, the intimate, and the emotional at the heart of the story of Italy's transformation during the 'economic miracle' years, showing how the lives of young Italians were shaped by changing understandings of love, marriage, masculinity, and family. New expectations of love and marriage in youth also coloured actual experiences of marriage, leading in some cases to dissatisfaction and even separation. The thoughts, feelings, choices, and experiences of individuals are at the heart of this story, although despite the growing emphasis on individual choice and feeling in films, magazines, novels, and newspapers, most continued to see their own feelings as bound up with the interests and welfare of their families. Even though the focus of the book has been on intimate life, from the arguments, discussions, and debates happening in courtrooms and in parliament, and as reported in newspapers, magazines, films, and television, it is equally clear that the personal and the emotional were intrinsically bound up in the life and self-image of the nation. Love and its darker companions, honour and jealousy, with their myriad and shifting meanings, had deep personal significance, but were at the same time intimately connected to late twentieth-century Italy itself.

Educational Attainment of First-person Writers (National Diary Archive Sample Set)

Men and women are charted separately since gender often dictated educational opportunities; training to become an elementary school teacher was a typically feminine career path, while men were more likely to undertake vocational or technical training. One of the men and three of the women also reported completing middle school education in later life; here they are counted as having an elementary school education as this was the qualification relevant up to early adulthood.

Qualification	Men	Women
Elementary school (3 years)	1	3
Elementary school (4 years)	0	1
Completed elementary school (5 years)	7	8
Elementary school (unclear if completed)	3	6
Lower middle school	8	9
Upper middle school	10	11
Liceo (classical secondary school), first 2 years	2	0
Liceo (completed)	2	3
Scuola magistrale (qualification to teach elementary school)	0	8
Vocational/technical education	7	4
Post-elementary schooling (undefined)	1	2
University attendance	1	2
University degree	11	24
Total	53	81

First-person Writers by Father's Profession
(National Diary Archive Sample Set)

Father's profession	Women	Men
Peasant	12	9
Manual labourer/working class	4	5
Artisan/skilled labourer	2	2
Commercial	5	1
Professional	5	7
Nobility	2	0
Total	30	24

A further five women and two men described coming from a rural peasant background, while four men described their background as an urban working-class one, four women mentioned an affluent family background, and four women a middle-class one, even though the father's profession was not named. At least three writers were brought up in religious institutions, either orphaned or abandoned.

Bibliography

Unpublished Primary Sources

Archivio Nazionale del Diario, Pieve Santo Stefano, Tuscany.
Files on personal separation cases, Tribunale civile e penale di Torino, Archivio di Stato di Torino.
UDI Archive (Unione Donne in Italia), Rome.

Published Primary Sources

Memoirs
Giovanna Cavallo, *Ho sognato i suoi occhi* (Milan, 1996).
Stefano Indrio, *Amatucci* (Ragusa, 2007).
Amalia Molinelli, *I pensieri vagabondi di Amalia* (Milan, 2002).
Luisa Puliti, *È nato un bambino di sesso femminile* (Viterbo, 1994).
Giuseppe Rigoni, *I Lunghi viaggi della speranza* (Brescia, 2015).

Newspapers
Corriere della Sera.
Giornale della Sicilia.
Il Mattino.
Il Resto del Carlino.
L'Ora.
L'Unita.
La Nazione.
La Stampa.

Magazines
ABC.
Annabella.
Arianna.
Effe.
Epoca.
Famiglia Cristiana.
Grand Hotel.
Grazia.
L'Espresso.
Tempo.

Other
Annuario Statistico Italiano.
Guido Baglioni, *I giovani nella societa industriale: Ricerca sociologica condotta in una zona dell'Italia del nord* (Milan, 1962).
Paolo Braghin (ed.), *Inchiesta sulla miseria in Italia* (Turin, 1978).

Ernesto De Martino, *La terra del rimorso* (Milan, 1961).

Ernesto De Martino, *Sud e magia* (Milan, 2012). First edition 1959; English translation: *Magic: A Theory from the South* (Chicago, 2015).

Goffredo Fofi, *L'Immigrazione meridionale a Torino* (Milan, 1964).

Charlotte Gower Chapman, *Milocca: A Sicilian Village* (London, 1973).

Lieta Harrison, *Le svergognate* (Rome, 1963); English translation: *The Wantons: A Searing Study of the Humiliation of Women in Modern Sicily* (London, 1966).

Lieta Harrison, *L'Iniziazione: Come le adolescenti diventano donne* (Milan, 1966).

Roberto Leydi, *Canti popolari italiani* (Milan, 1984).

Roberto Leydi (ed.), *Le tradizioni popolari in Italia: Canti e musiche popolari* (Milan, 1990).

Lorenzo Milani, Esperienze pastorali (Florence, 1957).

Brizio Montinaro (ed.), *Canti di pianto e dell'amore dell'antico Salento* (Bologna, 2000).

Gabriella Parca (ed.), *Le Italiane si confessano* (Florence, 1959).

Luisa Passerini, *Autoritratto di gruppo* (Florence, 1988); English translation: *Autobiography of a Generation* (Middletown, CT, 1996).

Julian Pitt Rivers, *People of the Sierra* (London, 1954).

Nuto Revelli, *Il mondo dei vinti: Testimonianze di vita contadina* (Turin, 1977).

Nuto Revelli, L'anello forte. *La donna: storie di vita contadina* (Turin, 1985).

Angela Sorgato, *Tu, io e il nostro amore* (Milan, 1971).

<https://secondhandsongs.com/performance/463879/versions>.

<http://bandaroncati.wiki.contaminati.net/index.php/Tango_della_Gelosia>.

Literary Sources

Dante Alighieri, *Vita Nova* (1295), translated by Andrew Frisardi (Evanston, IL, 2002).

Vittorio Brancati, *Il bell'Antonio* (Mondadori: Milan, 1949).

Dino Buzzati, *Un amore* (Milan, 1963).

Natalia Ginzburg, *Voices in the Evening* (London, 1963). Italian edition 1961.

Alberto Moravia, *La Romana* (Milan, 1947).

Vasco Pratolini, *Cronache di poveri amanti* (Florence, 1946).

Films

Adua e le compagne/Adua and Friends (Antonio Pietrangeli, 1960).

Amore vuol dire gelosia (Mauro Severino, 1974): 'Love Means Jealousy', no English title.

Bell'Antonio (Mauro Bolognini, 1960).

Belle ma poveri/Pretty but Poor (Dino Risi, 1958).

Bread, Love and Jealousy (Luigi Comencini, 1954).

Comizi d'amore/Love Meetings (Pier Paolo Pasolini, 1965).

Divorce, Italian Style (Pietro Germi, 1961).

Dramma della gelosia. Tutti i particolari in cronaca/Jealousy, Italian Style (Ettore Scola, 1970).

Girl with a Gun (Mario Monicelli, 1968).

Girl with the Red Scarf (Atif Yilmaz, 1978).

Jealousy (Pietro Germi, 1953).
The Magnificent Cuckold (Antonio Pietrangeli, 1964).
Marriage, Italian Style (Vittorio De Sica, 1964).
La mia signora/My Wife (Tinto Brass, Mauro Bolognini, and Luigi Comencini, 1964).
The Most Beautiful Wife (Damiano Damiani, 1970).
Poor Millionaires (Dino Risi, 1959).
Poveri ma belli/A Girl in Bikini (Dino Risi, 1957).
Rocco and His Brothers (Luchino Visconti, 1960).
Seduced and Abandoned (Pietro Germi, 1964).

Secondary Literature

Percy Allum, 'Uniformity Undone: Aspects of Catholic Culture in Post-war Italy', in Zygmunt Baranski and Robert Lumley (eds), *Culture and Conflict in Post-war Italy: Essays on Mass and Popular Culture* (London, 1990), pp. 79–96.
Benedict Anderson, *Imagined Communities: Reflections on the Origins and Spread of Nationalism* (London, 1983).
Enrica Asquer, *Storia intima dei ceti medi: Una capitale e una periferia nell'Italia del miracolo economico* (Rome, 2011).
Anna Badino, *Tutte a casa? Donne tra migrazione e lavoro nella Torino degli anni Sessanta* (Turin, 2008).
Beth Bailey, *From Front Porch to Back Seat: Courtship in Twentieth Century America* (Baltimore, MD, 1988).
Louis Bayman, *The Operatic and the Everyday: Post-war Italian Film Melodrama* (Edinburgh, 2014).
Masha Belenky, *The Anxiety of Dispossession: Jealousy in Nineteenth-century French Culture* (Lewisburg, 2008).
Rudolph M. Bell, *Fate, Honor, Family and Village: Demographic and Cultural Change in Rural Italy since 1800* (Chicago, 1979).
Sandro Bellasai, *La morale comunista: Pubblico e privato nella rappresentazione del Pci (1947–1956)* (Rome, 2001).
Sandro Bellassai, *La mascolinità contemporanea* (Milan, 2004).
Sandro Bellassai, 'The Masculine Mystique: Antimodernism and Virility in Fascist Italy', *Journal of Modern Italian Studies*, 10 (2005), pp. 314–35.
Lorenzo Benadusi, *The Enemy of the New Man: Homosexuality in Fascist Italy* (Madison, WI, 2012).
Richard Bessell and Dirk Schumann (eds), *Life after Death: Approaches to the Social and Cultural History of Europe During the 1940s and 1950s* (Cambridge, 2003).
Paul Betts, *Within Walls: Private Life in the German Democratic Republic* (Oxford, 2010).
Piero Bevilacqua, *Breve storia dell'Italia meridionale dall'ottocento a oggi* (Rome, 1993).
R. Howard Bloch, *Medieval Misogyny and the Invention of Western Romantic Love* (Chicago, 1991).
Anton Blok, *Mafia of a Sicilian Village: A Study of Violent Peasant Entrepreneurs* (Oxford, 1974).
Peter Bondanella, *A History of Italian Cinema* (London, 2009).

Richard Bosworth, *Mussolini: A Biography* (London, 2010).

Maud Bracke, *Women and the Reinvention of the Political: Feminism in Italy, 1968–1983* (London, 2014).

Anna Bravo, *A colpi di cuore. Storie del sessantotto* (Rome, 2008).

Sonia Cancian, *Families, Lovers and their Letters: Italian Postwar Migration to Canada* (Winnipeg, 2010).

Eva Cantarella, 'Homocides of Honour: The Development of Italian Adultery Law over Two Milennia', in David Kertzer and Richard Saller (eds), *The Family in Italy from Antiquity to the Present* (New Haven, CT, 1991), pp. 229–44.

Carlo Carotti, *Le donne, la famiglia, il lavoro nel cinema di Pietro Germi* (Milan, 2011).

Maria Casalini, *Famiglie comuniste: Ideologie e vita quotidiana nell'Italia degli anni '50* (Bologna, 2010).

Maria Casalini, 'The Family, Sexual Morality and Gender Identity in the Communist Tradition in Italy (1921–1956)', *Modern Italy*, 13:3 (2013), pp. 229–44.

Franco Cassano, *Il pensiero meridiano* (Rome, 2007).

Natasha Chang, *Shaping the New Woman: Body Politics and the New Woman in Fascist Italy* (Toronto, 2015).

Nancy Chodorow, *The Power of Feelings* (New Haven, CT, 1999).

Catriona Clear, *Women's Voices in Ireland: Women's Magazines in the 1950s and 1960s* (London, 2016).

Rebecca Clifford, 'Emotions and Gender in Oral History: Narrating Italy's 1968', *Modern Italy*, 17:2 (2012), pp. 209–21.

Rebecca Clifford, Robert Gildea, and Anette Warring, 'Gender and Sexuality', in Robert Gildea et al. (eds), *Europe's 1968: Voices of Revolt* (Oxford, 2013), pp. 239–57.

Guido Crainz, *Storia del miracolo economico: Culture, identità, trasformazioni* (Rome, 2005).

Niamh Cullen, 'Morals, Modern Identities and the Catholic Woman: Fashion in *Famiglia Cristiana*, 1954–1968', *Journal of Modern Italian Studies*, 18:1 (2013), pp. 33–52.

Niamh Cullen, 'Changing Landscapes of the Emotions? *Grand Hotel* and Representations of Love and Courtship', *Cultural and Social History*, 11:2 (2014), pp. 285–306.

Niamh Cullen, 'The Case of Franca Viola: Debating Gender, Nation and Modernity in 1960s Italy', *Contemporary European History*, 16:1 (2016), pp. 97–115.

Maria Rosa Cutrufelli, Elena Doni, Paola Gaglianone et al., *Il novecento delle italiane: una storia ancora da raccontare* (Rome, 2002).

Elisa Danese, 'Costumi sessuali e genere femminile nell'Italia degli anni sessanta: Inchieste cinematografiche e televisive', *Storia e futuro*, 13 (2007).

John Davis, *Land and Family in Pisticci* (London, 1973).

John Davis, 'Family and State', in David Gilmore (ed.), *Honour, Shame and the Unity of the Mediterranean* (Washington DC, 1987), pp. 22–34.

Ernesto de Cristofaro, 'Retorica forense e valori della comunità: Questioni d'onore in alcuni processi siciliani', in Francesco Migliorini and Giacomo Pace (eds), *Gravina, Cultura e tecnica forense tra dimensione siciliana e vocazione europea* (Bologna, 2013), pp. 371–410.

Michela de Giorgio, *Le Italiane dall'Unità ad oggi* (Rome, 1992).

Victoria de Grazia, *How Fascism Ruled Women* (Berkeley, CA, 2000).

Patrizia de Landi, '"La rivista ideale della donna italiana": I primi passi di "Grazia" tra innovazione e informazone', in Raffaelle de Berti and Irene Piazzoni (eds), *Forme e modelli del rotocalco italiano tra fascismo e guerra* (Milan, 2009).

John Dickie, *Darkest Italy: The Nation and Stereotypes of the Mezzogiorno 1860–1900* (London, 1999).

John Dickie, *Cosa Nostra: A History of the Sicilian Mafia* (London, 2004).

John Dickie, *Delizia! The Epic History of Italians and their Food* (London, 2010).

Jenny Diski, *The Sixties* (London, 2009).

Thomas Dixon, *From Passions to Emotions: The Creation of a Secular Psychological Category* (Cambridge, 2003).

Christopher Duggan, *Fascist Voices: An Intimate History of Mussolini's Italy* (London, 2012).

Carol Dyhouse, *Heartthrobs: A History of Women and Desire* (Oxford, 2017).

Mary Evans, *Missing Persons: The Impossibility of Auto/biography* (London, 1999).

Nicola Figlioli, *Dal caso Viola al delitto d'onore: le grandi svolte degli anni '60 viste dai giornali* (Tesi di laurea: Palermo, 2004).

Sarah Fishman, *From Vichy to the Sexual Revolution: Gender and Family Life in Postwar France* (Oxford, 2017).

John Foot, *Pedalare, Pedalare: A History of Italian Cycling* (London, 2012).

David Forgacs, 'Sex in the Cinema: Regulation and Transgression in Italian Films, 1930–1943', in Jacqueline Reich and Piero Garofalo (eds), *Re-viewing Fascism: Italian Cinema, 1922–1943* (Bloomington, IN, 2002), pp. 141–72.

David Forgacs, *Italy's Margins: Social Exclusion and Nation Formation Since 1861* (Cambridge, 2013).

David Forgacs and Stephen Gundle, *Mass Culture and Italian Society from Fascism to the Cold War* (Bloomington, IN, 2007).

Mauro Forno, *La stampa del ventennio: Strutture e trasformazioni nello stato totalitario* (Soveria Mannelli, 2005).

Eros Francescangeli, 'The Bride in Red: Morality and Private Relationships in the Italian Revolutionary Left—the Case of the Maoist group Servire il popolo', *European Review of History: Revue européenne d'histoire*, 22:1 (2015), pp. 101–19.

Ute Frevert, *Emotions in History: Lost and Found* (Budapest, 2011).

Rachel Fuchs, *Contested Paternity: Constructing Families in Modern France* (Baltimore, MD, 2008).

Stefano Gallo, *Senza attraversare le frontiere: Le migrazioni interne dall'Unità a oggi* (Rome, 2012).

Benno Gammerl, 'Emotional Styles: Concepts and Challenges', *Rethinking History: Special Issue on Emotional Styles*, 16:2 (2012), pp. 161–75.

Diana Garvin, 'Singing Truth to Power: Melodic Resistance and Bodily Revolt in Italy's Rice Fields', *Annali d'Italianistica*, 34 (2016), pp. 373–400.

Anthony Giddens, *The Transformation of Intimacy: Sexuality, Love and Eroticism in Modern Societies* (London, 1993).

Robert Gildea, James Mark, and Anette Warring (eds), *Europe's 1968: Voices of Revolt* (Oxford, 2013), pp. 239–57.

David Gilmore (ed.), *Honor and Shame and the Unity of the Mediterranean* (Washington, DC, 1987).

Paul Ginsborg, *A History of Contemporary Italy, 1943–1980* (London, 1990).

Paul Ginsborg, *Family Politics: Domestic Life, Devastation and Survival 1900–1950* (New Haven, CT, 2014).

Maureen Giovannini, 'Female Chastity Codes', in David Gilmore (ed.), *Honour, Shame and the Unity of the Mediterranean* (Washington, DC, 1987), pp. 61–74.

Robert Gordon, *Forms of Subjectivity* (Oxford, 1996).

Leo Goretti, '"Un posto che gl'andava a morire": Genere e generazioni nella fine della mezzadria in Toscana', *Zapruder*, 26 (2011), pp. 44–58.

Leo Goretti, 'Irma Bandiera and Maria Goretti: Gender Role Models for Communist Girls in Italy (1945–56)', *Twentieth Century Communism*, 4:4 (2012), pp. 14–37.

Naomi Greene, *Pier Paolo Pasolini, Cinema as Heresy* (Princeton, NJ, 1992).

Stephen Gundle, *Bellissima: Feminine Beauty and the Idea of Italy* (London, 2007).

Stephen Gundle, *Death and the Dolce Vita: The Dark Side of Rome in the 1950s* (Edinburgh, 2011).

Alana Harris, 'Love Divine and Love Sublime: The Catholic Marriage Advisory Council, the National Marriage Guidance Movement and the State', in Alana Harris and Timothy Jones (eds), *Love and Romance in Britain, 1918–1970* (London, 2015), pp. 188–224.

Ruth Harris, *Murders and Madness: Medicine, Law and Society in the Fin de Siècle* (Oxford, 1989).

Ulrich Herbert and Karin Hunn, 'Guest Workers and Policy on Guest Workers in the Federal Republic: From the Beginning of Recruitment in 1955 until its Halt in 1973', in Hanna Schissler (ed.), *The Miracle Years: A Cultural History of West Germany, 1949–1968* (Princeton, 2001), pp. 187–218.

Dagmar Herzog, *Sex after Fascism: Memory and Morality in Twentieth Century Germany* (Princeton, NJ, 2007).

Dagmar Herzog, *Sexuality in Europe: A Twentieth Century History* (Cambridge, 2011).

Danielle Hipkins, *Italy's Other Women: Gender and Prostitution in Italian Cinema, 1940–1965* (Oxford, 2016).

David Kertzer, *Comrades and Christians: Religion and Political Struggle in Communist Italy* (Cambridge, 1980).

Marcia Landy, *Folklore of Consensus: Theatricality in the Italian Cinema, 1930–1943* (Albany, NY, 1998).

Claire Langhamer, 'Adultery in Post-war England', *History Workshop Journal*, 62:1 (2006), pp. 86–115.

Claire Langhamer, 'Love and Courtship in Mid-twentieth Century England', *Historical Journal*, 50:1 (2007), pp. 173–96.

Claire Langhamer, 'Love, Selfhood and Authenticity in Post-war Britain', *Cultural and Social History*, 9:12 (2012), pp. 277–97.

Claire Langhamer, *The English in Love: The Intimate Story of an Emotional Revolution* (Oxford, 2013).

Robert Lumley, *States of Emergency: Cultures of Revolt in Italy from 1968 to 1978* (London, 1990).

Fiamma Lussana, *L'Italia del divorzio: La battaglia fra stato, Chiesa e gente comune, 1946–1974* (Rome, 2014).

Martyn Lyons, *The Writing Culture of Ordinary People in Europe, c. 1860–1920* (Cambridge, 2013).

Martyn Lyons, 'Questo cor che tuo si rese': The Private and the Public in Italian Women's Love Letters in the Long Nineteenth Century', *Modern Italy*, 19:4 (2014), pp. 355–68.

Millicent Marcus, *Italian Film in the Light of Neorealism* (Princeton NJ, 1986).

Mary Jo Maynes, *Taking the Hard Road: Life Course in French and German Workers' Autobiographies in the Era of Industrialisation* (Chapel Hill, 1995).

Mary Jo Maynes et al., *Telling Stories: The Use of Personal Narratives in the Social Sciences and History* (Ithaca, NY, 2008).

Kevin McAleer, *Dueling: The Cult of Honor in Fin-de-Siècle Germany* (Princeton, NJ, 1997).

Patrick McCarthy, 'The Church in Post War Italy', in Patrick McCarthy (ed.), *Italy Since 1945* (Oxford, 2000), pp. 133–52.

Josie McLellan, *Love in the Time of Communism: Intimacy and Sexuality in the GDR* (Cambridge, 2011).

Piero Melograni (ed.), *La famiglia italiana dall'ottocento ad oggi* (Rome, 1988).

Nelson Moe, *The View from Vesuvius: Italian Culture and the Southern Question* (Berkeley, CA, 2005).

Beatrice Monroy, *Niente ci fu* (Molfetta, 2012).

Penny Morris (ed.), *Women in Italy 1945–60: An Interdisciplinary Study* (New York, 2006).

Penny Morris, 'A Window on the Private Sphere: Advice Columns, Marriage and the Evolving Family in 1950s Italy', *The Italianist*, 27:2 (2007), pp. 304–32.

Penny Morris, 'Feminism and Emotion: Love and the Couple in the Magazine Effe', *Italian Studies*, 68:3 (2013), pp. 378–98.

Penny Morris, Francesco Ricatti, and Mark Seymour (eds), *Modern Italy: Special Issue on the Emotions*, 17:2 (2012), pp. 151–285.

Paolo Murialdi, *La Stampa italiana del dopoguerra 1943–1972* (Rome, 1973).

Nico Naldini, *Breve vita di Pasolini* (Parma, 2000).

Mauro Pasqualini, 'Politics of Emotions in the Italian Left: Gender, Consumption and Intimacy in Lorenza Mazzetti's Advice Columns and Novels, 1961–1969', *The Italianist*, 32: 3 (2012), pp. 415–36.

Luisa Passerini, *Women and Men in Love: European Identities in the Twentieth Century* (New York, 2009).

Silvana Patriarca, *Italian Vices: Nation and Character from the Risorgimento to the Republic* (Cambridge, 2010).

J. G. Peristiany (ed.), *Honour and Shame: The Values of Mediterranean Society* (Chicago, 1966).

Marta Petrusewicz, *Latifundium: Moral Economy and Material Life in a European Periphery* (Ann Arbor, MI, 1989).

Karen Pinkus, *The Montesi Scandal* (Chicago, 2003).

Donald Pitkin, 'Marital Property Considerations Among Peasants: An Italian Example', *Anthropological Quarterly*, 33:1 (1961), pp. 33–9.

Mariapia Pizzolante, 'Il Pompeo Magno da "piccolo gruppo" a "collettivo"', *Snodi: Pubblici e privati nella storia contemporanea*, 5 (2010), pp. 99–108.

Jan Plamper, 'The History of the Emotions: An Interview with William Reddy, Barbara Rosenwein, and Peter Stearns', *History and Theory*, 49:2 (2010), pp. 237–65.

Alessandro Portelli, 'The Peculiarities of Oral History', *History Workshop Journal*, 12:2 (1981), pp. 96–107.

Maria Porzio, *Arrivani gli alleati! Amori e violenze nell'Italia liberata* (Rome, 2011).

Rebecca Pulju, 'Finding a Grand Amour in Marriage in Postwar France', in Kristin Celello and Hanan Kholoussy (eds), *Domestic Tensions, National Anxieties: Global Perspectives on Modern Marriage Crises* (Oxford, 2015), pp. 126–46.

Gerd Rainer-Horn, *The Spirit of Vatican II: Western European Progressive Catholicism in the Long Sixties* (Oxford, 2015).

William Reddy, *The Navigation of Feeling: A Framework for the History of the Emotions* (Cambridge, 2001).

William Reddy, *The Making of Romantic Love: Longing and Sexuality in Europe, South Asia and Japan, 900–1200 CE* (Chicago, 2012).

Linda Reeder, *Widows in White: Migration and the Transformation of Rural Italian Women, Sicily, 1880–1920* (Toronto, 2003).

Jacqueline Reich, *Beyond the Latin Lover: Marcello Mastroianni, Masculinity and Italian Cinema* (Bloomington, IN, 2004).

Aida Ribero, *Una questione di libertà: Il feminismo degli anni settanta* (Turin, 1999).

Luca Salmieri, 'Genere e conflitto. Separazioni giudiziali a Napoli', *Polis*, XVI:1 (2002), pp. 5–34.

Martina Salvante, 'Less than a Bootrag: Procreation, Paternity and the Masculine Ideal in Fascist Italy', in Pablo Dominguez Anderson and Simon Wendt (eds), *Masculinities and the Nation in the Modern World* (London, 2015), pp. 93–112.

Emanuela Scarpellini, *Material Nation: A Consumer's History of Italy* (Oxford, 2011).

Emanuela Scarpellini, *Food and Foodways in Italy from 1861 to the Present* (London, 2016).

Monique Scheer, 'Are Emotions a Kind of Practice (And is that What Makes Them Have a History)? A Bourdieuian Approach to Understanding Emotions', *History and Theory*, 51:2 (2012), pp. 193–220.

Jane Schneider, 'Of Vigilance and Virgins: Honor, Shame and Access to Resources in Mediterranean Societies', *Ethnology*, 10: 1 (1971), pp. 1–24.

Jane Schneider, 'Trousseau as Treasure: Some Contradictions of Late Nineteenth Century Change in Sicily', in Eric B. Ross (ed.), *Beyond the Myths of Culture: Essays in Cultural Materialism* (New York, 1980), pp. 323–56.

Jane and Peter Schneider, *Culture and Political Economy in Western Sicily* (New York, 1976).

Jane and Peter Schneider, *Festival of the Poor: Fertility Decline and the Ideology of Class in Sicily 1860–1980* (Tucson, 1996).

Mark Seymour, *Debating Divorce in Italy: Marriage and the Making of Modern Italians, 1860–1974* (London, 2006).

Mark Seymour, 'Epistolary Emotions: Exploring Amorous Hinterlands in 1870s Southern Italy', *Social History*, 35:2 (2010) pp. 148–64.

Mary Seymour, 'Emotional Arenas: From Provincial Circus to National Courtroom in Late Nineteenth-Century Italy', *Rethinking History*, 16:2 (2012), pp. 177–97.

Jade Shephard, '"I Am Not Very Well I Feel Nearly Mad When I Think of You": Male Jealousy, Murder and Broadmoor in Late-Victorian Britain', *Social History of Medicine*, 30:2, (2017), pp. 277–98.

Renate Siebert, *È femmina però è bella. Tre generazioni di donne al sud* (Turin, 1991).

Giulia Sissa, *Gelosia: Una passione inconfessabile* (Rome, 2015).

Sidonie Smith and Julia Watson (eds), *Women, Autobiography, Theory: A Reader* (Madison, WI, 1998).

Birgitte Søland, 'Employment and Enjoyment: Female Coming-of-age Experience in Denmark, 1880s to 1930s', in Mary Jo Maynes, Birgitte Søland, and Christina Benningham (eds), *Secret Gardens, Satanic Mills: Placing Girls in European History, 1750–1950* (Bloomington, IN, 2005), pp. 254–68.

Peter and Carol Stearns, 'Emotionology: Clarifying the History of Emotions and Emotional Standards', *American Historical Review*, 90:4 (1980), pp. 813–36.

Carolyn Steedman, *Landscape for a Good Woman: A Story of Two Lives* (London, 1986), p. 44.

Simonetta Piccone Stella, *Ragazze del sud: Famiglie, figlie, studentesse in una città meridionale* (Rome, 1979).

Simonetta Piccone Stella, *La prima generazione: Ragazze e ragazzi del miracolo economico italiano* (Turin, 1993).

Simon Szreter and Kate Fisher, *Sex Before the Sexual Revolution: Intimate Life in England 1918–1973* (Cambridge, 2010).

Molly Tambor, *The Lost Wave: Women and Democracy in Postwar Italy* (Oxford, 2014).

Luisa Tasca, 'The "Average Housewife" in Post-world War II Italy', *The Journal of Women's History*, 16:2 (2004), pp. 92–115.

Anna Tonelli, *Per indegnità morale: Il caso Pasolini nell'Italia del buon costume* (Rome, 2015).

Anna Tonelli, *Comizi d'amore: Politica e sentimenti dal '68 ai Papa boys* (Rome, 2007).

Anna Tonelli, *Gli irregolari: Amori comunisti al tempo della Guerra Fredda* (Rome, 2014).

Hester Vaizey, *Surviving Hitler's War: Family Life in Germany, 1939–1948* (London, 2010).

Angelo Ventrone, 'Tra propaganda e passione: "Grand Hôtel" e l'Italia degli anni '50', *Rivista di storia contemporanea*, Vol. 17: 4 (1988), pp. 602–31.

Fabrice Virgili, *Shorn Women: Gender and Punishment in Liberation France* (London, 2002).

Thomas Glyn Watkin, *The Italian Legal System* (Aldershot, 1997).

Perry Willson, *Peasant Women and Politics in Fascist Italy: The Massaie Rurali* (London, 2002).

Perry Willson, *Women in Twentieth Century Italy* (London, 2009).

Perry Willson, 'The Nation in Uniform? Fascist Italy 1919–1943', *Past and Present*, 221 (2013), pp. 239–72.

Index

ABC (Magazine) 162–3, 191–2
Abortion 74–5, 77, 101–2, 178, 184
A Love Affair (Novel) 142–3, 153–4
Adua and Friends (Film) 63
Adultery 153–4, 167–8, 187–9
    Adultery Law (559) 153–4
Aerre 150–1
Agnorelli, Bruno 146
A Love Affair (Novel) 142–3, 153–4
Alcamo, Sicily 110–11
Annabella (Magazine) 155–8, 191–2,
    198–9
Archivo Diaristico Nazionale (National Diary
    Archive) 7–10, 178–9
Arianna (Magazine) 153–4
Article 587 (Honour) 107, 123

Baldassi, Francesco 79, 84–5
Bartoletti Stella, Massimo 85–6
Bartolomeo, Lucio 71–2, 86–7
Bartolozzi, Giovanna 178, 182–3
Battistini, Elisabetta 75, 81, 175–7
Bernhard, Cristina 73–4
Bertini, Mario 25–6, 61–2, 71–2
Bignozzi, Bruna 75–6
Blengino, Maria 60
Bracanti, Vittorio
    Il bell'Antonio (Novel) 69–70
Bread, Love and Jealousy (Film) 135–6
Buzzati, Dino 142–3

Calabria 129–30
Cardinale, Claudia 136–7
Catholic Action 4–5, 71–2, 86–7
Catholicism 4–5, 23, 35–6, 61–2, 86–7, 173–4,
    191–2
    Catholic Church 4–5, 137, 191
    Catholicism and women 49–50, 72–3, 101–2
    Catholicism and sexuality 4–5, 49–50,
        66–9, 72–3, 77–8, 101–2, 160–1
    Catholicism and masculinity 71–2, 87,
        90–1, 195
Caravello, Giuseppina 170–1, 190–1
Cavallo, Giovanna 38, 81–3
Cavinato, Lauretta 34–6, 44, 171–3, 195–7
Christian Democrats 111, 153–4
Cirillo, Lydia 104–6
Clavadolo, Mattia 123
Cohabitation, *see* Common-law marriage

Colasanti, Livia 2, 15, 190–1
Common-law marriage 75–6, 190–1
Communism 4–5, 54, 61, 76–8, 154–5,
    180–5, 195
Companionate Marriage 83, 173–4, 177
Comencini, Dino 135–6
Coppi, Fausto 160–1, 189
Corredo 38–42
Corriere della Sera (newspaper) 111–12, 114,
    117, 119–22, 125–6, 138
Courtship 25–7, 35–6
    Glances 87–9, 92–7, 117
    Rituals 55–8

Damiani, Damiano 124–5
Dei, Alda, Maria 19, 41–2, 57–8, 149–50
Dissipatore, Rosaria 144–5
Divorce 131–2, 135, 189–90
    Divorce campaign in Italy 131–2, 190–1
    1970 Law 131–2, 161–2, 173–4, 178–9, 191
    1974 Referendum 131–2, 153–4, 161–2,
        164, 191
Divorce Italian Style (Film) 101, 105–6, 136–7
Domestic violence 133, 143–6, 167
Dowry 37–8
Due cuori felici (Film) 135

Effe (Magazine) 156–8
Elopement 49, 97–9
    Fuitina ('Elopement for love') 109–12
Engagement 57–62

Famiglia Cristiana (Magazine) 35–6, 65–6,
    72–3, 101–2
Family Law Reform Act, 1975 131–2, 144–5,
    153–4
Fauciana, Rocco 125–6
Feminism 156–7, 174–5, 179–83, 186
Ferrarini, Walter 22–3
Fortuna, Loris 162–3
Frasca, Giovanni 65
Free love 184–5
Fresu, Maria 88
Fuitina, *see* Elopement
Furnari, Gaetano 107–9

Gani, Iris 146
Gelosia (Song) 133–4
Gelosia (Film) 135–6, 140–1

Germi, Pietro 105–6, 127–8, 135–6, 140–1
Ginzburg, Natalia
 The Voices in the Evening (Novella) 53–4,
  57, 65–6
Girl with a Gun (Film) 123, 127–8
Girl with the Red Scarf (Film) 97–8
Giornale di Sicilia (Newspaper) 107–9,
 112–16, 119, 125–7
Goretti, Maria 72–3, 101–2
Gower-Chapman, Charlotte 99–101
Grand Hotel (Magazine) 20–1, 28–9, 31–2,
 35–6, 44–5, 71, 82–3, 132–3, 136–9,
 152–3, 161–2, 188–9
 Agony aunts 45, 55–6
Grazia (Magazine) 28–9, 139–40, 188–9
Guarnieri, Anna Maria 191–2
Guerrini, Maria 43–4

Harrison, Lieta 69–70, 89–90, 106–7, 162–3
Homosexuality 6–7
Honour crime 11, 102–3, 105–19, 121, 125,
 198–9
 In Sicily 102–3, 107–19, 121, 125, 128
 Kidnapping 109–19, 125

Il bell'Antonio (Film) 69–70, 195
Il Mattino (Newspaper) 114–16
Il Resto del Carlino (Newspaper) 114, 117,
 119–21
Il Signor Max (Film) 135, 142–3
Indrio, Stefano 184–5
Iotti, Nilde 183–4
Italian Communist Party, *see* Communism
Italian Women Confess (book) 139, 148–9

La Dolce Vita (Film) 153–4
La mia Signora (Film) 138
Lamonica, Maria 31–2, 96–7, 103
La Nazione (newspaper) 144–6
La Perla, Giovanni 144–5
La Stampa (Newspaper) 119, 140, 143–4
La Zanzara (Magazine) 162–3
L'Ora (Newspaper) 112–16, 119, 125–6
Loren, Sophia 189–90
Lorenzini, Carlina 168–70
Love Meetings (Film) 129–30, 153–4
Luna Park (Magazine) 139
L'Unità (Newspaper) 120–2
Lush, Sidney 104–5

Mafia 111, 117
Marianini, Vittorio 46–7
Mariotti, Aldo 57–9
Marriage
 Age 24
 Arranged 34–5, 42–3, 49, 60–1, 65, 74–5,
  81–4, 111–12, 116, 140–1, 148–9, 170, 194

As escape 31–3
Class as barrier 46–7
Forced Marriage 168–70
Illness as barrier to 45–7
Reparatory Marriage 123
Legal separation 165–8, 170–3, 175, 183
Marriage, Italian Style (Film) 135–7
Martinelli, Sara 32, 46
Masculinity, *see* Sicily and Catholicism
Maselli, Maria 133–4, 151
Massini, Laura 27–31, 41–2, 46–7, 193–7
Mastroianni, Marcello 195
Melodia, Fillipo 107–9, 111–25, 197–9
Menichetti, Anna di Montegnacco 74–5
Merlin, Senator Angelina
 Law to outlaw brothels 63
Migration 24–5, 102–3, 144–6
 To America 60–1
 Female 31–2, 35–6, 60, 87–8, 103
 To Northern Europe 59–60, 116–17
 To Switzerland 83–4
 To Turin 60, 87–8, 103, 147–8
Molinelli, Amalia 1–2, 30–1, 35
Montagnara, Rita 183–4
Morselli, Guido 183–4
Musso, Lidia 33, 42–3, 46

Napoleonic Code 131–2

Occhini-Locatelli, Giulia 160–1

Paola, Maria 65–6
Parca, Gabriella 156–7
 See also Italian Women Confess
Parrella, Vincenza 179–81
Partito Comunista Italiano (PCI), *see* Italian
 Communist Party
Pasolini, Pier Paolo 129–30, 157–8
Passerini, Luisa 143
Pedacci, Adriana Libutti 34
Pettinari, Angelo 25, 79–81
Pezzino, Graziella 37–8, 138–9, 151
Physical Intimacy 65–9, 75–6
Pietrangeli, Antonio 135–6, 140–1
Pitt-Rivers, Julian 97–101
Poor but Beautiful (Film) 135–6
Pregnancy 2, 73, 75–7, 105–6, 148–9, 160–1,
 169, 174–80, 186, 190–1
Prostitution 63
Puliti, Luisa 64, 77, 154–5, 184, 189

Rape 117–19, 168–70, 179–80
Rebecca, Luisa 41–2
Reale, Orazio (Justice minister) 107
Reeder, Linda 99–101
Rigoni, Giuseppe 83–4
Risi, Dino 135–6

Rocco and his Brothers (Film) 135–6, 145–6
Romani, Vittorio 25–6, 56–7, 87
Rossi, Giobatta 25–6, 64–5
Rotundi, Vincenzo 71–2

Sansone, Luigi 161–2, 175
Sardinia 88–9
Schneider, Jane 99
Schneider Peter 99
Sciascia, Leonardo 107
Seduced and Abandoned (Film) 101, 105–6,
   127–8
Sereni, Emilio 76–7
Sereni, Marina 76–7
Sicily 19, 31–2, 94
  Corredo 39–41
  Courtship practices in 87–8, 94–6,
    102–3, 117
  Masculinity 117, 122, 136–7, 144–5, 195,
    197–9
  Society 110–11
  Violence 111, 113–14
Soprani, Anna 57, 81

Tale of Poor Lovers (Film) 63
Tariscio, Sebastiana 87–8, 103
Tempo (Magazine) 154–5, 157–8
The Communist (Novel) 183–4
The Magnificent Cuckold (Film) 135–7,
   140–3, 157–8
The Most Beautiful Wife (Film) 124–5
The Woman of Rome (Film) 63
Togliatti, Palmiro 183–4
Torrisi, Carmelina 125–7, 197
Treno Popolare (Film) 66–9
Trousseau, see *Corredo*

Unione Donne Italiane (UDI) 153–4,
   180–1

Vandano, Brunello 140
Vanzi, Maria 58–9, 173
Varanini, Riccardo 184–7
Varini, Amato 46–8, 61, 77–8
Viola, Bernardo 109, 113, 116–17, 122
Viola, Franca 94, 107–27, 197–9
Visconti, Luchino 135–6, 145–6